THE END OF MEMORY

THE STOB LECTURES 2002

A portion of this book was offered as the annual Stob Lectures, presented each fall on the campus of Calvin College or Calvin Theological Seminary in honor of Henry J. Stob. Eerdmans is pleased to present the book as part of its ongoing publication of books deriving from this series.

Dr. Stob, with degrees from Calvin College and Calvin Theological Seminary, Hartford Seminary, and the University of Göttingen, began his distinguished career as a professor of philosophy at Calvin College in 1939 and in 1952 was appointed to teach philosophical and moral theology at Calvin Theological Seminary, where he remained until retirement. He died in 1996, leaving many students influenced greatly by his teaching.

The Stob Lectures are funded by the Henry J. Stob Endowment and are administered by a committee including the presidents of Calvin College and Calvin Theological Seminary.

For more information on Dr. Stob and The Stob Lectures, see *www.calvin.edu/stob.*

THE END OF MEMORY

Remembering Rightly in a Violent World

Miroslav Volf

WILLIAM B. EERDMANS PUBLISHING COMPANY

GRAND RAPIDS, MICHIGAN / CAMBRIDGE, U.K.

Published 2006 by

Wm. B. Eerdmans Publishing Co.

2140 Oak Industrial Drive N.E., Grand Rapids, Michigan 49505 /

P.O. Box 163, Cambridge CB3 9PU U.K.

Printed in the United States of America

11 10 09 08 07 06   7 6 5 4 3 2 1

Library of Congress Cataloging-in-Publication Data

Volf, Miroslav.

The end of memory: remembering rightly in a violent world / Miroslav Volf.

p.   cm.

ISBN-10: 0-8028-2989-9 / ISBN-13: 978-0-8028-2989-4 (cloth: alk. paper)

1. Memory — Religious aspects — Christianity.

2. Reconciliation — Religious aspects — Christianity.   I. Title.

BV4597.565.V65 2006

241'.4 — dc22

2006029024

www.eerdmans.com

To Tim

Contents

⸻ ⧜ ⸻

vii

CONTENTS

PART ONE

Remember!

CHAPTER ONE

Memory of Interrogations

—◁◁◁◁◁▷▷▷▷▷—

I have a confession to make: I was once considered a national security threat. For months I was interrogated — not only about details of my own life but also for incriminating information about other people suspected of posing a threat to the state. No wonder, then, that the photos of mistreated Abu Ghraib detainees in Iraq shocked me to the core. I still remember where I was when I first saw the image of a person hooded and hooked to electrical wires standing helplessly with arms stretched out in what looked like a modern-day crucifixion. Terrible as these windows into mistreatment were in their own right, they also flooded my mind with scenes from my own — albeit less severe and humiliating — interrogations of more than twenty years ago.

Charges and Threats

It was the year of our Lord 1984, though to me it seemed more like the year of his archenemy. In the fall of 1983 I was summoned to compulsory service in the military of then-communist Yugoslavia. There was no way out of it. I had to leave behind my wife and a soon-to-be-born Ph.D. dissertation to spend one year on a military base in the town of Mostar, sharing a room with forty or so soldiers and eating stuff like cold goulash with overcooked meat for breakfast at 5:00 a.m. But as I stepped onto the base, I sensed that not just discomfort, but danger, awaited me.

My wife was an American citizen and therefore, in the eyes of my commanders, a potential CIA spy. I had been trained in the West in a "subversive" discipline that studies everything as it relates to God, who is above all worldly gods — including those of totalitarian regimes. I was writing a dissertation on Karl Marx, whose account of socialism and how to achieve it could only serve to de-legitimize the kind of socialism the Yugoslav military was defending. I was the son of a pastor whom the communists had almost killed as an enemy of the people after World War II and whom the secret police suspected of sedition and regularly harassed. I was innocent, but Big Brother would be watching me. I knew that. I just didn't know how very closely.

Unbeknownst to me, most of my unit was involved in spying on me. One soldier would give me a politically sensitive book to read, another a recent issue of *Newsweek* or *Time,* while a third would get his father, who worked for the Croatian magazine *Danas,* to give me a subscription. All this was designed to get me to talk about religion, ethnic belonging, politics, the military — anything that would expose my likely seditious proclivities. I had a Greek New Testament with me, and some soldiers pretended to be interested in discussing its contents, a topic prohibited on the base. I was named the administrative assistant to the captain, an otherwise attractive job, but given to me so that I would spend most of my time in a single room that was bugged. For a few months, almost every word I said was noted or recorded and every step I took, both on and off the base, was monitored.

My ordeal started not long after I stumbled onto a soldier translating to the security officer a letter my wife had written to me. I was summoned for a "conversation." "We know all about you," said Captain G., the security officer. He was flanked by two other officers, their faces expressionless and menacing at the same time. They had plenty of "proof" of my subversive intentions and activities. A foot-thick file lay on the Captain's desk — transcripts of conversations I'd had in my office, reports of what I'd said to this or that soldier elsewhere, photos of me entering buildings in town, sometimes taken from somewhere high above. Obviously, they knew a great deal about me. And they didn't seem to like any of it.

Like the court in Franz Kafka's *The Trial,* my interrogators were going to pull out "some profound guilt from somewhere where there was originally none at all."[1] I had engaged in religious propaganda on the base — I must therefore be against socialism, which in Yugoslavia was linked officially with atheism. I had praised a Nazarene conscientious objector for acting according to his principles — I was therefore undermining the defense of our country. I had said something unkind about Tito — I was therefore an enemy of the people. I was married to an American and had studied in the West — I was therefore a spy. The charges should have been embarrassing for the interrogators. Restricting freedom of speech, not engaging in it, should have been viewed as morally reprehensible. And some of the charges were just plain silly. Is every expatriot American a potential spy? But the officers were utterly serious: I must be out to overthrow the regime. The real issue, which they sensed rightly, was that the seams holding Yugoslavia together were at their breaking point. An enemy could be hiding under any rock, behind any bush.

Threats followed the charges against me. Eight years in prison for the crimes I'd committed! I knew what such threats meant. Had I been a civilian, I could have counted on the help of competent lawyers and public opinion, both within the country and abroad. But I was in the military, so there would be a closed military tribunal. I would have no independent lawyer. To be accused was to be condemned, and to be condemned was to be ruined . . . unless I confessed. And "confessed as quickly as possible and as completely as possible."[2] Unless I admitted everything they assured me they already knew, I was doomed. And so it went, session after session, week after week. I was force-fed large portions of terrifying threats with an occasional dessert of false hope. Except for Captain G., who was always present, new interrogators kept coming, their ranks reaching all the way up to that of general.

1. Franz Kafka, *The Trial,* trans. Breon Mitchell (New York: Schocken, 1998), 149.
2. Arthur London, *The Confession,* trans. Alastair Hamilton (New York: William Morrow and Company, 1970), 56.

All this attention, to be sure, gave me a sense of importance — the kind of importance felt by a fox being hunted by a king and his entourage, with their fine horses, sleek hounds, and deadly weapons! But one overwhelming emotion drowned almost all others: fear. Sometimes paralyzing fear — fear that makes your body melt, not just your soul tremble. Though I was never physically tortured, I was firmly held in my interrogators' iron hand and completely dependent on their mercy. They could do with me anything they wanted; and their eyes, as they pummeled me with threats, told me they would relish seeing me suffer. I did not fear so much the threatened imprisonment — I feared the seeming omnipotence of these evildoers. It felt as though a ubiquitous evil eye was watching me, as though an evil mind was twisting for its own purposes what the evil eye saw, as though an evil will was bent on tormenting me, as though a powerful, far-reaching hand lay at the disposal of that will. I was trapped and helpless, with no ground of my own on which to stand. Or from which to resist. Trembling before the false gods of power, I was something, all right. But as a person, I was nothing.

Memory of Abuse

The "conversations" stopped as abruptly as they had begun — and without an explanation. After my term in the military was up, security officers made a lame attempt at enlisting me to work for them. "Considering what you've done, we have treated you well," an officer told me. "You know what you deserved. You can show your gratitude by working for us." Gratitude? For months of my life stolen by interrogations just because I am a Christian theologian and married to an American? For all the mental torment? For fear, helplessness, and humiliation? For colonizing my interior life even after I was discharged from the military? For causing me month after month to view the world through the lens of abuse and to mistrust everyone?

My interrogations might be categorized as a mid-level form of abuse — greater than an insult or a blow, but mild compared to the torture and suffering many others have undergone at the hands of tormentors, especially those schooled in Red Army methods.[3] No prolonged isolation, no sleep deprivation, no starvation, no painful body positions, no physical assault or sexual mistreatment. Yet, even afterward, my mind was enslaved by the abuse I had suffered. It was as though Captain G. had moved into the very household of my mind, ensconced himself right in the middle of its living room, and I had to live with him.

I *wanted* him to get out of my mind on the spot and without a trace. But there was no way to keep him away, no way to forget him. He stayed in that living room and interrogated me again and again. I knew that it would not be wise to forget anyway, even if I could. At least not right away. Psychological as well as political reasons spoke against it. So gradually I pushed the Captain a bit to the side and arranged to live my life around him. When little else was going on, he would still catch my eye and make me listen for a while to his charges and threats. But mostly I had my back turned to him, and his voice was drowned in the bustle of everyday activities. The arrangement worked rather well. It still does — in fact, now he is confined to the far corner of my dark basement and reduced to a dim shadow of his former self.

My success at sidelining the Captain, however, left the main worry about my relationship to him almost untouched. That worry had surfaced as soon as the interrogations started: I was being mistreated, so how should I respond? The way I *felt* like responding was one thing. I wanted to scream and curse and return in kind. In his novel *The Shoes of the Fisherman*, Morris West reports the musings of the interrogator Kamenev: "Once you have taken a man to pieces under questioning, once you have laid out the bits on the table and put them together again, then a strange thing happens. Either you love him or you hate him for the rest of your life. He will either love you or hate you in return."[4] I don't know what my interrogator felt for me, but I felt absolutely no love for him. Only cold,

3. See, for instance, first-person accounts of internment and interrogations by Arthur London *(The Confession)* and Elena Constante (*The Silent Escape: Three Thousand Days in Romanian Prisons,* trans. Franklin Philip [Berkeley: University of California Press, 1995]).

4. Morris L. West, *The Shoes of the Fisherman* (New York: William Morrow and Company, 1963), 46.

enduring anger that even vengeance, if it were possible, would not alter. But I sensed — maybe more subconsciously than consciously — that if I gave in to what I felt, I would not be responding as a free human being but reacting as a wounded animal. And it did not matter whether that reaction happened in the physical world (which was impossible) or in my imagination. To act as a human being is to honor feelings, even the thirst for revenge, but it is also to follow moral requirements stitched by God into the fabric of our humanity. Fear-ridden and humiliated as I was, I was determined not to lose what I believed was best in the human spirit — love of one's neighbors, even if they prove to be enemies.

The more severe the wrongdoing, the more likely we are to react rather than respond, to act toward wrongdoers the way we *feel* like acting rather than the way we *should* act. Would I have clung to the principle of loving one's enemies had I been as severely abused as the Abu Ghraib detainees — or worse? I might not have. The force of the abuse might have overwhelmed my capacity even to think of loving my abusers — of wishing them well, of seeking to do good for them, of working to establish a human bond with them. Would, however, my inability have canceled the requirement to love my enemy? I think not. It would simply have postponed its fulfillment until some power beyond my own had returned me to myself. Then I would be able to do what deep down I knew I should do. Then I would be able to echo in my own way the struggle and the victory given voice in the sermon by nineteenth-century abolitionist and women's rights activist Sojourner Truth titled "When I Found Jesus":

> Praise, praise, praise to the Lord! An' I begun to feel such a love in my soul as I never felt before — love of all creatures. An' then, all of a sudden, it stopped, an' I said, Dar's de White folks dat have abused you, an' beat you, an' abused your people — think o' them! But then there came another rush of Love through my soul, an' I cried out loud — "Lord, I can love even de White folks!"[5]

5. Sojourner Truth and Olive Gilbert, *Narrative of Sojourner Truth: A Bondswoman of Olden Time, with a History of Her Labors and Correspondence Drawn from Her Book of Life; also, A Memorial Chapter,* ed. Nell Irvin Painter (New York: Penguin, 1998), 107-8.

Fortunately for me, it was only Captain G. that I had to love, not "de White folks," not people who hack others to death, not monsters out to exterminate entire ethnic groups.

To triumph fully, evil needs two victories, not one. The first victory happens when an evil deed is perpetrated; the second victory, when evil is returned. After the first victory, evil would die if the second victory did not infuse it with new life. In my own situation, I could do nothing about the first victory of evil, but I could prevent the second. Captain G. would not mold me into his image. Instead of returning evil for evil, I would heed the Apostle Paul and try to overcome evil with good (Romans 12:21). After all, I myself had been redeemed by the God who in Christ died for the redemption of the ungodly. And so once again, now in relation to Captain G., I started walking — and stumbling — in the footsteps of the enemy-loving God.

How, then, should I relate to Captain G. in my imagination now that his wrongdoing was repeating itself only in my memory? How should I *remember* him and what he had done to me? Like the people of God throughout the ages, I had often prayed the words of the psalmist: "Do not remember the sins of my youth or my transgressions; according to your steadfast love remember me, for your goodness' sake, O Lord" (25:7). What would it mean for me to remember Captain G. and his wrongdoing in the way I prayed to God to remember me and my own wrongdoing? How should the one who *loves* remember the wrongdoer and the wrongdoing?

That is the issue I have set out to explore in this book. My topic is the *memory of wrongdoing suffered by a person who desires neither to hate nor to disregard but to love the wrongdoer.* This may seem an unusual way of casting the problem of memory of wrongs suffered. Yet, to embrace the heart of the Christian faith is precisely to be pulled beyond the zone of comfort into the risky territory marked by the commitment to love one's enemies. There memory must be guided by the vow to be benevolent and beneficent, even to the wrongdoer.

Many victims believe that they have no obligation whatsoever to love the wrongdoer and are inclined to think that if they *were* in fact to love the wrongdoer, they would betray rather than fulfill their humanity.

9

From this perspective, to the extent that perpetrators are truly guilty, they should be treated as they *deserve* to be treated — with the strict enforcement of retributive justice. I understand the force of that argument. But if I were to share this view, I would have to give up on a stance toward others that lies at the heart of the Christian faith — love of the enemy, love that does not exclude the concern for justice but goes beyond it. In this book, I do not make the argument for a love of the enemy that at the same time affirms justice and goes beyond it; I simply assume it to be a given of the Christian faith.[6]

In looking at the kinds of questions that arise when a victim seeks to remember in accordance with the commitment to love the wrongdoer, I will refer throughout the book to my own interrogations, since in large measure these have been the crucible for my exploration of this topic. For me they have also been a window into the experiences of countless others both today and in the past, especially the sufferings of people in the last century, the bloodiest of them all. In Chapter Two, I will join the larger ongoing conversation among psychologists, historians, and public intellectuals about the importance of memory, a conversation that started largely in response to the great catastrophes of the last century, such as two world wars, Armenian genocide, the Holocaust, purges by Stalin and Mao, and the Rwandan genocide. I will argue that it is important not merely to remember, but also to remember *rightly.* And in the rest of the book I will explore from a Christian standpoint what it means to remember rightly. But here, in the second part of this current chapter, I will register how the struggle to remember rightly looks from the inside, in the experience of a person who was wronged but who strives to love the wrongdoer. So now that I have sketched the memory of my interrogations, I turn to examine critically — even interrogate — that very memory.

---

6. For a more extensive treatment of the topic, see Miroslav Volf, *Free of Charge: Giving and Forgiving in a Culture Stripped of Grace* (Grand Rapids: Zondervan, 2005) and *Exclusion and Embrace: Theological Reflections on Identity, Otherness, and Reconciliation* (Nashville: Abingdon, 1996).

Remembering Rightly

The summons to remember, directed at victims and the wider populace alike, has in recent decades become almost ubiquitous in Western culture. When I first encountered this injunction after my ordeal in 1984, I took it to be superfluous to my own interior life. I remembered all too well — I didn't need anyone to prod me to do so. I deemed the injunction to remember perilously one-sided, however, if it was simply urging me to make public what happened to me in secret — which seemed to be the main intent of the injunction's proponents.

To remember a wrongdoing is to struggle against it. The great advocates of "memory" have rightly reminded us of that. But it seemed to me that there were so many ways in which I could remember wrongly that the injunction verged on being dangerous. I could remember masochistically, to use the phrase coined by Milan Kundera in his novel *Ignorance,* by remembering only those things from the incident that make me displeased with myself.[7] Or I could remember sadistically, guided by a vindictive desire to repay evil for evil. Then I would be committing a wrongdoing of my own as I was struggling, with the help of memory, against the wrongdoing committed against me. I would be granting evil its second victory, its full triumph.

So from the start, the central question for me was not *whether* to remember. I most assuredly would remember and most incontestably should remember. Instead, the central question was *how to remember rightly.* And given my Christian sensibilities, my question from the start was, How should I remember abuse as a person committed to loving the wrongdoer and overcoming evil with good?

What does "remembering rightly" actually involve? This book as a whole tries to answer that question. But note here that whatever "rightly" ends up meaning, it cannot refer just to what is right for the wronged person as an individual. It must mean also what is right for those who have wronged that individual and for the larger community. The reason is simple. Remembering rightly the abuse I suffered is not a

7. Milan Kundera, *Ignorance,* trans. Linda Asher (New York: HarperCollins, 2002), 74.

private affair even when it happens in the seclusion of my own mind. Since others are always implicated, remembering abuse is of public significance. Let me take in turn each of these three relations in which the one who has been wronged stands.

First, there are aspects of remembering rightly that concern primarily the wronged person. Their impact on others is indirect. I asked myself, for instance, could these months of abuse that live on in my memory be somehow rendered meaningful? Could my life be meaningful even if those experiences were remembered as meaningless? What place would the memory of abuse occupy in my interior life? Would Captain G. continue to sit in its living room, or could I succeed in moving him to a side room or locking him up in a basement?

Such questions about the relationship between the memory of abuse and the victim's own interior "space" are closely linked with questions about the relationship between the memory of abuse and the victim's interior "time." How much of my projected future would Captain G. colonize, given that the memory of abuse kept projecting itself into my anticipated future? Would he define the horizon of my possibilities, or would he and his dirty work shrink to just one dark dot on that horizon and possibly even disappear from it entirely? These kinds of questions about remembering rightly — which I explore further in Chapter Four — I would have to answer on my own. But the way I answered them would not only shape my relationship to Captain G. but also affect my relationship to every social setting in which I found myself.

Second, consider the relationship of the memory of abuse to the wider social setting out of which the abuse arose or to which it might be applied. From the beginning, I did not experience my interrogations simply as an isolated case of mistreatment. As with most persons who have been wronged, my experiences immediately became an *example,* and they continued to function as an example in my memory. But what were they an example of? I could see them as an example of a pervasive form of human interaction that is often hidden behind the veil of civility but is ready to show its ugly face as soon as the social peace is sufficiently disturbed. Or I could see them as socialism exhibiting its true nature, the way some people think of September 11 as showing the true nature of radical Islam. I could also see them as an example that I would be wise to emulate in some sense if indeed I live in a world of brute power, while of course making certain that I wound up in Captain G's shoes, not my own unlucky pair. If I remembered my interrogations as a window into the brute power that rules the world, would I have remembered rightly? Or would I have remembered wrongly by first focusing on the negative and then allowing it to color the whole surrounding landscape? Would I be allowing the abuse to whirl me down into the dark netherworld, the memory of abuse having darkened my world, and the darkened world having made me remember the abuse even more negatively?

Alternatively, maybe my interrogations were in a deep sense at odds with the way the world is essentially constituted, an example of our world gone awry. What framework would I need to bring to the memory of Captain G's misdeeds so that I remembered them as an evil anomaly in a good world, rather than as a symptom of a world beyond good and evil? In what overarching account of reality would I need to insert his misdeeds to remember them as something worth fighting against — and worth fighting against not primarily with reactive blows but with the power of goodness? In Chapter Five, I explore such questions touching the exemplary character of mistreatment suffered.

Mostly, however, the struggle to remember rightly my ordeal of 1984 was not about my own inner healing or about how I should act in the larger social environment. It was the struggle to do justice and show grace to Captain G. So third, what does it mean to remember rightly in regard to the wrongdoer? If we are tempted to interject, "Who cares about him?" the response is surely that it is the wrongdoer whom God calls me to love. Whether I remembered publicly or privately, *what* I remembered concerned him profoundly; after all, I was remembering *his* wrongdoing.

To help myself be fair, I imagined Captain G. observing and listening in as I narrated in my memory what happened between us — a difficult decision, given how unfair he had been toward me. In my imagination, I also gave him the right to speak — another difficult decision, given that his terrorizing had reduced my speech to a stammer. I did not give him the last word. But neither did I give it to myself! Knowing how faulty memories generally are, and being aware of victims' proclivities and blind spots, I could not fully trust even myself. The last word was to be spoken on the Last Day by the Judge who knows each of us better than we know ourselves. Before then, the Captain would be allowed to speak and I would listen — with ears attuned to detect any attempts to whitewash his crimes. Still, I would listen to his protests, corrections, and emendations about the way I remembered him and his wrongdoing as I continued to hold firmly the reins of my remembering. During interrogations, Captain G. had repeatedly twisted my truth and reduced me to nothing; in contrast, I should listen to his truth and honor his personhood as I sought to tell rightly the story of his mistreatment of me.

Did he in fact do to me what I remember his having done? If my wounded psyche passed on to my memory injuries that he did not inflict, or exaggerated those he did, *I* would be wronging *him,* irrespective of the fact that it was he who in the past had overwhelmingly wronged me. And then there was the complicated but important matter of intentions, not just of observable actions. I was sensitive to intentions. The most maddening aspect of my interrogations was the sinister spin my interrogators gave to my straightforward speech and actions; they read into my words and deeds intentions that I never had. The devil was not in "facts," large or small, but in their interpretation. It was as though a warped mind was reading a plain text and coming up with most bizarre interpretations that somehow managed to account for the facts.

Now, if I was not careful as I remembered the ordeal, I could take my turn by spinning what Captain G. had said and done to me. For instance, I could isolate his deeds from the political and military system in which he worked and attribute the whole extent of the abuse to his evil character. More charitably, but equally untruthfully, I could make him disappear in the system and relieve him of all responsibility. The system was tormenting me, not the Captain; he was merely its mechanical arm. Or I could suggest that, paradoxically, he was truly doing evil and enjoying it as evil precisely because the system legitimized it for him as part of a greater good. Perhaps he feared the revival of the animosities in Bosnia between people of different faiths that had led to atrocities during World War II — a revival that, arguably, did in fact materialize and generated the further atrocities of less than a decade after my interrogations. Many other ways of interpreting Captain G.'s actions are conceivable, and choosing among them should not proceed simply according to my preference. For to misconstrue a wrongdoing would be to commit a wrongdoing of my own — a theme I explore in Chapter Three.

But to remember wrongdoing *truthfully* is already justifiably to condemn. And condemn it I did! But what is the right way to condemn? That may seem like a strange question. If the condemnation is truthful, it seems right. Justifiable. End of story. But not for the one who loves the wrongdoer. How does one seeking to love the wrongdoer condemn *rightly?* In the Christian tradition, condemnation is an element of reconciliation, not an isolated independent judgment, even when reconciliation cannot be achieved. So we condemn most properly in the act of forgiving, in the act of separating the doer from the deed. That is how God in Christ condemned all wrongdoing. That is how I ought to condemn Captain G.'s wrongdoing.

"One died for all" — including me! Wrapped up with that piece of good news is a condemning accusation: I too am a wrongdoer. How does the history of my own wrongdoing figure in my condemning memory of Captain G.? Not at all? Then I would always stand radically outside the company of wrongdoers as I remember his wrongdoing; he would be in the darkness and I in the light. But would that be right? Moral judgments are not only absolute judgments; they are also comparative judgments. So to remember Captain G.'s abuse rightly, must I not remember it as the act of a self-confessed wrongdoer rather than that of a self-styled saint?

Should I not also try to remember his wrongdoing in the context of his whole life, which might exhibit a good deal of virtue? In memory, a wrongdoing often does not remain an isolated stain on the character of the one who committed it; it spreads over and colors his entire character. Must I not try to contain that spreading with regard to Captain G.'s wrongdoing? How could I do so, if I didn't remember his virtues along with his vices, his good deeds along with the evil ones? Occasionally during my interrogations I seemed to see a warm sparkle in his otherwise icy eyes. Was this some genuine goodness trying to find its way out from underneath the debris of his misdeeds or the warped political structure for which he worked? Should I not remember those moments of seeming goodness, however dubious they were?

Furthermore, what effect, if any, does the death of Jesus Christ to save the ungodly have on Captain G. as an abuser? Christ "died for all," says the Apostle Paul; therefore, in some sense "all have died," not just those who believe in Christ (2 Corinthians 5:14). Captain G. too? Then how should I remember his abuse, given that Christ atoned for it? Or does Christ's atonement have no impact on my memory of his wrongdoing?

If One died for the salvation of *all,* should we not *hope* for the salvation of all? Should I actively hope for Captain G.'s entry into the world to come? Moreover, Christ died to reconcile human beings to one another, not only to God. Were Captain G. and I then reconciled on that hill outside the gate of Jerusalem? Will we be reconciled in the New Jerusalem, or must I at least hope that we will be? If so, my memory of wrongdoing will be framed by the memory and hope of reconciliation between wrongdoers and the wronged. What consequences would this have for the way I should remember his wrongdoing? In Chapter Six, I explore the impact of Christ's death on remembering wrongdoing.

The banquet is an image the New Testament frequently uses to describe that reconciled world. Captain G. and I sitting together at the table and feasting with laughter and camaraderie? A very scary thought, but not an impossible scenario! What would it mean to remember his wrongdoing *now* in view of such a potential future? What would life in *that* world — the world of perfect love and perfect enjoyment in God and in one another — do with the memory of abuse? Will I still remember the wrongdoing then? If so, for how long? Why wouldn't I just let it slip out of my mind? What good would the memory of it do there? Would it not stand as an obstacle *between* us? Can I imagine a world — can I *desire* a world — in which I would no longer label Captain G. as an "abuser" every time I saw him? The entire last section of the book (Chapters Seven through Ten) explores the fate of the memory of wrongdoing in God's new world of love.

Difficult Decision

In a sense, the most momentous decision in writing this book was to pose the original question, "How does one seeking to love the wrongdoer remember the wrongdoing rightly?" and let it guide the whole exploration. That decision was also the most difficult to make. It is not that I agonized about whether or not this was the *right* decision. I believe it was. The problem came in sticking with it. When I granted that I ought to love Captain G. — love not in the sense of warm feeling but in the sense of benevolence, beneficence, and the search for communion — much of what I wrote in the book followed, at least in rough outline if not in detail. But every time I wrote about "loving" Captain G. a small-scale rebellion erupted in my soul. "I love my parents and relatives, I love my wife and children, I love my friends, I love pets and wild geese. I might even love nosy neighbors and difficult colleagues, but I *don't love* abusers — I just don't and never will," screamed the leader of my internal insurrection. And at times as I wrote it would not have taken much to make me switch sides ... except that loving those who do me harm was precisely the hard path on which Jesus called me to follow him — a path that reflects more than any other the nature of his God and mine. Not to follow on that path would be to betray the One who is the source of our life and miss the proper goal of all our desires. It would also be a reckless squandering of my own soul.

My soul was at stake in the way I remembered Captain G. But I was not left to remember him on my own. I was (and still am) part of a community of memory — a Christian church — that from the start framed my memories. (In Chapters Five and Six I will say more about the relationship between my memory of wrongdoing and the defining memories of the Christian church.) I also inhabited a larger cultural environment in which struggles for memory and debates about memory raged. Captain G. was one of thousands of small props of the communist ruling elite in the former Yugoslavia; he and they were paid to defend the regime that ruled it, but a false memory was enlisted to legitimize its rule. The servants of false memory — historians, journalists, public intellectuals — made some things disappear from the nation's past and others materialize in it from out of thin air. And what the manipulators of memory neither erased nor invented, they warped and twisted to fit within the crooked lines of self-glorifying history. In Yugoslavia then, as in many countries in the world today, some thoughts could only be whispered in the intimate circle of family and friends — thoughts that were the stuff of submerged, "politically incorrect" memory. Telling the truth was a subversive act.

But the Yugoslavian communist elite was far from the worst manipulator of memory in the unhappy twentieth century. Other communist regimes treated the past with much less respect, just as they treated their citizens with more cruelty. And the Nazis, with their abhorrent and deadly racist ideology, were not only the most celebrated evildoers but also the most celebrated whitewashers of crimes. Remembering truthfully in such environments is an act of justice; and in order to expose crimes and fight political oppression, many writers, artists, and thinkers have become soldiers of memory.

So how does my struggle to remember rightly relate to this public remembering enlisted to serve the cause of justice? In the privacy of my interior life, the memory of Captain G.'s wrongdoing immediately showed itself Janus-faced, looking both in the direction of virtue and peace and in the direction of vice and war. And so it happens with public remembering: the protective shield of memory often morphs into a vicious sword, and the just sword of memory often severs the very good it seeks to defend. The next chapter explores this dangerous moral fickleness of memory.

CHAPTER TWO

Memory: A Shield and a Sword

"We remember Auschwitz and all that it symbolizes because we
believe that, in spite of the past and its horrors, the world is
worthy of salvation; and salvation, like redemption, can be found only in
memory."[1] Elie Wiesel spoke these words in the German Reichstag in an
address delivered on November 10, 1987, fifty years after the infamous
Kristallnacht, when mobs infiltrating the streets of Nazi Germany destroyed Jewish property and helped propel Germany closer to the horrors of the Holocaust. The words sum up a theme that runs like a bright
thread through Wiesel's work: the saving power of remembering suffered
wrongs. As he himself put it, faith in the saving power of memory — faith
that it will heal the individuals involved and help rid the world of violence — is his central "obsession."

Wiesel's work centers on the memory of the Holocaust; he is a survivor of that genocide. The scope of his work is, however, larger than the
memory of the Holocaust. It concerns the memory of all significant
wrongdoing. Recognizing how singular a phenomenon the Holocaust

---

1. Elie Wiesel, *From the Kingdom of Memory: Reminiscences* (New York: Summit,
1990), 201.

was, I will build here on the broader thrust of his work and leave its throbbing heart untouched.

Among our contemporaries, Wiesel may be the person most eloquently exploring the memory of wrongdoing. But belief in the redemptive power of such memory is widespread today. Psychologists and novelists, historians and philosophers, cultural critics and politicians are repeating the injunction "Remember!" like a reassuring drumbeat. But is memory such an unambiguous good? How strong is the link between memory and well-being? Isn't the memory of wrongs suffered itself suffused with pain and suffering? Hasn't it sometimes pushed those who remember to inflict pain and suffering on others? Doesn't it then have a link to perdition and not just to protection? And if memory of wrong suffered is integral to personal and social well-being but can also lead to the opposite, *how* should we remember for our memory to foster flourishing? At the periphery of his complex thought, Wiesel has raised such questions. To explore them is crucial, especially for those who, like me, believe with Wiesel in the redeeming power of memory.

In unfolding the relationship of memory, salvation, and perdition, I will mainly consider the memory of wrongs suffered. We recall many other kinds of things — stories from our childhood, adolescent dreams and disappointments, successes and failures in our work, the history of our ancestors or ethnic group, religious instruction, and more. Though all such memories are central to who we are and how we live, I will not address them in this book. My theme is not memory in general, but the memory of wrongs suffered. Moreover, in this chapter I will examine only the question of whether such memory is in some significant way "saving" in the sense of contributing to our well-being and that of our neighbors. There may be other reasons to remember wrongs irrespective of whether or not our remembrance is saving — perhaps sheer duty toward sufferers, the unyielding demands of justice, or simply that to be human involves remembering such things. But here I will leave aside these reasons for remembering, though I will return to them in the course of the book. For now I will focus on memory and well-being.

The Pleasure and Pain of Memory

Salvation lies in memory, suggests Elie Wiesel, borrowing religious vocabulary for urgent everyday concerns. Is it obvious, however, that we should associate the memory of wrongs with salvation — or with anything positive, for that matter? I dread, for instance, reliving in memory my long hours of terrifying interrogations in the winter of 1984. The reason is obvious: to relive those experiences is painful, even in memory. When we remember the past, it is not only past; it breaks into the present and gains a new lease on life.

Of course, we enjoy remembering *pleasant* experiences from the past. Consider, for example, the memories of Johannes, the fictitious author of Søren Kierkegaard's "Seducer's Diary." He is keeping the diary not simply to record his past conquests but also to recollect them and, in recollecting them, make them an occasion for "the second enjoyment."[2] We may object that his conquests are exploitive and his memory compulsive. But from his perspective as an aesthete whose main goal is to make life "interesting," the point of remembering is clear: memory multiplies pleasure because it re-presents the original experience. Often memory fails, of course, and the record of the past is erased. Distant events fade into the background and disappear. Pleasure experienced in the past remains just that — pleasure past, swallowed up by the night of non-remembrance and lost forever. But the more vivid the memory, the more the past pleasure becomes a present delight.

Just as the memory of pleasure re-presents past pleasure, so the memory of pain replicates past pain. "The moment, here in a flash, gone in a flash . . . does, after all, return as a ghost once more and disturbs the peace of a later moment," wrote Friedrich Nietzsche in one of his *Unfashionable Observations,* titled "Utility and Liability of History."[3] Consider

2. Søren Kierkegaard, *Either/Or,* ed. Howard V. Hong and Edna H. Hong (Princeton: Princeton University Press, 1987), 2:305. Johannes strives to describe the events from the past "as if they were taking place right now and with such dramatic vividness that it sometimes seems as if everything were taking place before one's eyes" (304).

3. Friedrich Nietzsche, "Utility and Liability of History," in *The Complete Works,* ed. Richard T. Gray (Stanford: Stanford University Press, 1995), 2:87.

traumatic memories. We tend to repress them when the suffering under-gone seems unbearable. Yet often what we repress resurfaces in flash-backs beyond our control, and then we experience anew the horror of past pain. Even if we doubt the reality of repression, as scholars increas-ingly do,[4] the point still stands: to remember suffering endured is to keep one's wounds open. The larger the wound and the better the recollec-tion, the more past and present merge and past suffering becomes pres-ent pain. If memory repeats and revives original suffering, how can sal-vation lie in memory?

One could argue that not all memory of pain is in itself painful. At the end of his masterpiece *City of God,* in talking about the blessed in the world to come, Augustine distinguishes between two kinds of knowledge of evil, which he correlates with two kinds of memory. In one kind of knowledge, evil is "accessible to apprehension by the mind," and in the other "it is a matter of direct experience."[5] The first is like a medical doctor's knowledge of a particular disease and the second like the knowledge of a patient suf-fering from that same disease. Augustine is talking here about the memory of wrongs the blessed have *committed,* not about the memory of wrongs they have *suffered.* In his view, the blessed will not remember having *suf-fered* wrongs at all — a thought to which I will return in Part Three of this book.[6] They *will* remember having wronged *others* — remember in the way a medical doctor apprehends a disease she has never suffered from. But they will have "no sensible recollection of past evils" suffered; such recol-lection "will be completely erased from their feelings."[7] Even though Au-gustine does not explain how such an erasure will happen in the world to come, the underlying conviction that leads him to speak of it is plausible

4. See Richard J. McNally, *Remembering Trauma* (Cambridge, Mass.: Harvard Uni-versity Press, 2003).

5. Augustine, *City of God,* trans. Henry Bettenson (Harmondsworth: Penguin, 1976), XXII.30.

6. According to Augustine, the saints in the world to come will have no memory of offenses that *others* have perpetrated against them. Augustine writes of the freed will in the Heavenly City: "It will be freed from all evil and filled with all good, enjoying unfail-ingly the delight of eternal joys, forgetting all offenses, forgetting all punishments" (*City of God* XXII.30).

7. Ibid.

enough: If in memory we are re-experiencing evil committed and suffered, we are not yet fully freed from its effects.

To see more clearly how remembering may be seen as the very opposite of salvation, consider the question whether one can remember past sufferings without remembering the feelings that accompanied our experiences. Depending on the mood of the moment, I can either remember my father's funeral simply as a fact, or I can be deeply saddened by the realization that this extraordinarily good man has disappeared from my life. So one can recall an event without re-sensing the emotion that originally accompanied it. But such emotionless recollection makes for a significantly altered memory. As Avishai Margalit argued in *Ethics of Memory,* the "sensibility" (feelings) tied to an original event is an essential component of the memory of that event. "The amazement and horror in watching the collapse of the twin towers in New York ... is the kernel of the memory of the collapse and not ketchup added on top of it."[8] Memories of suffering unaccompanied by corresponding feelings of pain or deep sympathy inevitably involve forgetting. I can remember my father's funeral without sadness only if I allow my memory of it to be altered by forgetting the emotional dimension of the event.

This is, in fact, exactly how Augustine thought about the matter of memory and sensibility. The two ways of knowing evil — knowing by apprehension of mind and knowing by experience — have "two corresponding ways of forgetting evil," writes Augustine. "The learned scholar's way of forgetting is different from that of the one who has experienced suffering. The scholar forgets by neglecting his studies; the sufferer, by escaping from his misery." With this distinction of forgetting in mind — forgetting of facts and forgetting of misery — Augustine then claimed that in the world to come past evils will be "completely erased from their [the saints'] feelings."[9] According to Augustine, the life of the blessed involves not only remembering past wrongs but also forgetting — forgetting how suffering and evil *felt.*

8. Avishai Margalit, *The Ethics of Memory* (Cambridge, Mass.: Harvard University Press, 2002), 62-63.

9. Augustine, *City of God* XXII.30.

With regard to salvation, the excision from memory of a pain endured is as significant as remembering the event that caused the pain. If well-being lies in memory, then must the memory not be of the kind that at its heart includes the forgetting of pain? For surely, as long as the pain is felt salvation remains incomplete.

Identity

But perhaps we should not be so preoccupied with the pain of memory — at least not before we have reached the state of the blessed in the world to come, whose memories Augustine thought purged of any sensible recollection of evil. For memories do not merely replicate pleasure or pain; they also decisively shape our identities.

Inwardly, in our own self-perception, we *are* much of what we remember about ourselves. I am who I am largely because I remember growing up in Novi Sad in communist Yugoslavia, doing this or that mischief (including the stealing of numerous car "tags" — a crime not dissimilar to Augustine's famous and gratuitous stealing of pears),[10] and enduring ridicule by my schoolteachers and fellow students because my father was a Pentecostal minister. In similar fashion, outwardly, in the way others perceive us, we *are* what others remember about us. I am who I am partly on account of what my parents remember about me as a child, how my colleagues and students "remember" or view me based on my actions and reactions, and how my readers remember my books and articles. Memory, as the argument goes, is central to identity. To the extent that we sever ourselves from memories of what we have done and what has happened to us, we lose our true identity. If suffering has been part of our past, pain will be part of our identity. We must hold fast to our memories along with their pain; otherwise we will not be true to ourselves. So salvation lies in memory insofar as that memory prevents us from distorting our essential selves and living a lie.

10. See Augustine, *Confessions*, trans. Henry Chadwick (New York: Oxford, 1992), II.4.9.

But what exactly is the relationship between memory and identity? Let's accept for the moment that we *are* to a significant degree what we and others remember about us. Don't we remember about ourselves many intensely discordant actions, feelings, and experiences — betrayals and fidelity, pain and delight, hatred and love, cowardice and heroism — as well as thousands of bland moments unworthy of note? The memory that helps make us up is a veritable patchwork quilt stitched together from the ever-growing mountain of discrete, multicolored memories. What will be stitched into the quilt and what will be discarded, or what will feature prominently on that quilt and what will form a background, will depend greatly on how we sew our memories together and how others — from those who are closest to us all the way to our culture as a whole — sew them together for us. We are not just shaped *by* memories; we ourselves *shape* the memories that shape us.

And since we do so, the consequences are significant; for because we shape our memories, our identities cannot consist simply in *what* we remember. The question of *how* we remember also comes into play. Because we can react to our memories and shape them, we are larger than our memories. If our reactions to our memories were determined simply by the memories themselves, then we would be slaves of the past. But unless we have been severely damaged and are in desperate need of healing, we have a measure of freedom with regard to our memories. To the extent that we are psychologically healthy, our identities will consist largely in our free responses to our memories, not just in the memories themselves.

Moreover, are we not also what we hope for in the *future?* It is true, the past can rob us of the future, just as it can rob us of the present. But here again the psychologically healthy person's *dreams* for the future cannot be mere forward projections of her memories, for then she would be cemented in her past, of which her future would be only the boring and oppressive extension. A person with a healthy sense of identity living in freedom and security will let the future draw her out of the past and the present and will play with new possibilities and embark on new paths. With regard to our past, present, and future, then, we are a great deal more than our memories, and how memories shape our identity depends not only on the memories themselves but also on what we and others do with those memories.

To return to my own experience in the Yugoslavian army, I can view myself primarily as a person who was terrorized by powerful people against whom I was helpless and whose intentions I could not discern. Or I can see myself primarily as a person who, after some suffering, has been delivered by God and given a new life, somewhat like the ancient Israelites, who in their sacred writings saw themselves not primarily as those who suffered in Egypt but as those who were delivered by Yahweh. I can be angry about suffering. I can be thankful for deliverance. I can be both. I can also let that year of suffering recede somewhere into a distant background and stretch myself toward the future — for instance, I can pour my energies into the exciting work of the Yale Center for Faith and Culture, which I direct, and I can engage more fully in shaping the lives of Nathanael and Aaron, my two sons.

To be sure, not all experiences of pain will be sidelined so easily. Some will stubbornly insist on being at the heart of our identity; the memory of them will define us without our having much say in the matter. But clearly these are exceptions and not the rule; and the more psychologically healthy a person is, the more exceptional such memories will be. In either case, if salvation lies in the memory of wrongs suffered, it must lie more in what we *do* with those memories than in the memories themselves. And what we do with our memories will depend on how we see ourselves in the present and how we project ourselves into the future.

So far, I have discussed Wiesel's claim that salvation lies in the memory of wrongs from the standpoint that such memory is a *component* of well-being, which is to say that salvation lies literally in memory. But the claim can also be taken to mean that remembering is essential for *achieving* the well-being that lies outside memory. In fact, this is how Wiesel primarily intended the claim (though he very much insists on the importance of remembering wrongs for personal identity).[11] We can un-

---

11. See Elie Wiesel, "Ethics and Memory," in *Ernst Reuter Vorlesungs im Wissenschaftskolleg zu Berlin* (Berlin: Walter de Gruyter, 1977), 14-15.

derstand memory as a *means to* well-being in at least four distinct though closely related ways.

Healing

One way to think about memory as a means to salvation is to relate it to *personal healing.* Psychological wounds caused by suffering can be healed only if a person passes through the narrow door of painful memories. In other words, she must endure the pain of remembering to reach a cure — one of Sigmund Freud's basic insights. An unexpressed traumatic experience is like an invasive pathogen "which long after its entry must continue to be regarded as an agent that is still at work."[12] And healing is possible only when a person recalls a wounding event along with the emotional reaction that accompanied it. By drawing them both into the light of consciousness, therapy provides an opportunity "for the normal discharge of the process of excitation."[13] In other words, since in recollection the feelings accompanying the event are set free from "strangulation," as Freud puts it, healing can take place.

We may interpret Freud as meaning that, at least to some degree, healing will result from the mere act of remembering formerly repressed events and the emotional reactions to them. Shine the light of knowledge into the dungeon where memories of suffering and wrongdoing are locked up, and you will be freed from their clandestine and subversive work! But this cannot be correct. If your mere remembering of a traumatic experience produced healing, you wouldn't have been wounded by the experience in the first place; for remembering the trauma replicates it — and by default its effects! — in an altered form. So repetition *as such* is a problem, not a solution.

As trauma literature consistently notes, the healing of wounded psyches involves not only *remembering* traumatic experiences; it must also

12. Sigmund Freud, *Studies on Hysteria*, vol. 2 of *The Standard Edition of the Complete Works of Sigmund Freud* (London: Hogarth, 1955), 6.

13. Sigmund Freud, *Five Lectures on Psycho-Analysis*, vol. 11 of *The Standard Edition of the Complete Works of Sigmund Freud* (London: Hogarth, 1955), 19.

include *integrating* the retrieved memories into a broader pattern of one's life story, either by making sense of the traumatic experiences or by tagging them as elements gone awry in one's life. Personal healing happens not so much by remembering traumatic events and their accompanying emotions as by *interpreting* memories and *inscribing* them into a larger pattern of meaning — stitching them into the patchwork quilt of one's identity, as it were.

For example, as I relive in memory the humiliation and pain of my interrogations by military police, I can tell myself that that suffering has made me a better person — say, in the way it has drawn me closer to God or made me more empathetic with other sufferers. Or I can decide that my experience has contributed in some small way to exposing the injustice of a regime that controlled its citizens, curtailed their freedoms, and sacrificed their well-being out of a commitment to an unworkable ideology. In either case, healing will come about not simply by *remembering* but also by viewing the remembered experiences in a new light. Put more generally, the memory of suffering is a *prerequisite* for personal healing but not a means of healing itself. The *means* of healing is the *interpretive* work a person does *with* memory. So salvation as personal healing must involve remembering, but mere remembering does not automatically ensure personal healing.

Acknowledgment

A second way to understand memory as a means of salvation concerns *acknowledgment.* The interrogations to which I was subjected would not have been possible without the cooperation of some of my fellow soldiers. They sought to lure me into conversations about politically sensitive topics (such as pacifism!) and provided me with literature potentially subversive to the communist regime to elicit my responses, which the police then secretly taped. To those unfamiliar with what was going on behind the scenes, these soldiers would have looked like perfectly decent human beings; yet they were willingly participating in an effort that could have ruined the life of an innocent person.

If no one remembers a misdeed or names it publicly, it remains invisible. To the outside observer, its victim is not a victim and its perpetrator is not a perpetrator; both are misperceived because the suffering of the one and the violence of the other go unseen. A double injustice occurs — the first when the original deed is done and the second when it disappears.

This injustice of hiding wrongs fuels the strong urge many victims feel to make known what they have suffered, even if some are hesitant to speak up. Since the public remembering of wrongs is an act that acknowledges them, it is therefore also an act of justice. This holds true at both the personal and broader levels. Commenting on the work of the South African Truth and Reconciliation Commission, André du Toit writes:

> The victims of political killings cannot be brought back to life, nor can the harm and trauma of torture and abuse somehow be negated. What can be done, though, is publicly to restore the civic and human dignity of those victims precisely by acknowledging the truth of what was done to them. This was the function and purpose of the victims' hearings where people were enabled to tell their own stories, and to have them publicly acknowledged in non-adversarial procedures.[14]

Acknowledgment is essential to personal and social healing. Notice, however, what acknowledgment means here. According to du Toit, the Truth and Reconciliation Commission was supposed to acknowledge not the unqualified remembrances of victims but "the *truth* of what was done to them." No doubt our first duty is simply to attend to the experiences

---

14. André du Toit, "Moral Foundations of the South African TRC: Truth as Acknowledgement and Justice as Recognition," in *Truth vs. Justice: The Morality of Truth Commissions,* ed. Robert I. Rotberg and Dennis Thompson (Princeton: Princeton University Press, 2000), 134. In our judicial system, adversarial procedures are meant to get at "the truth of the matter." But it is not clear that this is in fact their effect. Money can buy a perpetrator a good deal of "reasonable doubt," as well as being used to place on the shoulders of the accused a crime he has not committed, with the consequence that truth gets trampled underfoot.

and memories of victims as they present them to us. But ultimately we cannot put aside the question of truth, even if that question is a very complicated one, as I will show in Chapter Three. Scholars who study memory unanimously agree: Memories are notoriously unreliable.[15] There is no reason to think any differently of the memories of victims. Though they often do remember correctly, the pain of their undeniable suffering and understandable rage can easily distort their memories.

My own memory of interrogations by Captain G. and his superiors is a case in point. As I've remembered and occasionally retold the story, the interrogators' brutality has tended to grow, even as basic facts remained the same. Or I might conveniently leave out the fact that my fellow soldiers did not act out of malice toward me but out of a desire to please superiors in exchange for small benefits, such as longer hours off base. I've found myself portraying the perpetrators as greater villains than I know, in my more honest moments, they in fact were. In my memory I have at times treated them unjustly, and "injustice" *is* the proper term here, even though we do feel reluctant to suggest that a victim may be guilty of it. If a victim's telling of truthful stories is a form of justice, then a victim's skewing of painful memories must be a form of injustice. And an unjust remembrance of wrongdoing is not a means of salvation. *Truthful* and therefore *just* memory is. Untruthful memories are unjust memories and therefore add to the evil from which they seek to subtract. So in order for acknowledgment to foster well-being, it does not suffice simply to remember mistreatment; the memory of it must be truthful.

Solidarity

A third way that memory can serve as a means to salvation consists in generating *solidarity* with victims. Remembering suffering awakens us from the slumber of indifference and goads us to fight against the suffering and

15. See Brian L. Cutler and Steven D. Penrod, *Mistaken Identification: The Eyewitness, Psychology, and the Law* (Cambridge: Cambridge University Press, 1995); Elizabeth Loftus and Katherine Ketcham, *Witness for the Defense: The Accused, the Eyewitness and the Expert Who Puts Memory on Trial* (New York: St. Martin's Press, 1992).

oppression around us — or so the argument goes. To struggle against evil, we must empathize with its victims. And to empathize with victims, we must know either from experience or from witnesses' stories what it means to hunger, thirst, shiver, bleed, grieve, or tremble in fear. The memory of past horror will make us loathe to tolerate it in the present.

It is true that we must recall *past* wrongs in order to struggle against *present* ones. At the most elemental level, we cannot know what it means to be wronged unless we remember either our or someone else's having been wronged. Neither can we spring into action against a wrongdoing if we lack a vivid sense of what it means to be wronged any more than we can spring into action if we do not see present suffering happening. So memory is important not just in that it offers a general *sense* of what it means to be wronged. Memory of a particularly egregious wrongdoing can provide additional *motivation* for solidarity with those who suffer wrong today. We see emaciated bodies of Serbian concentration camp inmates behind barbed wires, we remember pictures of people reduced to human shadows in Nazi concentration camps, and we are motivated to help present victims. Remembering past suffering seems both indispensable and conducive to generating solidarity.

It is not clear, however, that the memory of past suffering *necessarily* leads to such good ends. Might it not also have the opposite effect? Consider those who have been wronged in deeply painful ways. Their indifference to the suffering of others — precisely on account of their own suffering — is also a possible, even understandable response. Why expect those who are nursing their own wounds and mending their own shattered lives to minister to the needs of others? There *are* good reasons for them to do so, but these reasons do not stem from memory itself, but rather from a broader set of convictions about the nature of reality and our responsibilities within it. Though the memory of our own suffering can be a motivating force to alleviate the suffering of others, it can also turn our eyes away from other sufferers. By itself, the memory of wrongs seems insufficient to generate solidarity.

In sum, when it comes to generating solidarity with victims, memories of wrongs are indispensable, but they are also insufficient and even potentially dangerous. They *can* engender empathy and mitigate oppression, but they can also lead to indifference and even trigger renewed violence — hardly means of salvation. To be means of salvation, memories themselves must be redeemed.

Protection

The fourth way in which memory can serve as a means of salvation is by *protecting* victims from further violence. As Elie Wiesel put it in his Nobel lecture, the "memory of evil will serve as a shield against evil, . . . the memory of death will serve as a shield against death."[16] Though Wiesel describes this belief as existential and not based on controlled observation, at least in one of its aspects the belief seems immediately plausible, namely, that exposing evil prevents or at least deters its perpetration. A notable feature of evil is that it seeks to cloak itself with a mantle of goodness in order to hide its true nature; whenever possible, Satan will appear as the angel of light precisely because it enhances his satanic work. Evil thrives when concealed and languishes when exposed. When evildoers fear that the light of memory will shine on them, they are likely to retreat out of fear of exposure; when the light of memory is switched off, more wrongdoing is likely to follow.

It would seem that memory's power to serve as a protective shield for victims is undeniable. Yet even this apparent truth is more complicated than it first appears. Though in many cases memory may rein in evildoers, in others it may goad them on. Some evildoers, convinced of the rightness of their abominable cause, commit atrocities *in order to be remembered*. This is in part the motivation of terrorists. The memory of their deeds is their glory — the reason that in many ancient cultures, including Israel's, blotting out the memory of perpetrators was not a crime against their victims, as we are inclined to think today, but a punishment of tormentors.[17]

---

16. Wiesel, *From the Kingdom of Memory,* 239.
17. During the trial of Timothy McVeigh, some argued that he ought not to be executed, for killing him would satisfy his wish to die for a cause and elevate his stature

A more significant problem with the protective function of memory than its occasionally opposite effect is that protection itself can be a deeply problematic endeavor. As victims seek to protect themselves, they are not immune to becoming perpetrators. Indeed, as the deft and gloomy aphorist Emil M. Cioran has observed, the great persecutors are often "recruited among the martyrs not quite beheaded."[18] The memory of their own persecution makes them see dangers lurking even where there are none; it leads them to exaggerate dangers that do exist and overreact with excessive violence or inappropriate preventive measures so as to ensure their own safety. Victims will often *become* perpetrators precisely *on account of* their memories. It is *because they remember* past victimization that they feel justified in committing present violence. Or rather, it is because they remember their past victimization that they justify as rightful self-protection what to most observers looks like violence born of intolerance or even hatred. So easily does the protective shield of memory morph into a sword of violence.

The Problem: The Moral Fickleness of Memory

How then can salvation lie in remembering wrongdoing and suffering? Instead of simply protecting a person, memory may wound another. Instead of generating solidarity with victims, it may breed indifference and reinforce cycles of violence. Instead of truthfully acknowledging wrongdoing, it may bolster a victim's false self-perceptions and unjust demands. Instead of healing wounds, it may simply reinjure. Remembering wrongs will forge an identity, but the identity may be that of a person imprisoned in his own past and condemned to repeat it. Notice the word "may" in the previous sentences — the memory of wrongs *may* wound, *may* breed indifference, *may* reinforce false self-perceptions, *may* reinjure. I am not arguing that remembering wrongs *must* produce all

---

among his followers. Instead, it was advocated, he should be left to rot in some prison without publicity, thereby erasing the memory of him.

18. Emil M. Cioran, *A Short History of Decay,* trans. Richard Howard (London: Quartet, 1990), 4.

these results, or even that as a rule it does produce them. In no way do I want only to associate remembering wrongs with perdition. My point *is,* however, that the memory of wrongs suffered is from a moral standpoint *dangerously undetermined.*

Elie Wiesel is well aware that the memory of wrongs suffered — even the memory of the Holocaust, marks of which he bears on his own body — can have widely divergent effects, some of them pernicious. At least as well as anyone, he knows the pain of memory and therefore the deeply felt need of many victims to wipe out from their minds all traces of days that are blacker than nights, as he puts it in *Forgotten.*[19] He writes vividly, in *The Accident* for instance, about how holding on to the dead in memory can rob us of the ability to give ourselves in love to the living.[20] And he clearly knows the potential misuses of memories through their tendency to create a false sense of identity, generate hatred, breed indifference, and lead to violence rather than justice.[21] Wars in the former Yugoslavia in the 1990s have led this passionate prophet of memory to see clearly that memory itself can be made into "an abomination." In Bosnia, "that tormented land," he writes, "it is memory that is a problem. It's because they remember what happened to their parents or their sister or their grandparents that they hate each other."[22] He even concedes in an interview that the negative use of memory has loomed larger throughout history than has its positive use. At the edges of his work, Wiesel points to the need to redeem memories if they themselves are to be redeeming. Yet perhaps understandably, he leaves this problem for others to explore and instead cries out in as many creative ways as he can the one dominant injunction: "Remember!"

If his injunction should be obeyed and if the negative use of memory has loomed larger throughout history than its positive use has, then it is essential to explore ways of *redeeming* memories of wrongs suffered.

19. Elie Wiesel, *Forgotten* (New York: Schocken, 1992), 297.

20. Elie Wiesel, *The Accident,* trans. Anne Borchardt (New York: Hill and Wang, 1962).

21. See Wiesel, "Ethics and Memory," 11-28.

22. Elie Wiesel and Richard D. Heffner, *Conversations with Elie Wiesel,* ed. Thomas J. Vincigoerra (New York: Schocken, 2001), 144-45.

What does it take to remember for good, to remember in salutary rather than destructive ways? How can we help memory become a bridge between adversaries instead of a deep and dark ravine that separates them? How can former enemies remember together so as to reconcile, and how can they reconcile so as to remember together? These questions, I believe, pose the most important challenges to remembering in our conflict-ridden world. This book attempts to engage them.

PART TWO

How Should We Remember?

CHAPTER THREE

Speaking Truth, Practicing Grace

M emories of wrongs suffered are morally ambiguous, I have argued in Chapter Two. They can serve to restore health and dignity, protect, and prompt the pursuit of justice. At the same time, such memories can also lead people to abase their humanity by nursing resentments and committing misdeeds. Though today many people rightly take the medicine of remembering wrongs against turmoil of the soul and violence in society, such "medicinal" memories often poison their patients with the very diseases they are meant to cure. Medicine and poison — memories of wrongs seem to be both.

Currently added to this dangerous moral ambiguity of memories is a powerful sense of their importance. There is today something of a memory boom, a widespread desire to memorialize events — at times almost an obsession with remembering. This memory boom has, I surmise, two principal causes (plus many subsidiary ones). Almost paradoxically, the first is the fast-paced, novelty-obsessed, entertainment-saturated culture in which we live. On the one hand, it makes most of us quick to forget — forget even those things that once meant a great deal to us. As the media nail us to a narrow strip of the extended present, and as the new replaces the old with breathtaking speed, the past seems like a landscape viewed from a fast-moving train — a blur that quickly fades to black. On the other hand, as we lean forward in time we extol memory and memorialize experiences to counter the slipping of the past into oblivion, to prevent our memories from faltering "like old veterans parading," as E. L. Doctorow put it in *City of God*.[1]

Witness the readiness in the U.S. to erect memorials to events that have only just happened. Debate about the appropriate monument for the victims of "9/11" was running full speed only a few weeks after the terrorist attack, when we could not possibly have had enough time to absorb the impact of the disaster and reflect on its meaning![2] We demand immediate memorials as outward symbols because the hold of memory on our inner lives is so tenuous. And then, because we have tangible, observable memorials, we feel absolved of the obligation to remember on our own; we feel free, in good conscience, to immerse ourselves in the blur of the present. Thus does the memory boom try to compensate for an actual memory bust.

Second, in the wake of the great social catastrophes of the twentieth century, beginning with World War I, there has emerged in the West a broad cultural consensus that we must remember major wrongs suffered — remember them all and remember them always.[3] By remembering, goes the claim, we fight manufactured oblivion that serves to mask the character and deeds of oppressors, whether they are totalitarian dictators, such as Stalin and Hitler, or personal tyrants, such as abusive parents or impossible bosses. By remembering, we pay a debt of honor to those who have been wronged and have suffered. To forget their violation would be to fail in our most basic obligation to do justice. To forget their killing would be tantamount to taking their lives for the second time.[4] In a

1. E. L. Doctorow, *City of God* (New York: Plume, 2001), 178.

2. On the topic of memorialization, see James Young, *The Texture of Memory* (New Haven: Yale University Press, 1993), 4.

3. On the connection between the great catastrophes, especially World War I, and the heightened importance of memory, see Jay Winter, *Sites of Memory, Sites of Mourning: The Great War in European Cultural History* (Cambridge: Cambridge University Press, 1995); *War and Remembrance in the Twentieth Century*, ed. Jay Winter and Emmanuel Sivan (Cambridge: Cambridge University Press, 1999).

4. See Avishai Margalit, *The Ethics of Memory* (Cambridge, Mass.: Harvard University Press, 2002), 20-21.

fast-paced culture plagued with widespread wrongdoing, it seems necessary to continue taking the medicine of memory. The risks involved on account of its moral indeterminacy, its tendency to do no less harm than good, are the price we must pay.

The two previously mentioned aspects of remembrance — the importance assigned to memories of wrongdoing and the real dangers of such memories — are uncomfortable bedfellows. They squeeze us between the imperative to remember and the warning that by doing so we risk mistreating others and betraying ourselves. To uphold the importance of memories of wrongs responsibly, we need to filter out the poison from the medicine of memory. But how? How can we remember rightly? How can memories that, on the one hand, help define and protect us and aid us in doing justice cease, on the other hand, to wound, separate, and even drive us to aggression? How can they instead heal, bind together, and foster common flourishing?

Redeeming the Past

For Christians, the question of rightly remembering wrongs suffered is part of the larger issue of redemption, particularly the redemption of the past. And what does redemption of the past mean?

In *Thus Spoke Zarathustra*, Nietzsche makes a startling statement about redemption: to redeem people from the ill will "against time and its 'it was,' that alone should I call redemption."[5] His emphatic "alone" shortchanges the definition of redemption, however; for it is not only the past that needs redeeming. The present, which Nietzsche insisted ought to be left untouched, cries out for redemption, too! Our defective and enfeebled bodies, our wounded souls, even our eyes and ears as organs of perception need to be made whole. The future also needs redeeming — not future events that haven't yet happened of course, but our projected future, toward which we stretch ourselves in dreams and

5. Friedrich Nietzsche, *Thus Spoke Zarathustra*, in *The Portable Nietzsche*, trans. and ed. Walter Kaufmann (New York: Penguin, 1976), 251-52.

labors. For unhealthy dreams and misdirected labors often become broken realities.

Not only did Nietzsche slight the redemption of the present and the future, but he also misconceived what it means to redeem the past. He did so by advocating acceptance of the past in a heroic act of *amor fati* — love of fate. For acceptance is *putting up with* the past, not *redeeming* it. Still, Nietzsche was correct in insisting on the importance, indeed the necessity of redeeming the past; for even with a redeemed present and future, redemption is incomplete without the redemption of the past — both our individual pasts and the past of the world, of which we are part and which is part of us. What we have suffered weighs us down like a heavy load we long to have lifted; like an indefatigable enemy, it assails us relentlessly. The wreckage of history — a trail of shattered beauty, defiled goodness, twisted truths, streams of tears, rivers of blood, mountains of corpses — must somehow be mended. That the past must and will be redeemed is a conviction essential to the Christian notion of redemption.

Redemption and Right Remembrance

Learning to remember well is one key to redeeming the past; and the redemption of the past is itself nestled in the broader story of God's restoring of our broken world to wholeness — a restoration that includes the past, present, and future. So what is the relationship between remembering well and redeeming the past? Questions such as those that stem from my interrogations by Captain G. and his crew can help point us toward an answer. Will I look at those experiences with resentment and a desire to get even, or will I find peace about the matter and maybe even strive to reconcile with the perpetrators? Will inner peace and commitment to reconciliation lead me to remember charitably, or will resentment and fear draw in my mind meaner sketches of those experiences than reality supports? Will I leave the terrors behind and pursue my present projects, though perhaps continue to worry about other militaries that brutally interrogate innocent citizens?

I could remember my interrogations in any of the ways suggested by these questions and many more. Which options I pursue will depend partly on what I believe will happen to me and on how I — and others — relate to that troubling episode of my life. Will I feel secure in the midst of abiding insecurities in the world, or will I always feel exposed to threats? Will the wounds heal, or will they remain open, painful, festering? Will the wrong be somehow righted? Will I have to take the righting of the wrong into my own hands if I do not wish to settle for the triumph of evildoers, or is there hope for the righting of wrongs by an impartial judge in the here and now or at the end of history? Will the ordeal be rendered somehow meaningful, or will it remain a random intrusion of fruitless suffering that casts a shadow of malaise over the whole of my life? Can this episode be integrated into a larger story of redemption that includes whole communities, indeed the whole world, or must I suffer and overcome suffering solely within my own "ego-history"?[6] Is there reasonable hope for reconciliation not only with my wounded past but also with those who have wronged me, or will they — should they! — remain forever excluded from the company of those who belong to the community I consider mine? Answering such questions is crucial to remembering rightly the wrongs we have suffered.

These general questions can be particularized to fit the experiences of any of us. The answers to many of them will depend on convictions that concern the core of our being and the basic fabric of reality. Who are we as individuals, communities, and humanity as a whole? What are we here for? Where are we going? As I examine how to remember rightly in this and the following chapters, I will draw on answers grounded in the Christian faith. And what are the core convictions of that faith? Consider the following five propositions.

First, we don't just happen to be in the world as products of chance or necessity; the God of love created each one of us, together with our world.

Second, we are not in the world just to fend for ourselves while pursuing lives filled with as little pain and as much pleasure as possible; God

6. For the term "ego-history" see Piere Nora, *Essais d'ego-histoire,* [contributions de] Maurice Agulhon . . . [et al.], réunis et présentés par Pierre Nora (Paris: Gallimard, 1987).

has created us to live with God and one another in a communion of justice and love.

Third, humanity has not been left by itself to deal with the divisive results of our deadly failures to love God and neighbor — a fissure of antagonism and suffering that taints all human history and scars individual lives; in Christ, God entered human history and through his death on the cross unalterably reconciled human beings to God and one another.

Fourth, notwithstanding all appearances, rapacious time will not swallow us into nothingness; at the end of history God, who took on our finitude in Jesus Christ, will make our fragile flesh imperishable and restore true life to the redeemed, so that forever we may enjoy God, and each other in God.

Fifth, the irreversibility of time will not chisel the wrongs we have suffered into the unchangeable reality of our past, the evildoer will not ultimately triumph over the victim, and suffering will not have the final word; God will expose the truth about wrongs, condemn each evil deed, and redeem both the repentant perpetrators and their victims, thus reconciling them to God and to each other.

In very rough outline, this is the broad Christian story — the story of creation, redemption, and final consummation. For me this story frames what it means to remember rightly, and the God of this story makes remembering rightly possible.

Suspicions about Truthfulness

A key aspect of remembering rightly is remembering truthfully. To some, a Christian text on memory and truthfulness need say no more than the simple injunction, "Remember truthfully!" Simply apply to the past the ninth commandment as it has been traditionally understood — "You shall not bear false witness!" (Exodus 20:16) — and you will say all that needs to be said on the matter. That we should remember truthfully is at first glance as obvious as that in general we should tell the truth rather than offering distortions of it, half-truths, or outright lies. We may debate whether in some situations we might be exempt from such an obli-

44

gation, such as when telling the truth may result in significant harm to others or ourselves. But even if we allow the validity of such exemptions, they remain exceptions, not the rule. The rule is simple: be truthful in telling what you remember no less than in telling what you experience or intend to do. Does it not then seem that we could dispense with long discourses on memory and truthfulness?

Not so fast. For our memories are particularly vulnerable to distortion. Shortly, I will address the limits of human knowing in general — limits that memories share. But memories also have a peculiar limit that makes them even less reliable than other forms of knowing, namely, that by definition *what* we remember has happened in the past and is not unfolding before us. If I tell you that I am looking at a heron in the marsh outside my window, I am telling you about something that I'm seeing in the immediate present. Or if I tell you that I plan to ride my bike this afternoon if it doesn't rain, I am telling you of the intention that I'm entertaining right now. It's different with memories. If I tell you that I *saw* a heron a week ago at noon, or that three days ago I intended to ride my bike, my seeing and my intending are not taking place as I speak; they belong to the past. There is temporal distance between my present self and my former seeing and intending; I have to *re*member what transpired. That temporal gap and the work of memory needed to bridge it leave space for falsehood to slip in, for imagination to supply what memory is lacking. I am not talking about intentional lying. I can purposely lie about what I remember, of course, just as I can lie about what I perceive or intend. But here I am talking about the unintentional blurring that often happens because of a gap in time. Did I see heron a week ago at noon, or five days ago closer to 10:00 a.m.? Was it really a heron, or was it some other large bird — maybe a stork?

The likelihood of error increases when memories recall accounts of complex events rather than just simple perceptions or intentions. As William James noted at the end of the nineteenth century,

> The most frequent source of false memory is the accounts we give to others of our experiences. Such accounts we almost always make both more simple and more interesting than the truth. We

quote what we should have said or done rather than what we really said or did; and in the first telling we may be fully aware of the distinction. But ere long the fiction expels the reality from memory and reigns in its stead alone. This is one great source of the fallibility of testimony meant to be quite honest.[7]

In a word, we are prone to embellish our memories — and we do so often and quite innocently, especially in storytelling.

Even honest embellishments, suggested James between the lines, may be motivated by a subconscious desire to present ourselves in a better light. We *should* have said or done something, but we didn't. Helped by the passage of time, we improve upon the original by remembering that we *have* said and done what we *should have* said and done but clearly have not. Here memory is only tenuously related to what actually happened; for out of it has grown a fictive image or story fed by attitudes we find desirable and practices we find useful. For instance, to justify some unappeased anger toward Captain G., the psychological torture that I experienced might in my memory morph into physical torture, to which I was never subjected. I want him to look worse than he does, so I make him to look worse in memory.

Living as we do in a culture of suspicion and spin, today many suggest that memories are rarely truthful. Even worse, in large swaths of our culture there is a vague sense that memories *cannot* be truthful in the sense of at least roughly corresponding to what actually happened. Alternatively, some believe that since all stories about the past are told from a particular perspective, all stories have their own truthfulness, but one that is independent of what actually happened — a kind of fictitious truth, in other words. All the versions are just about equally true. Finally, some doubt that it would even be *desirable* to strive to remember truthfully, for by doing so we might do more harm than good.

Clearly, then, the simple injunction "Remember truthfully" leaves far too much unsaid about the relationship of memory and truthfulness. In the following pages I will examine this relationship by looking at the in-

7. William James, *The Principles of Psychology* (New York: Dover, 1890), 1:373-74.

ner logic of remembering, the moral obligation and desirability of truthfulness in remembering, and finally the conditions that make such remembering possible.

A Claim to Truthfulness

Suppose a friend asks me, "Do you remember at what time the first plane crashed into the north tower of the World Trade Center on September 11?" and I reply, "Certainly. I was in New York when it happened. It was at 9:46 a.m." If my friend checks on the internet, only to find out that the attack happened at 8:46 a.m., she may tell me, "Your memory is no better than mine! You got the time wrong! In fact, your memory's even worse than mine! At least I knew that I didn't remember!" In so saying, she would be a bit rough on me, but she would also be right. To remember something incorrectly is, in an important sense, not to remember at all — we *do not remember* to the precise extent that *what* we remember is incorrect. Our minds find the file in which the needed information is stored and read its contents without realizing that it has been tampered with. A sense of familiarity with the *process* of remembering makes us think that we remember the *facts,* but we don't;[8] for our imagination has clandestinely come to the aid of our faltering memory so that we unwittingly pass fictions for truths.

The so-called false memory syndrome — a condition in which a person's identity and interpersonal relationships are centered around a memory of a traumatic experience that is objectively false but in which the person strongly believes — illustrates my point well. A person may remember that as a child he was mistreated by his father, though that idea has been planted in his mind by someone else, say, a misguided therapist. Is he remembering? Though he *believes* he is remembering, he is not. We cannot remember what has not happened, and if we sin-

---

8. On the distinction between "remembering" and "seeming to remember" see Susan J. Brison, *Aftermath: Violence and the Remaking of a Self* (Princeton: Princeton University Press, 2002), 72.

cerely claim to remember a fictitious event, then strictly speaking we do not remember falsely but instead falsely *believe* we remember what is a product of imagination, perhaps sparked by the power of suggestion and nourished by the feeling of resentment. The fact that a person suffering from false memory syndrome cannot distinguish imagined fictions from true memories makes little difference. To the extent that we remember, we remember truthfully. When we say at the beginning of our narration, "Here is what I remember . . . ," or when we subtitle our book "A Memoir" we *commit ourselves to render truthfully what happened in the past.*[9]

When dealing with complex events, such as the 9/11 terrorist attacks or my interrogations by security officers, we may well remember some aspects of an experience but not others. Still what we remember, we remember truthfully. What we don't "remember" truthfully, we aren't remembering but imagining. We know that reality is too complex for any of us to perceive even a simple segment of it fully, let alone remember it truthfully. So in given situations we are lenient with regard to what we consider sufficiently truthful to qualify as remembering. If you had any personal knowledge about my interrogations, and if I told you that my interrogators placed a hood over my head and tied electric wires to me or that they stripped me naked and sexually abused me, you would rightly accuse me of falsely exaggerating my sufferings and might suspect that, for whatever reason, I was projecting onto my own experience the abuses suffered by Abu Ghraib detainees in Iraq. For nothing like that happened to me. But if I described in detail the face of a general from Sarajevo who came to interrogate me only once, you might be impressed by how truthful my memory is, even if I have gotten wrong the color of his alternatingly friendly and menacing eyes. The more complex the events and the more distant the past, the more forgiving of memory's inaccuracies we are likely to be.

A memory always only approximates the remembered event. In our

9. Paul Ricoeur has argued that, when it comes to memory, "a specific search for truth is implied in the intending of the past 'thing,' of *what* was formerly seen, heard, experienced, learned" (*Memory, History, Forgetting,* trans. Kathleen Blamey and David Pellauer [Chicago: University of Chicago Press, 2004], 55).

everyday use, "remembering" involves a mixture of truthful description and imagined construction. Still the tie between remembering and truthfulness holds. In a strict sense, to remember is to remember truthfully. In the everyday sense, to remember is to render the past event truthfully to the best of our knowledge.

Can Memories Ever Be Truthful?

Let's assume that my argument has so far been persuasive: We make claims to truth when we say that we remember. Still, it's one thing to make a claim to truth, but quite another to make good on that claim by in fact remembering truthfully.

In certain circles today, truth isn't what we used to think of it as, namely, the formal correspondence between mind and reality. Apart from bits of factual information — names, dates, phone numbers — there is no objective truth, some argue. The "truth" about the past is merely the story we find compelling, whether because it is attractive and useful or because it has been surreptitiously imposed on us by subtle persuasion or social constraint. Calling such a story "true," however, does not say anything about its epistemic status, about its relation to what in fact happened, for the simple reason that it is impossible for any story to correspond formally to events of the past. Instead, to call a story true is to indicate that it is pleasing, or that it offers a window into a desirable way of being in the world, or that it has succeeded as a move in the struggle for power — a struggle in which all human beings are involved, not only as possessors of things but as speakers of languages.[10]

This is not the place to engage in extended philosophical debates

10. Friedrich Nietzsche continues to be the most significant advocate of such an account of "truth." He is also the most successful teller of stories that are true in this sense. His *Genealogy of Morals* is one of them. It is not intended to be true in the sense of giving us a historically accurate description of the emergence of Western morality — just rhetorically persuasive to certain audiences with certain sensibilities about life. See Alasdair MacIntyre, *Three Rival Versions of Moral Enquiry* (Notre Dame, Ind.: University of Notre Dame Press, 1990), 42-47.

about whether or not such a radically perspectival and functionalist notion of truth, including truth about the past, can be plausibly maintained. The position is, I believe, philosophically incoherent.[11] But without expounding the arguments against it, suffice it to say that for me, as a Christian theologian with a nearly classical notion of the divine being, truth is a transcendental category and is underwritten by an all-knowing God. If something is true — say, that the base at which I was interrogated was in Mostar, a town in present-day Bosnia and Herzegovina, or that part of the reason for the interrogations consisted in my refusal as a soldier to pledge to kill the enemy in wartime — it is true independently of the situation in which I as a narrator find myself, independently of the goals I pursue or the struggles in which I am engaged. It is true everywhere, always, and under all circumstances. It is true universally.

Granted, we human beings always remember and tell our stories from a particular perspective, just as we perceive events from a particular perspective. We do so for two principal reasons. First, we are spatially limited. We can be in one place only and can therefore see things only from that one place. Our perception is enhanced if we examine a particular scene from different perspectives, like circling around a mountain peak to see it from all sides — but the limitation remains. And it remains partly because we are, second, temporally limited — we cannot see the mountain peak from all sides all at once. We live not only in the "here" but also in the "now" and can perceive and remember only from within that "now," which is always moving forward. So we fail to perceive fully what preceded any given event, what in the past contributed to its making; and we are mainly in the dark about the effects it will have in the future.

To be sure, we do get many things right — perhaps dates and places, the basic details of individual episodes, some accompanying sounds, smells, and feelings, and so on (though even in their regard we often need reminders to jog our memory). But for the most part we remain ig-

11. For a recent compelling argument against relativism and constructivism, see Paul Boghossian, *Fear of Knowledge: Against Relativism and Constructivism* (Oxford: Clarendon Press, 2006).

norant of the causes of any given event and the motivations for it. Our memory cannot situate it properly in its larger frame of reference; and we can more or less only guess what it might mean. We can remember only fragments of it. When Milan Kundera observes in his novel *Ignorance* that what is remembered is often "the plausible plastered over the forgotten,"[12] he may be exaggerating, but not by much.

We always perceive and remember less than we have witnessed or experienced. Yet this inescapably subjective and limited character of human knowing does not mean that "truth" is no more than an opinion supported by one or the other form of power. Perspectives and interests notwithstanding, we can speak meaningfully of truthful memories. When we claim to remember, we are claiming that, to the best of our knowledge, our memory is true in the sense that it corresponds in some way to events as they occurred.

The Moral Obligation to Remembering Truthfully

When we say that we remember, we not only claim to remember truthfully; we also have a *moral obligation* to remember truthfully. It has been much discussed in recent years whether we have a moral obligation to remember egregious wrongs. I will return to this question later in the book,[13] but for now my topic is not the moral obligation to remember, but rather, the moral obligation to be *truthful* when we remember.

Our ability to fulfill this obligation is limited, for memory only approximates, as I have just noted. We always remember partially. Second,

---

12. Milan Kundera, *Ignorance,* trans. Linda Asher (New York: HarperCollins, 2002), 126. For a scholarly assessment that resonates with Kundera's judgment, see Chris Westbury and Daniel C. Dennett, "Mining the Past to Construct the Future: Memory and Belief as Forms of Knowledge," in *Memory, Brain, and Belief,* ed. Daniel L. Schacter and Elaine Scarry (Cambridge, Mass.: Harvard University Press, 2000), who argue that recollection is "never more than the most plausible story we come up with (or, perhaps, only a story which is plausible enough) within the context of the constraints imposed by biology and history" (19).

13. See Chapter Ten.

we do not have complete control over our memories. Sometimes they simply pop into our minds without the involvement of our will in any significant way. At other times we deliberately store memories in our minds, from which we retrieve them in the work of recollection. Yet there are some memories that our minds refuse either to *commit* into storage or *retrieve* from it, no matter how hard we try. Remembering often happens *to* us rather than being done *by* us. As rememberers we are passive as well as active. Thus as our ability to *fulfill* the moral obligation to remember truthfully is limited, so that moral obligation is itself limited. Still, when we remember we ought to remember truthfully — as truthfully as we can.

Suppose that I am talking with friends about the 9/11 terrorist attacks. I tell them that I was in New York that very morning giving a lecture on reconciliation at a prayer breakfast held at the United Nations. I mention in passing that only minutes before the attacks I concluded by reciting Paul Celan's "Deathfugue," which speaks of "a grave in the air" where "you won't lie too cramped." One friend, who happened to have attended the breakfast, looks at me with mild disapproval and says, "No. Don't you remember!? You *started* your talk with that poem!" The untruth is just a simple case of incorrectly rendering a sequence of events. But my friend's intervention suggests that if I remember and relate what happened, I have a moral obligation toward others and myself — in this case a light moral obligation, to be sure! — to remember and relate what happened *truthfully.* I may not be culpable if I misremembered unintentionally; but I am responsible to remember correctly. The obligation to remember truthfully is just one dimension of the general obligation to tell the truth — biblically speaking, not to "bear false witness" (Exodus 20:16) and to "let your 'yes' be 'yes' and your 'no' be 'no'" (James 5:12) — as it applies to the past.

I can tell a fictional story, of course, or I can engage in the creative retelling of events designed to elicit laughter or make a point. In such instances, the obligation to tell the truth does not apply in the same way; for the intent is to entertain, not accurately inform. In contrast, when one wants to relate what happened in the past, "one unavoidably invokes the idea of a certain correspondence between the narrative and what really happened," as Paul Ricoeur put it.[14] Such correspondence is what distinguishes memory and history from imagination and fiction.

Granted, remembered correspondence is always a *re*construction that is "a different construction than the course of events reported."[15] But memory is properly reconstructive to the extent that it aims to reproduce. The reproductive aim of memory does not exclude the possibility that sometimes what really happened — not only the events themselves but also the emotions of the actors involved — can be best remembered by employing fiction. Recall the story the prophet Nathan told to King David. The king had just seen to it that a good man got killed in order to cover up his own adultery and take the man's wife into his royal harem. The prophet comes to David and tells him about a rich man who took from a poor man his only ewe lamb, which was "like a daughter to him," to prepare a feast for a guest. It is because this fictive story corresponded to David's personal history that Nathan could say, "You are the man!" after the anger of the unwittingly self-condemning king burned against the story's rich and greedy oppressor (2 Samuel 11:1–12:23). If I tell a story of what happened either in a realistic or fictional narrative, my construction must respect the original event and therefore always be, at the core, an attempt at a reconstructive reproduction.

In relation to the past, the narrator bears an "unpaid debt"; so Ricoeur correctly argued. He explained, "This idea of debt, which may seem strange at first, appears to me to emerge out of an expression common to the painter and to the historian: both seek to 'render' a landscape, a course of events. Under the term 'render' can be recognized the intention of 'rendering its due to what is and to what was.'"[16] Ricoeur introduced the notion of "debt" in relation to history, but it applies as well to memory, though in a somewhat different sense. When we remember, we bear the moral obligation to pay to others the debt of giving events their "due" by remembering them truthfully.

---

14. Paul Ricoeur, *The Reality of the Historical Past* (Milwaukee: Marquette University Press, 1984), 25-26.

15. Ibid., 26.

16. Ibid., 26-27.

Truthfulness as an Obligation of Justice

Our moral obligation to tell the truth is heightened if a story reflects *well or badly* on our own character or that of another person. Return with me to those reminiscences with my friends about the attacks of 9/11. Imagine if after the conversations on our way home, that same friend who corrected me about "Deathfugue" said to me, "Come on, that was no lecture you gave, and you know it! A two-minute reflection was all you did, and you quoted only the first line of Celan's poem about drinking 'black milk of daybreak.' You said nothing about a 'grave in the air.' You're inflating your part to puff yourself up." Or imagine that sitting with those same friends I had said, "After we were escorted out of the UN building as it was being evacuated, we went to the nearby offices of the organizers of the event. As we waited to leave the city, I suggested that we have water ready for pedestrians streaming out of Manhattan and, since we were clergy, offer to pray with those who were fleeing." But my friend remembered things rather differently. "Wait a second — you did no such a thing. It was *I* who suggested that we serve the crowds fleeing the city on foot."

Let's assume here that in both of the above cases my friend's account was accurate. Now his intervention would be more significant than his objection to my claim to have recited sections of "Deathfugue" at the end of my UN lecture. For now my reminiscences were unjustly bolstering my reputation. It matters whether I gave a lecture or offered just a few remarks, and whether I recited Celan's line about a "grave in the air"; it matters which one of us suggested serving the people fleeing the city. The memory of such events entails comparative judgments about my friend and me; therefore, my moral obligation to remember and retell what I remember truthfully — to give due credit both to others and to myself — is heightened. (And in case you're wondering, I did give a lecture at the UN that fateful day and did recite the contested lines before the first plane hit,[17] but I did not suggest serving the fleeing crowds; my friend did.)

17. For the text of the talk see http://www.christianembassyun.com/speech_by _dr__volf.htm.

The obligation to act justly by remembering truthfully is most acute in cases that involve *one party's violation of another.* Were the attacks of 9/11 acts of terror against innocent civilians (as I believe they were) or deserved punishment on corporate America for sucking the blood of the Muslim poor (as some Islamists claim)? In the first case, the men who crashed those four doomed planes would be justly blamed and appropriately called terrorists and vile evildoers. In the second case, the blame would mostly fall on American executives and their business partners, including those who were sent to their "grave in the air," and the men who caused the conflagrations would be viewed as heroic freedom fighters or soldiers in a just war. In such cases, truthfulness is absolutely crucial even if it will be strongly influenced by one's point of view.

Or return to the example of my interrogations: What if I fabricated the whole account of my interrogations by Captain G. because I needed a good personal story as an illustration in this book, or because I wanted to gain moral capital — in some circles, at least — by portraying myself as a victim of Yugoslavia's Communist regime? Then I would be accusing an innocent man of seriously wronging me. The same would be the case if I exaggerated the extent of his wrongdoing against me, say, by suggesting that he placed me in solitary confinement. Alternatively, I could remember untruthfully at my own expense, perhaps by minimizing the extent of the wrongdoing against me. In this case I would be failing to give due credit to myself, and unless I were doing so out of mature generosity aimed at forgiveness and reconciliation, I might harm myself in the process. For untruthful memories do not just fail to give due credit to the people and events remembered; they often *injure* those involved in the remembered activity.

So the obligation to truthfulness in remembering is at its root an obligation to do justice, even in such a seemingly simple act as the "naming" of what one person has done to another. If someone were to look into the records of my interrogations (which I have not done), my guess is that they would be described as "conversations." This is how I was occasionally summoned. "Captain G. wants you to come for a conversation," I would be told by a soldier or an officer sent to call me to a session of interrogations. The euphemism was designed to mask the injury about to be committed. Remembering my interrogations as "conversations," however, would be justifying the unjustifiable. That act of injustice would violate a basic moral obligation to truthfulness: doing justice.

A Step toward Reconciliation

But more than justice is threatened in remembering — or more accurately *retelling* — untruthfully. For when perpetrators "remember" untruthfully, their stories are a continuation of wrongful deeds in an altered form. They add the insult of misrepresentation to the injury of the original violation. And when victims "remember" untruthfully, their stories are often attacks on perpetrators in response to injuries suffered; they retaliate illicitly. To "remember" untruthfully is not only to continue but also to deepen in memory the conflict created by the initial injury. It is to add fuel to the fire of the already existing conflict. To remember truthfully, on the other hand, is to render justice both to the victim and to the perpetrator and therefore to take a step toward reconciliation.

Those who recognize the moral obligation to reconcile have, as a result, an additional reason for remembering truthfully. Above and beyond the fact that truthful remembering is a way to treat others justly, such remembering is an indispensable precondition of reconciliation between parties estranged by the transgression of one against the other. For peace can be honest and lasting only if it rests on the foundation of truth and justice.

Dangerous Truth?

Especially in academic circles in the field of the humanities, there is widespread resistance to the idea that we have a moral obligation to remember truthfully. Truth, it is said, is *dangerous*. Take the last examples we've discussed — conflicts on account of wrongdoing. In any of these cases, if both parties claim to know the *truth* of what transpired between them, but their "truths" clash, they will have all the more reason to cross swords.

As formulated, the objection seems on the whole correct. When "truths" clash, conflicts are exacerbated. Yet in its main thrust the objection rests on confusion. Notice that it concerns the *claim* of each party to *possess* the truth, not the *moral obligation* of both parties to *seek* the truth. The conflict is deepened not because truthfulness matters too much to one or both parties, but because it matters too little — so little, in fact, that they, as fallible human beings invariably tempted to pursue their own interests, can feel justified in simply *claiming* to possess the truth, the whole truth, and thus to forgo seeking it.

If I claim to possess the truth, I will be unlikely even to entertain the possibility that others may be right, or at least partly right, and I wrong, or at least partly wrong; unlikely to enter imaginatively into the world of others so as to learn to appreciate the force of their account of what happened; unlikely to take the road of inverted perspective so as to examine from their vantage point my memories as well as their own. In a phrase, I will be unlikely to exercise "double vision," which is essential to remembering truthfully in situations of conflict.[18] Claims to possess the uncontestable truth aren't always wrong, but they *are* always dangerous — especially dangerous when a person's *claim to possess* the truth matters more to her than the truth itself. But this takes us straight back to the moral obligation to remember truthfully. The obligation to remember truthfully, and therefore to seek the truth, counters the dangers involved in claims to possess the truth. Seekers of truth, as distinct from alleged possessors of truth, will employ "double vision" — they will give others the benefit of the doubt, they will inhabit imaginatively the world of others, and they will endeavor to view events in question from the perspective of others, not just their own.

Far from being dangerous, then, the moral obligation to truthfulness is salutary. What is positively dangerous is to give up the quest for truth about the past and instead to celebrate multiple, incompatible stories about the past, thus suggesting that no story corresponds more accurately to actual events than the other. Omer Bartov drew attention to

18. See Miroslav Volf, *Exclusion and Embrace* (Nashville: Abingdon, 1996), 212-20, 250-53.

Heinrich Himmler's infamous speech to the SS at Posen in 1943, in which Himmler lauded the project of exterminating the Jews as "a glorious page in our history which has never been written and which will never be written." Building partly on this telling comment, Bartov observed that efforts to come to terms with ambiguous reality by suggesting the multiplicity of equally valid perspectives "can play so easily into the hands of those who have no qualms about producing realities of the most horrific nature and then claiming that they had never taken place."[19] With no grip on the reality — the truth — of the past, accusatory and exculpatory stories end up getting the same weight. They neither confront perpetrators with the threat of exposure nor comfort victims with the promise of justice.

It is dangerous, I have said, to claim to possess the truth about the past, and it is dangerous to claim that all memories are equally valid in terms of their correspondence to actual events. The second danger is, moreover, greater than the first. For if there is no such thing as "*the* truth" about the past, and therefore, *a fortiori,* if there is no obligation to seek such truth, we are left only with clashing opinions and little hope for resolving them except through imposition (if one party has the overwhelming power) or compromise (if there is a rough parity of power). In either case, sooner or later rebellion is bound to ensue because one or both parties believe that falsehood substituted for truth, that justice was not done.

But if there *is* such a thing as "the truth" about the past, and if one party claims to possess it, yet without sufficient grounds, the possibility remains of questioning that claim and showing it to be mistaken or inadequate. In other words, the possibility of reform is built into the claim to possess the truth. So if I claim to possess the truth about the past, I must not summarily dismiss plausible claims that what I assert is the truth is in fact a half-truth or an untruth. Between the door of claims to truth and the room of truth itself lies the hallway — sometimes the maze — of plausibility and perspective. Entering that door and walking carefully through that maze toward the truth is salutary even if there are dangers to be avoided along the way.

19. Omer Bartov, "Intellectuals on Auschwitz: Memory, History, and Truth," *History and Memory* 5 (1993): 112.

Truthfully Remembering Wrongdoing

So far I have argued that the commitment to truthfulness is involved in the act of remembering, that we have a moral obligation to remember truthfully, and that seeking to remember truthfully is not dangerous but salutary (or at least more beneficial than remembering without seeking the truth), for truthfulness is a form of justice and an indispensable precondition of reconciliation. But is it practically *possible* for us to remember truthfully? I have already examined one side of this question, namely, whether memories in general can correspond in some sense to the reality of past events, and I have answered the question affirmatively. Indeed, strictly speaking, all remembering is truthful; we cannot remember what has not happened. But there is another side to the question — a more practical side that concerns specific kinds of memories. Granted that remembering truthfully is theoretically possible, can we as a matter of fact remember *wrongs suffered* in a truthful way?

When it comes to remembering wrongs, what often undermines the truth involves more than just inadequate perception, faulty retention, and incomplete understanding. Sometimes the sheer enormity of wrongdoing suffered overwhelms memory. I am not referring to cases of repression. Some victims remember every detail of their suffering and yet have a sense that their memory is failing. Primo Levi, a survivor of the death camp in Auschwitz, is a good example. He writes:

> Of my two years of life outside the law [the concentration camp] I have not forgotten a single thing. Without any deliberate effort, memory continues to restore to me events, faces, words, sensations, as if at that time my mind had gone through a period of exalted receptivity, during which not a detail was lost.[20]

---

20. Primo Levi, *Moments of Reprieve* (New York: Summit, 1986), 10-11. Other survivors of the Holocaust have made similar observations. See, for instance, Dori Laub, "Truth and Testimony: The Process and the Struggle," in *Trauma: Explorations in Memory*, ed. Cathy Caruth (Baltimore: Johns Hopkins University Press, 1995), 61-75.

And yet he believed that memory is a "fallacious instrument"[21] and that, in any case, it was not the few privileged survivors who could tell the truth about the concentration camps but instead the many ordinary people who were murdered.[22]

But memory may stumble even under a much less crushing burden than the atrocity of genocide, and stumble in worse ways than the ones Primo Levi might have had in mind. For example, resentment for humiliation endured may distort the memory even of a run-of-the-mill wrongdoing endured. The victim's imagination may then spin a tale of sinister malevolence or callous carelessness at work against him, when in fact the wrongdoing was simply the fallout of the perpetrator's own unsuccessful struggle against a personal weakness.

Or consider what a victim's memory might do when faced with a perpetrator editing the past so as to whitewash his crimes, even make them disappear. A victim will want to resist him; and so a battle of memories ensues. The perpetrator wants to minimize his wrongdoing and spread the blame; the victim wants the blame placed squarely on the perpetrator's shoulders. In the heat of battle, the perpetrator's blame grows in the victim's eyes beyond anything that is warranted by what actually happened. So the wrongdoer becomes both the perpetrator who truly deserves blame and the scapegoat who carries more blame than is his due. When it comes to remembering wrongs, the temptation of unfairness is never far off.

Remembering anything truthfully is a difficult task. We are finite be-

21. Primo Levi, *The Drowned and the Saved*, trans. Raymond Rosenthal (New York: Vintage International, 1989), 23.

22. Could even they? If the dead could speak, they could tell their own truths — truths about what transpired in their tortured bodies and souls and in their immediate environments. But their own experiences would remain insufficiently informed on account of the enormity of the evil that victimized them. Their suffering was part of a larger system of suffering situated in a particular land with a particular history and cannot be adequately understood unless the whole of which they are a part is adequately understood. And even if they could perceive adequately and remember truthfully, to whom could they communicate their memories successfully? Who would be able to hear their truth, and hear it *as* truth, without domesticating it within their own more limited horizons or misusing it for the pursuit of their own interests?

ings, always here and not at the same time there, always living in the present and not simultaneously in the past, present, and future; we know and remember from a particular vantage point, and the passage of time opens a gap into which unintentional untruthfulness about the past may slip in the form of distorted memories. It is particularly difficult for us to remember truthfully the wrongs we have suffered. For the bit of our memories' integrity that our finitude has left untainted, our moral weakness and at times even moral perversity threatens to finish off. We seem to be faced with the impossibility of truthfully remembering precisely that which is most important to remember truthfully: suffered wrongs. For to retell suffered wrongs untruthfully is to practice injustice and prepare the soil from which that practice will abundantly bear its bad fruit.

But we are morally obliged to remember them truthfully! So does this seemingly unfulfillable moral obligation mean that we are condemned to grope blindly in the vast regions of our wounded past — regions both terrifyingly luminous and impenetrably dark? Are all of our truth-seeking attempts futile? They are not. For we *can* and *do* remember some things, and remember them sufficiently truthfully, even if never fully. Even the scraps of memory are vital. They often comprise the only hold we have on the reality of the past. As an archaeologist does with shards of ancient pottery, we piece together bits of memory as we reconstruct events, and we do so not just as professional historians but also as ordinary people engaged in the everyday activity of remembering. Some of these reconstructions we deem impossible or unlikely; others we advocate as likely or even almost certain. Our scraps of recollection allow us to dignify the reconstructive work we do by giving it the noble name of memory rather than dismissing it as mere biased fabrication. Memories constructed from such scraps can help heal and protect our wounded psyches and serve as powerful tools in the effort toward justice and reconciliation.

Looking beyond the earthly limitations of memory, we can hope for more than piecing together scraps of recollection. Over the centuries Christians have believed that the day is coming on which our past, marred by wrongdoing, will be bathed in the warm light of God's truthful grace. I am referring to what has been traditionally called the Day of

Judgment. True, the Judge will be the just God, whose knowledge knows no limits and whose memory is as complete as it is unfailing. All wrongdoing will be remembered in its full import and condemned for what it is: injury of neighbor and sin against God. The Christian tradition identifies the Judge not simply as God, however, but as Jesus Christ — the one who bore the sin and pain of the world as he, the Innocent One, died on the tree of shame outside the gates of Jerusalem. He who knows our guilty and wounded past and has borne it himself will reveal all truth about that past. Even more. Through his judgment of grace, we will be freed from the inescapable injustice of the suppressions, lies, evasions, and half-truths in which we, as bearers of memories, are presently ensnared, our best efforts notwithstanding. Christ the Judge, who bore the sin of the world, will enable us truthfully and fully to remember our past, as well as the past of those whose lives were intertwined with ours on account of wrongdoing.

In the here and now, we can only provisionally discharge our obligation to remember truthfully. Our attempts are a fallible way of participating in God's truth-telling about our lives at the end of history, yet an indispensable one as well.

Speaking Truth in Love[23]

Christian theologians have consistently interpreted the prohibition in the Decalogue against bearing false witness — the ninth commandment — as ruling out all untruthful speech. In the words of Thomas Aquinas, in this commandment God forbids us "to injure him [i.e., our neighbor] by word."[24] Since untruthful memories (an oxymoron!) are a form of false witness, the prohibition encompasses the injuring of one's neighbor by "remembering" untruthfully. So far in this chapter, I have applied the

23. The section "Speaking Truth in Love" incorporates material from a text I co-authored with Linn Tonstad for *The Ten Commandments,* ed. Roger Van Harn (Grand Rapids: Eerdmans, forthcoming).

24. Thomas Aquinas, *God's Greatest Gifts: Commentaries on the Commandments and the Sacraments* (Manchester, N.H.: Sophia Institute Press, 1992), 65.

ninth commandment to the problem of memory by showing both why we have the moral obligation to remember truthfully and why it is possible for us to fulfill that obligation in a limited though important way.

Many Christian theologians view the prohibitions of the Decalogue as the negative side of implied positive injunctions. For Martin Luther, the father of the Protestant Reformation, the ninth commandment does not only prohibit false witness; it also urges us to speak *well* of our neighbors. What fulfills the ninth commandment, he insisted, is not just "a manner of speech which harms no one," but further, a manner of speech that "benefits everyone, reconciles the discordant, excuses and defends the maligned."[25] The way we talk about neighbors should be more than just formally true; it should also benefit them individually, as well as help repair and sustain bonds between them. This broadened interpretation of the prohibition against false witness is a consequence of Luther's belief that we should be concerned as much with our neighbors' interests as with our own. We fulfill the prohibition against bearing false witness when we love our neighbors (including our adversaries) as ourselves by speaking well of them.

Apply now this positive implication of the ninth commandment to the question of the memory of wrongs. Though truthful memory is vitally important in its own right, remembering truthfully is part of the larger obligation to speak well of our neighbors and thereby to sustain and heal relationships between people. But how do we speak well of wrongdoers truthfully? Isn't the injunction to do so a self-contradiction that requires us in one breath to name a wrong as wrong and to praise its perpetrator?

Perhaps so. But then again, there is more than one way to tell the story of a wrongdoing. For example, in remembering we could isolate the wrongdoing without situating it in the context of the perpetrator's overall character and deeds. Such remembering would not be strictly untruthful. But it would be unloving. It would mislead people to believe that the perpetrator is a worse person than he actually is. A memory that

25. Martin Luther, *Luther's Works*, vol. 43, ed. Harold J. Grimm (Philadelphia: Fortress, 1957), 23.

is formally true would, because of its incompleteness, be also untrue. Those who love do not remember a person's evil deeds without also remembering her good deeds; they do not remember a person's vices without also being mindful of her virtues. Similarly, those who love do not remember a perpetrator's wrongdoing without also being mindful of their own failings (see Galatians 6:1-2). Thus the full story of wrongdoing becomes clear through the voice of love, that is, when we speak "the truth in love" (Ephesians 4:15).

In explaining what it means to speak well of a neighbor, Luther took one more radical step. He urged that a person "cover up" his or her "neighbor's sins and infirmities."[26] The instruction to "cover" the sins of our neighbors is based on the statement by the Apostle Peter that "love covers a multitude of sins" (1 Peter 4:8); yet it is rooted in the belief that we should love our neighbors not simply as we love ourselves, but love them as Christ, who laid down his life for our salvation, has loved us. We are to be "Christs" to our neighbors, believed Luther, by covering their sins in a way that reflects Christ's covering of our sins by means of his atoning death. But what could "covering" our neighbors' wrongdoing mean? Certainly not whitewashing it, for doing so would obscure the truth! Instead, after their sins have been confessed, condemned, and forgiven — *if* they have been confessed, condemned, and forgiven! — they should be "hidden," "covered," "dispersed," that is, "forgotten" out of love toward the forgiven transgressor.

In the meantime, what bearing does the injunction to "forget" forgiven sins have on remembering wrongs suffered? For starters, to "cover" or "forget" wrongs, we must remember them in the first place! And as we have already seen, we must remember them truthfully. But truthful memory does not have to be indelible memory. The purpose of truthful memory is not simply to name acts of injustice, and certainly not to hold

26. Luther, *Large Catechism* [electronic resource], trans. F. Bente and W. H. T. Dau (Grand Rapids: Christian Classics Ethereal Library/Boulder: NetLibrary, 1921). On multiple ways to "hide" sins, see Søren Kierkegaard, *Works of Love*, trans. Howard V. Hong and Edna H. Hong (Princeton: Princeton University Press, 1995), 280-89; idem, *Eighteen Upbuilding Discourses*, trans. Howard V. Hong and Edna H. Hong (Princeton: Princeton University Press, 1990), 55-78.

an unalterable past forever fixed in the forefront of a person's mind. Instead, the highest aim of lovingly truthful memory seeks to bring about the repentance, forgiveness, and transformation of wrongdoers, and reconciliation between wrongdoers and their victims. When these goals are achieved, memory can let go of offenses without ceasing to be truthful.[27] For then remembering truthfully will have reached its ultimate goal in the unhindered love of neighbor.

27. See Part Three.

CHAPTER FOUR

Wounded Self, Healed Memories

How should we redeem morally ambiguous memories of wrongs suffered? This is the question that guided my discussion of remembering truthfully in the previous chapter. Truthfulness, I argued, is important because it gives the events and people involved in them due credit, whereas untruthfulness does them injustice and may lead to practicing further injustice. "Remember truthfully!" is the first rule of salutary remembering. I also suggested that the rule has two aspects, one negative and one positive. In its negative aspect — "Don't speak falsely about the past!" — the rule provides an indispensable presupposition for employing memories as a shield rather than wielding them as a sword. In its positive aspect — "Speak lovingly the truth about the past!" — the rule supplies tools for remembering that repair relationships cracked or broken on account of wrongdoing.

Some people might think that the rule "Remember truthfully!" is all that needs to be said about the redemption of memories. What else could redeeming them mean but purging them from untruthfulness and turning them into tools for doing justice and showing grace? Truthful memories *are* redeemed memories, the argument could conclude. More would be needed, of course, to redeem a *past wrongdoing itself,* as distinct from the memory of it. From a Christian standpoint, both the wrongdoers and the wronged would need to appropriate in faith the reconciliation God has brought about in Christ and echo it in relationships with each other, while hoping for the Day of Light, when their reconciliation will be complete.[1] The wrongdoers would need to accept the consequences of their misdeeds, repent, restore as far as possible what their violation has taken from their victims, and mend their ways; the wronged would need to nurse their wounds and restore a measure of wholeness to their self, forgive those who have offended them, and seek to mend broken relationships with their offenders. All these steps would be essential for the redemption of the past wrongdoing, and each would require that the wrongdoing be remembered truthfully; but none would redeem specifically the *memory* of it. They wouldn't need to, so long as the memory was truthful and therefore already redeemed.

The argument seems persuasive, and yet it is faulty. It assumes that the cognitive side of memories — the fact that they are a form of knowing — is alone relevant. Consequently, the important issue is whether memories are true or false. But memories are also a *form of doing*, not just a form of knowing. They have a pragmatic side. In the attempt to blunt the blade of aggressive memories and stay the hand that wields them as a sword, we must examine their pragmatic side as it affects individuals as well as their relationships with other people. But first we need to say a bit more about the relationship between the cognitive and pragmatic sides of memories.

What Memories Know and Do

In his magisterial book *Memory, History, Forgetting*, Paul Ricoeur noted that we remember in two clearly distinct though closely intertwined ways. One way is passive. As noted in Chapter Three, sometimes remembering just happens to us. Memories get stored in appropriate "cham-

---

1. On human forgiving as echoing that of God, see Miroslav Volf, *Free of Charge: Giving and Forgiving in a Culture Stripped of Grace* (Grand Rapids: Zondervan, 2005).

bers" of our minds and occasionally pop into our consciousness, perhaps because of a trigger but with no intentional effort. The second way in which we remember is active. We intentionally store what we want to remember, and when the need arises, a particular memory becomes "an object of a search ordinarily named recall, recollection."[2] Remembering is now a matter of doing something rather than simply being affected. Consider the remembering of phone numbers, for example. Before the advent of cell phones with computerized contact lists and automatic dialing capacities, we habitually committed phone numbers to memory. We recalled them to contact various people or, in less humble instances, to demonstrate our impressive capacity to remember. We didn't memorize phone numbers just for the sake of remembering. So it is with most of what we remember, even if sometimes seemingly arbitrary thoughts get stuck in our memory, such as annoying tunes that we can't get out of our head.

Use is so much a part of memory in general that some scholars propose to define memory as "the ability to store useful information and to retrieve it in precisely those circumstances and that form which allows it to be useful."[3] If this is correct, then it is not quite accurate to say that we *add* use to the process of remembering. Remembering is tied to use from the get-go (even if, once we have remembered something, we can aimlessly play with the memory without using it as a means to a particular end).

Though use is integral to all remembering, it is particularly important in cases involving the memory of wrongs. For whether we remember as passive receivers or active pursuers of memories, *what* we remember often deeply affects what we *do*. If we are concerned primarily with *ourselves* as we remember wrongs suffered, we may remember in order to avoid getting into similarly injurious situations again; try to restore some measure of inner well-being disturbed by the traumatic event; ad-

2. Paul Ricoeur, *Memory, History, Forgetting,* trans. Kathleen Blamey and David Pellauer (Chicago: University of Chicago Press, 2004), 4.

3. Chris Westbury and Daniel C. Dennett, "Mining the Past to Construct the Future: Memory and Belief as Forms of Knowledge," in *Memory, Brain, and Belief,* ed. Daniel L. Schacter and Elaine Scarry (Cambridge, Mass.: Harvard University Press, 2000), 14.

just our expectations about the future; gain moral capital or draw economic and political advantage as victims; or withdraw into ourselves and nurse our wounds. If we are concerned primarily with *offenders* as we remember wrongs suffered, we may remember in order to exact revenge on culprits and keep them shamed, guilt-ridden, morally inferior, politically controllable, or economically exploitable. Or, if we are inclined to show grace to the offenders, we may remember so as to forgive their misdeeds, so as to release them from guilt and shame and from the just consequences of their actions. We have seen all these elements in the responses of people around the world remembering the terrorist attacks of 9/11, for example.

Almost equally significantly, as we use the memory of wrongs suffered for these and other purposes, we keep reconfiguring our identity. Whatever we do with our memories, our identity shifts, however slightly, in the process of using them. Again with reference to 9/11 as an example, many Americans have changed the way they perceive themselves because of how they remember the disaster, especially the motives and broader goals of the attackers and the responses of the world's population at large. In their minds, self assurance has given way to a sense of vulnerability, and a nation enjoying blessings of peace has become a nation at war. So in short, we don't just remember suffered wrongs; we *use* our memories of them.

Now consider memories of wrongs in their passive form — memories that happen to us, rather than memories that we actively pursue. For not only do *we act on* memories of wrongs suffered; these memories *act on us,* too. They steal our attention, and they assault us with inner turmoil marked by shame, guilt, and maybe a mixture of self-recrimination and self-justification. They envelop us in dark mists of melancholy, they hold us back so that we cannot project ourselves into the future and embark on new paths. They chain our identity to the injuries we have suffered and shape the way we react to others. Such memories are not just clusters of information about the past — not even clusters of information stored for future use. They themselves are powerful agents.

The dual potential of memories of wrongs for good and for ill — the starting point of this study — stems chiefly from their pragmatic rather than their cognitive side. That holds true whether we act on memories or they act on us.

Truthfulness and Use

We bear an obligation to remember truthfully wrongs that we have suffered, I argued in the previous chapter. So how does truthfulness relate to the use and abuse of memories? Recall, first, that distorted and false memories are unjust and injurious memories. Even when they are not employed to legitimize injustice (which often they are employed to do), to remember wrongs untruthfully is to act unjustly. Remembering untruthfully *constitutes* a misuse of memories. Inversely, truthful memories of wrongs suffered are just memories; they render due credit to both the wrongdoer and the wronged. To remember wrongs truthfully is to act justly. So simply by remembering wrongs suffered, we are already using them. We use such memories rightly if we remember truthfully; we misuse them if we remember untruthfully. Put more technically, the cognitive side of such memories has itself a pragmatic dimension.

The use of memories of wrongs is related to their truthfulness in one more way: the use of memory exerts pressure on *which* memories of wrongs we are willing to consider truthful, just as the memories of wrongs we consider truthful place constraints on the uses to which we can put them. Consider the impact of intended use on truthfulness. Freudian psychoanalysis presupposes the human tendency to suppress memories of what is unpleasant, such as events that caused excessive suffering or one's own morally reprehensible acts. The technical term for this propensity is "repression." But whether or not psychoanalysis is correct about repression, such convenient "forgetfulness" is at work not only in regard to events that cause neuroses or traumas; it is also a much more general occurrence, part of normal human functioning. By distorting memories of wrongs committed or suffered, we insulate ourselves from unpleasant truths about ourselves. Friedrich Nietzsche put the issue unforgettably in his well-known aphorism from *Beyond Good and Evil:* "'I have done that,' says my memory. 'I cannot have done that,' says my pride, and remains inexorable. Eventually, memory yields."[4] In most cases, memory does not yield in the radical sense of disappearing from consciousness. Instead, it gets distorted. Our minds latch onto an embellished version of the repugnant events so that we will not be shamed or plagued by guilt when we see ourselves in the mirror of memory.

Nietzsche's aphorism also implies the inverse: truthfulness about memories of wrongs suffered constrains their use. Otherwise, why would pride have to prod memory to yield? Months prior to my interrogations, a fellow soldier served as a catalyst to make me talk into a hidden microphone about forbidden subjects that would expose my supposedly subversive political and religious views. Imagine for a moment that this soldier was a longtime friend of mine (which he was not) and that I had contributed to his willingness to betray me by a lengthy history of exploiting our friendship for my own gain. If I accept the (hypothetical) truth of my own repeated transgressions against him, I will presumably be less inclined to use the memory of his betrayal to bolster my moral superiority, let alone to justify revenge against him; my truthful memory will tell me that I am no better than he is. So truthfulness places constraints on at least some injurious uses of memories. Indeed, it is *because* truthfulness constrains the uses to which memories can be put that an intention to misuse memories exerts pressure to play loose with truthfulness.

So far we have made two observations about the relationship between truthfulness and the use of memories: truthfulness constitutes a just use of memories, and it constrains their misuse. Truthfulness is also an important element of inner healing — of learning how to live with the past without its wounds being kept open by the blade of memory.

4. Friedrich Nietzsche, *Beyond Good and Evil: Prelude to a Philosophy of Future,* in *Basic Writings of Nietzsche,* trans. and ed. Walter Kaufmann (New York: Modern Library, 1968), #68. The Apostle Paul was familiar with the phenomenon when he noted that people tend to "suppress truth with ungodliness" (Romans 1:18).

Truthfulness and Healing

In the previous two chapters I have suggested that memories which deeply trouble us must pass through the narrow gate of truth to become memories which allow us to live at peace with ourselves.[5] No doubt we can achieve a sense of well-being — we can be "happy," as we like to put it — while simply leaving the truth about the past behind us. In the extreme, such "happiness" rests on a sovereign unconcern about the past in which memory gives way to obliviousness. Friedrich Nietzsche proposed that to be truly happy requires some such disregard of the past accompanied by deep immersion in the present. For him, the child is a symbol of happiness undisturbed by the burdens of the past. "Not yet having a past to disown," writes Nietzsche, a child "plays in blissful blindness between the fences of the past and the future." The image of the child moves us, he continues, "as though it were the vision of a lost paradise."[6]

Let us assume that Nietzsche is correct about a child's relation to the past. Can those beyond, say, toddlerhood enjoy such an unencumbered embrace of the present, however? Even if as adults we could remain blissfully unaware of the past and future, would it be desirable to do so? Complete immersion in the present might produce happiness — that is, if our present circumstances were happy ones — but our lives would be shallow, not to mention downright dangerous. Imagine chasing a stray ball across a busy highway without looking for oncoming cars because you "blissfully" ignore your knowledge about automobile accidents and fail to consider your mortality! Assuming we could survive, however, our lives would lose depth and richness for lack of memory and hope to

---

5. This in no way presumes that psychotherapeutic techniques such as psychoanalysis and psychodynamic theory, in which exploration of past trauma is critical to healing, are more effective in helping patients find wholeness than are cognitive behavioral approaches, which dwell exclusively in the present. Dealing with the past is only one part of personal healing.

6. Friedrich Nietzsche, "On the Utility and Liability of History for Life," in *Unfashionable Observations,* trans. Richard T. Gray (Stanford: Stanford University Press, 1995), 88.

bring the past and future into the present. For the way we experience time is similar to the way we hear a sound from a good stringed instrument. When we hear a sound from a good cello, for example, we don't hear a tone produced only by the base length of the string — co-present in that sound are tones from the string's half-length, fourth-length, eighth-length, etc. This is how a stringed instrument produces a complex tone. It is similar with the music of our lives. At any given time, we do not hear only the simple, solitary tone of the present; rather, in that present resonate many sounds of past actualities and future possibilities. This is how our present acquires depth.

If it would be a mistake to try to play in blissful oblivion between the fences of the past and future, what should we do with the burdens of the past? The answer: the past must be redeemed, for redemption of the past is one aspect of the Christian vision of salvation. The critical question is, however, whether we should strive to redeem the past by ignoring the questions of truth and of justice, as Nietzsche maintained. We should not. To do so would be to float blissfully above reality in the bubble of untruth about ourselves and unconcern for those who have wronged us. Sooner or later, the bubble would brush against the rough edges of reality, and its thin, rainbow-colored surface would abruptly pop. Depending on whether or not relationships with others mattered to us, our childlike happiness, undisturbed by the burdens of the past, would then either sink into deep melancholy or morph into callous indifference. With the past simply tossed into the trashbin of "blissful" oblivion rather than redeemed, our happiness would be both false and unstable.

Rarely do we simply disregard wrongs suffered, however. If we would rather not face their truth, we are more likely to distort them and maybe occasionally repress them. But neither repression nor distortion lead to genuine healing. Repressed memory does not simply disappear into the night of forgetfulness. If the advocates of the phenomenon of repressed memory are correct,[7] it is stored in subconscious memory, where it leads

---

7. See Bessel A. van der Kolk and Alexander C. McFarlane, "The Black Hole of Trauma," in *Traumatic Stress: The Effects of Overwhelming Experience on Mind, Body, and Society,* ed. Bessel van der Kolk et al. (New York: Guilford Press, 1996), 3-23.

a secret life that interferes with healthy functioning. Personality effects from these insurgents of subconsciousness run the gamut from a general numbing of responsiveness, to alterations of personal identity, to urges to reenact trauma as either victimizer or victim. In most cases by far, however, we *remember* mistreatment rather than repressing it.[8] But in memory we distort it, mostly giving its intolerable content a more acceptable form. Here too, however, the unacknowledged truth about our past will threaten the delicate bubble of false peace protecting our pleasant distortions and convenient lies.

In an essay titled "Trauma and Experience," Cathy Caruth notes that it is the "truth of traumatic experience that forms the center of its pathology or symptoms"; "it is not a pathology . . . of falsehood or displacement of meaning, but of history itself," Caruth continues.[9] If she is correct, then no genuine and complete healing will take place if the truth about the traumatic event doesn't dwell at least for a while in the chamber of memory. It will not do to relegate the search for truth to the courtroom but encourage unconstrained playfulness with the narrative of suffered wrongdoing in the therapist's office. This is the advice Susan Brison gives in her otherwise fine book *Aftermath*. In the courtroom, she suggests, you must keep a trauma narrative "straight" in order to get justice; in the therapist's office, however, you should play "with the past" and "rewrite it in a different way" "in order not to be held back" as you "spring away from it."[10] But if it is the truth of traumatic experience that forms the center of its pathology, how can the circumvention of truth bring healing?

Would "rewriting in a different way" the story of my interrogations truly help me to heal (quite apart from the likelihood that it would be an act of injustice toward my interrogators,[11] even if the "rewriting" re-

---

8. For a compelling critique see Richard J. McNally, *Remembering Trauma* (Cambridge, Mass.: Harvard University Press, 2003). Cf. Frederick C. Crews, "The Trauma Trap," *The New York Review of Books* 51, no. 4 (2004): 37-40.

9. Cathy Caruth, "Trauma and Experience: Introduction," in *Trauma: Explorations in Memory*, ed. Cathy Caruth (Baltimore: Johns Hopkins University Press, 1995), 5.

10. So Susan J. Brison, *Aftermath: Violence and the Remaking of the Self* (Princeton: Princeton University Press, 2002), 103.

11. See Chapter Three.

mained confined to the privacy of my mind and/or the therapist's office)? If I need to spin for myself a tale of what did not happen so as to "spring away" from what did happen, has not the past remained an untamed beast? Won't I instead be genuinely healed when I can move freely through life with a sense of peace about what in fact *did* happen — and when, with that same sense of peace about what happened, I can let it fade from my memory? Indeed so! For only *truthful* memories give access to the event with which peace needs to be made. Rewritten memories insulate from the event and make continued inner turmoil their likely outcome. They are not a means of genuine healing but a symptom of persisting disease and a method of coping — two sides of one corroded coin. We will have taken an important step toward healing when we neither fear to face the wound of wrongdoing in memory nor feel compelled to keep returning to it, even if in a rewritten form.

It takes knowing the truth to be set free from the psychic injury caused by wrongdoing. Christian tradition has always insisted on this tenet in relation to guilt — objective guilt, that is, not the mere feeling of guilt, appropriate or not. Freedom from guilt requires that the light of truth shine into the dark corners of our lives, whether in this life through uncoerced confession, private or public, or at the doorway to eternity during God's final judgment. The same is true in regard to the wounds caused by wrongdoing. We must name the troubling past truthfully — we must come to clarity about what happened, how we reacted to it, and how we are reacting to it now — to be freed from its destructive hold on our lives. Granted, truthful naming will not by itself heal memories of wrongs suffered; but without truthful naming, all measures we might undertake to heal such memories will remain incomplete.

But how is it possible to remember truthfully when distortions of memories are a deep wound's most frequent manifestation? As Cathy Caruth puts it, the traumatized "carry an impossible history within them,"[12] a history the truth about which is often too difficult to bear, since truthful memories echo the ripping that created the original wound. In Kaja Silverman's words, they "provide the disembodied

---

12. Caruth, "Trauma and Experience: Introduction," 5.

'wound' with a psychic residence."[13] How can we blunt the wounding blade of painful memories without sacrificing their truthfulness?

To answer this question we need to explore other elements of inner healing. Much may need to happen *outside* a person who has been seriously wronged before she may be able to achieve inner healing. Friends, family, or the public at large may need to acknowledge and condemn the wrongdoing; the offender may need to apologize and, if possible, offer restitution; the setting that made the injury possible may need to change so that the wronged person can feel safe; and more. Other requirements for inner healing must happen *inside* the wronged person. She will need to develop a sense that the wrongdoing has not closed off her horizon of future possibilities, that it does not exhaustively define her identity, and that her life continues to have meaning notwithstanding the wrongdoing, possibly even partly because of it. In the following pages, I will explore the three last-mentioned requirements for inner healing as they bear on the healing of memories — more specifically, on the ability to remember a wrongdoing truthfully without being either tormented or in some way damaged by memories.

Integration

One important way in which we achieve inner healing is by integrating remembered wrongdoing into our life-story. But what does it mean to "integrate" in this regard?

First, we integrate events into our life-story by giving them positive *meaning* within that story.[14] We may come to believe that through the violation we have gained important insights that otherwise would have remained hidden from us. Perhaps, for example, I might conclude that my interrogations have helped me identify with people similarly reduced to

13. Kaja Silverman, *The Threshold of the Visible World* (New York: Routledge, 1996), 189.

14. Psychiatrists who use psychotherapeutic techniques argue that giving meaning is "a central goal of therapy." Van der Kolk and McFarlane, "The Black Hole of Trauma," 19.

utter powerlessness. Or an ordeal may have taught us important lessons about humanity, as, for example, when we view survival in extreme adversity as a testimony to the indomitable human spirit. Or again, we may have grown closer to God through a trying event — perhaps the experiencing of intense pain, which leads us to identify in a deeper way with the Crucified Christ.[15] In these and other ways, we render the wrongdoings endured meaningful for us. We integrate them into our life-story by coming to understand how they contribute to the goodness of the whole. We perceive that, in one way or another, they have made us better people.

But what about *horrendous* wrongs? Can *they* be meaningful for us? To use Dostoyevsky's famous example, can a mother's experience of having to watch her own four-year-old child be thrown to devouring dogs be meaningful as part of that mother's life-story?[16] Like a disfigured foot too misshapen for a shoe, such events resist taking on positive meaning. Any positive meaning we might lend to them seems to rob them of their overwhelming horrendousness. The best we can do toward integrating such terrible wrongs into our life-story is to *label* them as senseless segments of our life-story. Once labeled, memories of horrendous wrongs are no longer loose beasts wreaking havoc in our inner being and external relationships; they are locked up in the basement of our mind. Though the imprisoned beasts may stomp and shriek, we can live in the rest of the house unthreatened.

As we remember such labeled wrongs, are we doomed, in the famous words of Maurice Blanchot, to keep "watch over absent meaning"?[17] Yes, we will keep watch over absent meaning, if for no other rea-

---

15. On this last way of reading suffering, see Marilyn McCord Adams, *Horrendous Evils and the Goodness of God* (Ithaca, N.Y.: Cornell University Press, 1999), 156-80.

16. Dostoyevsky uses the example when discussing the question of whether God can ever be justified in the face of overwhelming evil, a question related to that of giving events positive meaning but not identical with it. See *The Brothers Karamazov*, trans. Richard Pevear and Larissa Volokhonsky (New York: Farrar, Straus and Giroux, 1990), 242-43.

17. Maurice Blanchot, *The Writing of the Disaster* (Lincoln: University of Nebraska Press, 1986), 42.

son than to ensure that in our search for consolation we do not reach for cheap meaning that falsifies the wrongdoing suffered. But how can we keep this watch in hope rather than despair? First, if we accept the basic Christian convictions I have sketched in Chapter Three, we may hope that even the meaninglessness of horrendous wrongs cannot ultimately shatter the wholeness of our lives. Even if some segments of our lives remain irredeemable, we ourselves can and will be redeemed.[18]

Second, as we watch over absent meaning we can hope that the meaning of at least some horrendous wrongs for our lives will be revealed at the end of history, after our lives and the whole of history have run their courses and after we have been securely shielded from all evil in God's new world. But this is a hope for the future disclosure of meaning, not the present ascription of it. Such hope helps in the healing of memories, but it does not complete it.

In a sense, every time we ascribe positive meaning to wrongs suffered, we do so in hope. To be sure, our judgments on how such events contribute to some good are always provisional. For tomorrow may reveal insights about yesterday that are hidden from us today; and we can understand any given event adequately only from the perspective of the whole, which is to say when our lives and history have run their courses. Still, the endeavor of giving meaning to some wrongs endured and labeling others as segments of our life's journey gone awry is borne on the wings of hope — hope for full disclosure of the now incomplete meaning of some wrongs, and for ultimate redemption from others in the face of their apparent meaninglessness.

New Identity

For the healing of painful memories, however, faith in Christ offers even more than hope for life's wholeness and ultimate meaning. In his fine book *Imagining Redemption,* David Kelsey has pursued a very simple question: What earthly difference does Jesus make? Two of his answers

18. See Chapter Nine.

are relevant for the healing of memories: Jesus Christ gives new identity and opens new possibilities.

Consider first the *new identity* conferred by Christ on the wronged person. The greater the wrong suffered, the more it gets ingrained into the identity of the person who endured it. Such a person sometimes comes to view himself — and others also come to view him — primarily as a sufferer of that particular wrong, for example, as "a survivor of the Rwandan genocide" or as the "one who has been betrayed." It is as though the wrong suffered is the most defining event of his life — an event that trumps creative accomplishments, friendships, joyful events, whether old or new, and all else. When wrongdoing defines us, we take on "distorted identities, frozen in time and closed to growth,"[19] in Kelsey's words. In less severe cases, the wrongdoing may not define us fully; yet it lodges in our core self and casts a dark shadow on everything we think and do.

Christians believe, however, that neither what we do nor what we suffer defines us at the deepest level. Though the way we think of and treat ourselves and the way others think of and treat us does shape our identity, no human being can make or unmake us. Instead of being defined by how human beings relate to us, we are defined by how *God* relates to us. We know that fundamentally we are who we are, as unique individuals standing in relation to our neighbors and broader culture, because God loves us — to such a great extent that on the cross Jesus Christ, God incarnate, shouldered our sin and tasted our suffering.

Even more, by opening ourselves to God's love through faith, our bodies and souls become sanctified spaces, God's "temples," as the Apostle Paul puts it (1 Corinthians 6:19). The flame of God's presence, which gives us new identity, then burns in us inextinguishably. Though like buildings devastated by wind and flood, our bodies and souls may become ravaged, yet we continue to be God's temple — at times a temple in ruins, but sacred space nonetheless. Absolutely nothing defines a Christian more than the abiding flame of God's presence, and that flame bathes in a warm glow everything we do or suffer.

19. David Kelsey, *Imagining Redemption* (Louisville: Westminster John Knox, 2005), 60.

This new identity — not humanly acquired but divinely bestowed, even in the midst of our ruin — helps to heal wounded selves. We remember wrongs suffered as people with identities defined by God, not by wrongdoers' evil deeds and their echo in our memory. True, sometimes that echo is so powerful that it drowns out all other voices. Still, behind the unbearable noise of wrongdoing suffered, we can hear in faith the divinely composed music of our true identity. When this happens, memories of mistreatment lose much of their defining power. They have been dislodged from the place they have usurped at the center of the self and pushed to its periphery. They may live in us, but they no longer occupy us; they may cause pain, but they no longer exhaustively define. We are more than what we have suffered, and that is the reason we can do something with our memory of it — integrate it into our life-story, turn it into a junction from which we set out on new paths, for instance. And because we are more than what we have suffered, we may be able to embark, maybe at first haltingly, upon a journey of reconciliation with those who have wounded us.

Early on in my experience of military interrogations, I was greatly tempted to see myself at least partially as a victim, as an "interrogated-and-threatened" human being. Back then, some twenty-plus years ago, I would never have put things quite that way. But the wrongdoing tended to occupy a good deal of my interior space. And yet, since I knew myself as a person loved and indwelled by God, the memory of wrongdoing that gripped my life in such tenacious ways never reached the core of my being so as to govern my self-perception and thus define me. True, God's presence and love did not erase the memory of the wrong that I suffered; it still projected itself into the present through the gate of memory. But rather than enveloping me, it was eventually relegated to the periphery of my life. There were other factors that guarded my "center" against memories of the wrong I endured — factors such as the mere passage of time, living in a social environment in which human rights matter, and belonging to a community of faith. But these aids helped heal my memories because my identity in Christ served as a skeleton to which they could cling.

With the defining power of memories of wrongs now demonstrably broken, we need to revisit the first step in the healing of these memories:

integrating them into our life-story, either by labeling them as patches of absent meaning in the quilt of our life or by coming to see how they fit into its whole and contribute to some good. With a new identity in the center of that quilt, wrongdoings suffered are relegated to its periphery; they do not dominate the whole. Indeed, it is precisely because the memories of wrong endured do not dwell at the core of our identity that we can be effective in the healing task of integrating them into our life-story. And as we will see in Chapter Six, it is because memories of wrongs do not define us that we can remember not just as those who have been wounded but as those who are committed to loving the wrongdoer and seeking reconciliation.

New Possibilities

In addition to new identity, Christ also offers *new possibilities,* argues David Kelsey. Grievous wrongdoing doesn't just wound the body and soul, and it doesn't just worm its way into our identity. It also entraps us. Like a ball chained to a prisoner's leg, it drags heavily on our spirit and prevents it from roaming freely, stretching itself into the unknown, playing with new possibilities, imagining alternative futures. Susan Brison describes with deep insight how a wrongdoing endured robs a person of the future. "The past," she writes, "reaches toward the present and throttles desire before it can become directed toward the future."[20] As a victim of rape and near murder, she writes specifically of erotic desire. But other desires of those who have been seriously mistreated also have a hard time directing themselves to the future. Wrongdoing suffered makes us see what's behind us even when we look straight ahead. Memory metastasizes into the territory of the future, and the future, drained of new possibilities, mutates into an extension of the painful past.

20. Brison, *Aftermath,* 96. Distinguishing between postmemory (the usual sense of memory, according to which what we remember comes after the event) from prememory (memory of the past that projects itself into the future), she writes in a similar vein: "The backward-looking postmemory of rape thus, at every moment, turns into the forward-looking prememory of a feared future that someday *will have been*" (88).

In the Christian view of life, however, future possibilities do not grow simply out of the actuality of the past and present. As Jürgen Moltmann has powerfully argued in *Theology of Hope*, instead of arising simply from what was or what is, the future comes from the realm of what is not yet, "from outside" — from God. God's promise engenders new possibilities.[21] To a childless couple God says: "Your wife Sarah shall have a son" (Genesis 18:10). And from then on, the hopelessness of infertile bodies that have for years refused to produce offspring no longer defines the future of Abraham and Sarah. God's promise does. It is not that Sarah, who mocked, now never doubts; rather, though doubt may grip her, she continues to stretch out to the possibility opened by the promise. And so it is with all of us children of Abraham and Sarah.

Even more definitively, in Jesus Christ God has promised to every human being a new horizon of possibilities — a new life into which each of us is called to grow in our own way and ultimately a new world freed from all enmity, a world of love. To be a Christian means that new possibilities are defined by that promise, not by any past experience, however devastating. If the traumatized believe the promise — if they live *into* the promise, even if they are tempted at first to mock it — they will, in Kelsey's words, enter a world "marked by a genuinely open future that they could not have imagined in the living death of the old world they have constructed for themselves."[22]

When Christ's promise defines our possibilities, memories of the traumatic past become for us just that — memories of one segment of our past. They need not colonize the present nor invade the future by defining what we can do and become. Past wrongdoing suffered can be localized on the timeline of our life-story and stopped from spilling forward into the present and future to flood the whole of our life.

Unlike the sufferings of many, my mistreatment in interrogations was not of sufficient magnitude for their memory to rule my present completely or define my future. But as an encounter with the world of brutality, on occasion the experience threatened to push me into dark al-

21. Jürgen Moltmann, *Theology of Hope* (Minneapolis: Fortress, 1993).
22. Kelsey, *Imagining Redemption*, 39.

leys in which force is the only possible response to evil; the mistreatment seemed to close the door to a future defined by justice, let alone love and forgiveness. Yet when I viewed my interrogations in the light of God's promise in the death and resurrection of Christ, my memory of them became just that — a memory of a past occurrence with limited relevance for the possibilities in my future. It was a witness to the past, not a preview of the way the future must be. For in the light of Christ's self-sacrifice and resurrection, the future belongs to those who give themselves in love, not to those who nail others to a cross.

Again, my belonging to a community in which I was free from the fear of being suddenly summoned to interrogations helped a great deal in keeping my memory of them from dominating my present and my future. But what helped even more was the word of divine promise. For that word assured me that even if I were again to live in such a world, the horizon of my possibilities would not become dark. Even then, I could count on the future reality of a radically different world.

Afraid of not having hope — possibilities.

Memory, Self, and Others

Let's assume that we have truthfully remembered a wrong suffered, that we have integrated its memory into our life-story, that it has been dislodged from the center of our identity and assigned a proper place on its periphery, and that its hold over how we live in the present and how we project ourselves into the future has been broken. All this work has gone far in stifling the painful memory's ill effects on our own self. But we also use memory in relation to *others*.

These two uses of memory are intertwined. We cannot experience full internal healing from a wrongdoing suffered without "healing" the relationship with the wrongdoer. After all, it is in the relationship that we have been wounded. A physical wound will heal without the involvement of the person who inflicted it, for the body of the victim is a spatially distinct, individual entity and not intertwined with the body of the one who has injured it. The self, however, is always a social self, and a wrongdoing intertwines the wrongdoer and the wronged as little else

83

does. For the mistreatment consists not just in the pain or loss endured, but also in the improper relating of the wrongdoer toward the wronged. That improper relating is what we mainly remember as the wrongdoing suffered — and remember it not just with our mind but also with our body. Any healing of the wronged without involving the wrongdoer, therefore, can be only partial. To complete the healing, the relationship between the two needs to be mended. For Christians, this is what reconciliation is all about. Reconciliation with the wrongdoer completes the healing of the person who suffered the wrong.

Yet remembering so as to relate well to the self and remembering so as to relate well to others are distinct activities. In Chapter Five I will elaborate the ways to remember well with regard to our neighbors — both those who have wronged us and the wider social circle in which we live.

Frameworks of Memories

C ontemporary prophets of memory have convinced most of us: We have a duty to remember wrongs suffered. Forgetfulness betrays those who have been violated and delivers the powerless into the hands of evildoers. Yet as we observe how memories of wrongs have been used throughout history, we cannot but wonder whether such memory is as much a curse as a blessing. How can we enjoy the blessings of memory without suffering its curses? Can we disentangle the two, or are they so inextricably intertwined that blessings cannot be had without curses?

I have written this book with the conviction that memory can be re-deemed, at least partially. We can learn how to remember well. In the previous two chapters I explored two simple rules for keeping the abomi-nations of memory, as Elie Wiesel calls them, at bay:

> "Remember truthfully!" — a rule pressed upon us by histori-ans, philosophers, and theologians. In human relationships, truth is an elusive good. And yet it is indispensable. Deceitful memories — memories by which we deceive others and sometimes even ourselves — are unjust and injurious.
>
> "Remember so as to heal!" — a rule pressed upon us by psy-chotherapists and religious professionals entrusted with the care

of souls. Wrongs suffered create wounds that, left unattended and with the help of memory, can wreak havoc in people's lives and may even prompt them to harm others. Unhealed memories are potentially ruinous — for the wounded and for their neighbors.

But the two rules mentioned do not suffice to help us remember rightly. Consider the following two important phenomena and how they reinforce each other. First, the experience and memory of serious wrongs challenges some basic common assumptions about the character of the world, its order, and justice (just as, inversely, our deep convictions about the world shape how we experience and remember wrongdoing). Bad things should not befall good people, let alone be inflicted on them by others! That commonsense, bedrock assumption underpins much of our moral life. Suffering a serious wrong sometimes shatters this assumption in one blow. The experience can make us feel disoriented and push us down a slippery slide toward a moral netherworld in which everything is permitted.

Second, with a wounded self and a moral world in ruins, we sometimes seek to heal ourselves by harming others. Intentionally or not, we seek to "spring away" from an injury at others' expense. Our shattered sense of self-worth and wounded pride cry out for stories of our superior power and achievements. As we denigrate others and extol ourselves, we swell with energy and confidence. Or our self-righteous rage at having been violated gorges its insatiable appetite on vengefulness and the consequent ruination of other people's lives. If our aim for revenge cannot hit its proper target, we may project malevolence on all members of the group from which our offenders come and simply spray the field indiscriminately. As victims, we victimize. If in doing so we again feel good about ourselves, it is precisely because we have denigrated and violated others.

Consider my possible reaction to my military interrogations. As a person wronged by Captain G., I might deem all military officers or all socialists evil. I might think of them as "beasts" who understand no other language than that of brute force, and I might dream of avenging myself of the mistreatment to which I was subjected. If I were to follow

86

these dark and irrational whispers of resentment, I would be seeking to reaffirm my own power and goodness and to ensure my security by disparaging and injuring others. Both the wounding of my self and the resultant shattering of my moral universe would have contributed to a misguided effort to heal myself. The first would have pushed me to reach for the poison, and the second would have removed the warning label from the bottle. In short, as victims we can wield the memory of our suffered wrongs as a sharp blade that cuts uncaringly and unmercifully into the lives of those around us.

Literal and Exemplary Memory

To counter the misuse of memory in relation to others, Tzvetan Todorov advocates what he calls the *exemplary* use of memory. The best way to get at what he means by this term is to contrast it with what he calls *literal* memory, which he describes thus:

> Suppose an event — let us posit a painful segment of my past or of a group to which I belong — is preserved literally (which does not mean truly); it remains an intransitive fact, leading nowhere beyond itself. The associations that connect themselves to it are contiguous to it: I restore the causes and consequences of the event, I discover all the people anyone could conceivably associate to the initial author of my suffering and I condemn them in turn. I also establish continuity between the being I was and the one I am now, or between the past and the present of my group, and I extend the consequences of the initial trauma to each moment of my existence.[1]

According to Todorov the central feature of literal memory is focus on the individual or group engaged in remembering. We seek to remember in order to construct a plausible narrative of a wrong we have suffered, to

1. Tzvetan Todorov, "The Abuses of Memory," *Common Knowledge* 5, no. 1 (1996): 14.

understand precisely what happened and why, to comprehend its effects on our lives, to condemn the culprits, and through all these activities to recover psychic or social health and stabilize identity. The primary concern of literal memory is our own well-being.

In contrast, *exemplary* memory pushes us beyond the concern for our own well-being by helping us learn lessons from the past so as to apply them in new situations. Todorov describes exemplary memory in this way:

> Or suppose, without denying the singularity of the [traumatic] event itself, I decide to use it, once recovered, as one instance among others of a more general category, and I use it as if it were a model to understand new situations with different agents. The operation is dual: on the one hand, as in the work of psychoanalysis or of mourning, I diffuse pain caused by the memory by domesticating and marginalizing it; but, on the other hand — and this is where our behavior ceases to be purely private and enters into the public sphere — I open this memory to analogy and to generalization, I make of it an *examplum* and I extract a lesson from it; the past thus becomes a principle of action for the present.[2]

In both literal memory and exemplary memory, we pursue our own well-being; we remember the wrong suffered so as to benefit ourselves. But in exemplary memory we also seek to benefit others. Preoccupation with the self has given room to regard for others, and we remember for the sake of their good, not just our own. Memories of wrongs suffered are not just traces of the troubling past in need of healing, sometimes pursued at others' expense; they are catalysts for doing justice. Instead of being absorbed in "dressing his own wounds" and "nourishing his resentment against those who have committed against him an indelible offence,"[3] writes Todorov, a person engaged in the exemplary use of

2. Ibid.
3. Ibid., 19.

memory will "make use of lessons of injustice undergone in the past to fight injustices taking their course today."[4]

Confusing Lessons

Exemplary memory as proposed by Todorov is one more defining line in the sketch of redeemed memories of suffered wrongs — memories that apply balm to torn relationships instead of deepening conflicts. The sketch began with an examination of truthfulness in remembering. The second element added the suggestion that memories of wrongs suffered should be integrated into our life-stories, while at the same time pushed away from the defining center of our identity to its periphery and kept contained in the past rather than allowed to colonize the present and future. This "therapeutic" element of the sketch treats mainly the use of memories in relation to the self and leaves open the question of their use in relation to others. But the misuse of memories carries as great a potential for damage against others as against the self; so something like the idea of exemplary memory is needed to complete the picture of redeemed memories. For the purpose of exemplary memory is to forestall the misuse of memories of wrongs suffered in relation to others. But will the practice of exemplary memory succeed in its protective purpose? The answer depends on the ability of memories to deliver correct lessons in new situations, which is where the problems with exemplary memory begin. For it is possible to draw rather divergent, even conflicting lessons from the same experience of mistreatment.

There are two main reasons why memories of wrongs suffered speak from both sides of the mouth. First, it is often difficult to identify the correct situations in which to apply the lesson of a particular memory. Consider the memory of the Holocaust — a good example since we often claim to remember in order to prevent anything like it from ever happening again, whether to the Jews or to any other group. The memory of the Holocaust seems a near paradigm of exemplary memory. Yet over the

4. Ibid., 14.

past decades, vigorous cultivation of the memory of the Holocaust in the West has not nudged us far toward thwarting a number of genocides around the globe — some of them executed with almost unmatched brutality, such as the slaughter of the Tutsi population in Rwanda.

What accounts for the ineffectiveness of exemplary memory is not just a lack of will to get involved, though that lack is a major problem. The ineffectiveness stems also from the difficulty of identifying just which current situations match the past situation we claim a genuine commitment never to allow to happen again.[5] Consider one aspect of that problem: the distinction between victims and perpetrators. In the attempted genocide of the Jews during World War II, that distinction was clear beyond doubt. The same is true in many situations today. For example, on the individual rather than the group level, if a person innocently walking down the street gets robbed and killed, we can be confident that the pedestrian is the victim and his assailant the victimizer. In many situations that distinction is not so clear, however. When I consider Captain G.'s interrogations and threats against me, it is clear *to me* that I was wronged and that he did the wronging. But his actions could be interpreted differently. Someone who believed that the Christian faith fosters violence and serves as a cover for subversive activities in socialist societies might think that Captain G. was just doing his job well.

In addition, the more the histories of individuals and peoples are intertwined and the longer they engage in conflict, the more the lines between victim and victimizer blur. Yesterday's victims became today's victimizers and today's victimizers tomorrow's victims. In the conflicts between Bosnians, Croats, and Serbs during the recent war in the former Yugoslavia, between Jews and Palestinians in Israel, and between Catholics and Protestants in Northern Ireland, for instance, the situation is arguably less clear than it was in Nazi Germany between the Jews and the

5. Alain Finkielkraut formulates the problem in the following way: "In the name of 'Never that again!' we have leaned for support on one catastrophe [the Holocaust] in order to authorize another [Serbian aggression against Croatia and Bosnia]. . . . How do we explain that a memory so obsessed with barbarity can be, at the same time, so fallacious?" *Dispatches from the Balkan War and Other Writings,* trans. Peter S. Rogers and Richard Golsan (Lincoln: University of Nebraska Press, 1999), 116.

Germans, for the violence has been taking place over an extended period and has gone in both directions. The messier the conflict and the more difficult it is to write a moral narrative that can clearly distinguish the victims from the victimizers, the more disoriented exemplary memory becomes. If you cannot distinguish the committer of an injustice from the sufferer of it, the mere memory of the injustice will help you little in fighting an apparently similar injustice taking place in the present.

Let us assume, however, that we *have* been able to draw a correct analogy between the past and the present. We know that a given present situation is like a particular past wrongdoing. Exemplary memory still faces one more challenge: determining exactly what lesson the past wrongdoing teaches. Todorov assumes, for instance, that "injustice undergone in the past" teaches us "to fight injustices taking their course today."[6] But does it? Let us say that I believe I live in a dog-eat-dog world in which justice is impossible — a world in which we are unable either to know or to do what is just. Will then the memory of injustice lead me to fight injustice? It might in a sense, though I will neither remember nor fight injustice *as* injustice, but rather as an act that threatens my interests or my life. As an inhabitant of that dog-eat-dog world, I might simply do my best to be a dog who eats and avoids getting eaten. Belief in the possibility *of* justice is the condition of the struggle *for* justice, but the memory of wrong suffered is unable to generate that belief. Even worse, the memory of wrongs suffered may strengthen the belief in the impossibility of justice. After all, suffering inflicted by others is an assault against the conviction that we live in a moral universe. How then can such memory on its own teach us to fight current injustices?

Even if we grant Todorov's claim that the memory of wrongs suffered in the past teaches us to fight current injustices, that lesson, though valuable, is still morally too ambiguous. For the fight against injustices will compound the problem rather than resolve it if that fight itself is not carried on *justly*. It is possible to struggle for justice using unjust means, and it is possible to do so without contradiction if one believes that he lives in a world in which it is possible to *know* what is just but in which most peo-

6. Todorov, "The Abuses of Memory," 14.

ple *do not care* about acting justly. Imagine the following scenario: I know that I have been cheated by a particular merchant in the past. I see that my neighbor is being cheated by that same merchant today. I remember having been cheated myself, and that memory teaches me to come to my neighbor's aid. But I could fight against the injustice being done to her by helping her turn the tables on the unwitting merchant and cheat him in return, thus waging a "war" that is manifestly unjust.

So in and of itself, the memory of injustice suffered does not teach one to fight *justly* against injustice. Without in any way violating the memory of a wrong suffered, I can decide to use cunning, raw power, or brute force to fight the injustice — and invoke the memory of wrong suffered in support of my means. Of course, fighting justly against injustice would be both more moral and more prudent than doing so unjustly; for claims to justice legitimize the struggle, whereas sheer exertion of power arouses suspicion. But what would matter most would not be to fight justly against injustice, but to keep others in check by whatever means necessary to prevent them from committing injustice.[7] The memory of wrong suffered can teach us to struggle *justly* against injustice only if it is accompanied by a principled opposition to injustice. Where does a principled opposition to injustice come from? From a source other than the mere memory of wrong suffered.

A Framework for Remembering

We seem to have come full circle to where we were earlier in this chapter when we started drawing the third defining element in the sketch of salutary memories — the idea of exemplary memory. To advocate exem-

7. Some such reasoning lies behind the recently developed theory of a preventive war, which, according to just war criteria, cannot be just but is deemed necessary with regard to relations of power. By adopting such a perspective, one will likely learn the following lesson from past injustices: "If you don't get them, they'll get you; therefore a preventive strike is reasonable." So, since by definition "they" have in fact not yet "gotten you," injustice undergone in the past ends up teaching one to commit injustice in the present.

plary memory seems to offer as a *solution* what is no more than the original *problem* of applying in the present the memory of past wrongs. As a rule, it is not that we fail to draw lessons from such memories; we do draw lessons, but too often in a way that tramples justice underfoot and fans the fires of conflict rather than fighting injustice justly and promoting peace. We abuse memories of wrongs most egregiously precisely when we *do* treat them as examples but do so in a *wrong* way. Recall that truthfulness and successful healing of memories will not get us out of difficulty. They are important in their own right and may nudge us toward the proper use of exemplary memory, but they do not answer fully the question of how to use memory to benefit others rather than to diminish or destroy them.

The first three steps toward redeeming memories of wrongs suffered — "Remember truthfully!" "Remember therapeutically!" and "Learn from the past!" — are all necessary, but even as a group they leave us short of the goal. To get to our destination, we need to place remembering into a larger moral framework. But from where should that framework come and what should it be?

After noting that "not all lessons [of memory] are good," Todorov suggested that the lessons "are up for evaluation with the help of universal rational criteria that sustain human dialogue."[8] I rather doubt that such "universal rational" criteria exist, if by that designation he means criteria on which all rational beings would agree, independently of the contexts and traditions in which they have been reared and in which they stand. For all "universal" and "rational" criteria are formulated from a particular standpoint — whether that standpoint is secular or religious, contemporary or ancient, or some mixture of these features. We cannot escape particular standpoints, but we can compare and debate positions formulated *from* particular standpoints. It is with this conviction in mind that in what follows I explore a framework for the use of exemplary memory that is drawn from the traditions of the Christian Bible.

I will focus on the ways in which these traditions remember the two central events of redemptive history — Israel's exodus from Egypt and

---

8. Todorov, "The Abuses of Memory," 14.

Christ's death and resurrection on behalf of humanity. Memories of these pivotal events from sacred history, I suggest, should serve as the broad framework that regulates how we remember wrongs suffered in our everyday lives. Put differently, I propose to treat these redemptive events as regulative meta-memories. At least for Christians, "exemplary" in its primary sense refers not to the memory of any given wrong suffered, but specifically to the memory of the suffering and deliverance of God's people and of God's Anointed.

Dangerous Memories?

Some may find inappropriate, counterproductive, or offensive my suggestion to treat the memories of the Exodus and Christ's Passion (meaning here his death and resurrection) as regulative memories. Haven't memories of the Exodus and Passion been gravely misused? Doesn't their misuse rest partly on their regulative power as uncontestable sacred memories? After all, during some periods of Christian history Good Friday was a day of horror for the Jews. Deemed "Jesus killers," the Jews had to endure the murderous rage of Christians as they remembered the death of their savior.[9] Neither is the history of remembering the Exodus above reproach. Remembering that God killed the Egyptian firstborn, ordered the obliteration of the Amalekites, who attacked the Israelites from the rear during their desert sojourn (Deuteronomy 25:17-19), and drove out the Canaanites, who inhabited the Promised Land (Deuteronomy 4:37-38), some more radical and militaristic Jews and Christians have felt justified in mistreating non-Jews and driving them out of their homes and off of their land.[10]

9. See, for instance, the entries "Grenoble," "Languedoc," "Germany," "Kholm (Chelm)," and "Cracow," in *The Jewish Encyclopedia: A Descriptive Record of the History, Religion, Literature, and Customs of the Jewish People from the Earliest Times to the Present Day,* ed. Cyrus Adler, Isidore Singer, et al. (New York and London: Funk and Wagnalls, 1916).

10. See Michael Walzer, *Exodus and Revolution* (San Francisco: Basic Books, 1985), 141-44; and Tom Segev, *Elvis in Jerusalem: Post-Zionism and the Americanization of Israel* (New York: Metropolitan Books, 2002), 6. For examples see Ellen Cantarow, "Gush

By my suggestion, then, am I driving out one demon (abominations result-ing from everyday memories) with another, even more powerful and sinis-ter demon (abominations resulting from sacred memories)?

My argument here rests on the conviction that the memories of the Exodus and Passion, properly understood, are not the problem; rather, decontextualized, thinned-out, and distorted versions of these memo-ries are.[11] The misuse of the Passion memory, for example, often rests on reasoning similar to the following grossly simplistic syllogism. Premise 1: "The Jews killed Jesus." Premise 2: "Those who kill should be killed or at least punished." Conclusion: "We are justified in mistreating and killing Jews." Conveniently left out of Premise 1 is a recognition of the crucial role of the Romans (Gentiles!) in the crucifixion of Jesus, the fact that only some Jews demanded Jesus' crucifixion, and the principle that any guilt those Jews might bear is not transferable to all other Jews.[12] Equally significantly, forgotten is the deeper and more important theological truth that the whole of humanity — every sinful one of us — "killed" Je-sus. As to Premise 2, it flies in the face of what is at the heart of the Chris-tian understanding of the Passion. God came down to earth *not* to pun-ish or kill enemies (which we all are); instead, God gave God's own self as a sacrifice on their behalf, Jews and Gentiles alike. The syllogism that jus-tifies the mistreatment and killing of Jews is, therefore, totally mistaken, and acting on it is utterly wrong.[13]

My point is this: cut off the memories of the Exodus and Passion

Emunim: The Twilight of Zionism?" (http://www.corkpsc.org/db.php?aid=2401); Rabbi Meir Kahane, "Passover — Holiday of Vengeance" (http://www.kahane.org/meir/pass-over.html); Rabbi Meir Kahane, "The Arabs in Eretz Israel" (http://www.kahane.org/meir/arabs.html).

11. See Miroslav Volf, "Christianity and Violence," *Reflections* (Winter 2004): 16-22.

12. The two last points were made succinctly in the historic document of the Sec-ond Vatican Council, "Nostra Aetate": "Even though the Jewish authorities and those who followed their lead pressed for the death of Christ (see Jn 19:6), neither all Jews in-discriminately at that time, nor Jews today, can be charged with the crimes committed during his passion." *Vatican Council II: Constitutions, Decrees, Declarations,* ed. Austin Flannery, O.P. (Northport, N.Y.: Costello, 1996), 573.

13. See Miroslav Volf, "Johannine Dualism and Contemporary Pluralism," *Modern Theology* 21, no. 2 (2005): 198-200.

from the larger story in which they are embedded and employ them in situations of conflict, and you may turn these memories into deadly weapons! Respect the inner logic of these memories as shaped by the larger narrative contexts in which they are situated and let that logic govern how you act in situations of conflict, and these memories are likely to become instruments of peace. A closer look would show, I believe, that this is how they function for the majority of believers who take them seriously. That's also how they functioned for me, during and after those difficult months on the military base in the town of Mostar. The memory of the Exodus assured me that God is a God of justice; the memory of the Passion nudged me to try to love those who seemed to me to deserve the very opposite of love.

Sacred Memory

Jews and Christians have preserved their sacred memories of the Exodus and Passion in the Old and New Testaments. The sacred record of the history of the "Jews" — in this text, a specific reference to the Old Testament people of God — is also part of the Christian story, as the Hebrew Bible is the Christian Bible's Old Testament. Thus the Exodus is not only part of the Jewish story, but also part of the Christian story — differently so from the Passion, but nonetheless essentially so. Writing as a Christian, I will treat it as such.

In the Old Testament, memory is of central importance. In his classic book *Jewish History and Jewish Memory,* Joseph Yerushalmi writes:

> Only in Israel, and nowhere else, is the injunction to remember felt as a religious imperative to an entire people. Its reverberations are everywhere, but they reach crescendo in the Deuteronomic history and in the Prophets. "Remember the days of old, consider the years of ages past" (Deut. 32:7). "Remember these things, O Jacob, for you, O Israel, are my servant; I have fashioned you, you are my servant; O Israel, never forget me" (Isaiah 44:21). "Remember what Amalek did to you" (Deut. 25:17). And, with

hammering insistence: "Remember that you were a slave in Egypt" (Deut. 5:15; 15:15; 16:12; 24:18).[14]

The "hammering insistence" on memory, especially the memory of redemption from suffering and mistreatment, is not just a feature of Jewish religious life. In many of their key convictions and practices, Christians have inherited from the Jews an emphasis on the centrality of memory. Every single Christian confession is an exercise in memory — even the confession that seemingly narrates nothing about the past but simply states, "Jesus is Lord!" for it invokes the name of a person who lived in a given time and place. Every celebration of Holy Communion is an event of memory; it is conducted "in remembrance" of Jesus Christ, of what he has done and of what he will do. Four formal features shared by memories of the Exodus and Passion are important to note before we examine the content of these memories and its bearing on our everyday memories, especially those of wrongs suffered: identity, community, the future, and God.

Sacred Memory: Identity

Memory *defines the identities* of Jews and Christians. To be a Jew is to remember the Exodus. To be a Christian is to remember the death and resurrection of Christ. Of course, Jews and Christians don't just remember; they also act in the present (for example, they seek to love their neighbors as themselves), and they hope for the future (for example, they hope for the just and peaceful rule of the Messiah). But take away the memories of the Exodus and Passion, and you will have excised the pulsating heart that energizes and directs their actions and forms their hopes.

To bring more clearly into focus the identity-shaping character of the memories of the Exodus and Passion, compare "history" and "memory." According to Yerushalmi, history is a matter of intellection, and its

14. Yosef Hayim Yerushalmi, *Zakhor: Jewish History and Jewish Memory* (Seattle: University of Washington Press, 1982), 9-10.

vehicle is historiography; memory, at least as "sacred memory," is a matter of identification, and its vehicles are commemorative rituals and liturgies. What memory draws from the past, he writes, is not "a series of facts to be contemplated at a distance." This is what history does. In contrast, "memory draws from the past a series of situations into which one could somehow be existentially drawn."[15] Though Yerushalmi contrasts too sharply "a series of facts" to contemplate and "a series of situations" into which to be drawn, since in its own way memory is also concerned with facts, his main point is well taken: sacred memory shapes identity by drawing worshipers existentially into the sacred past.

The Passover Seder is the paradigmatic Jewish memory in this regard. Its purpose is not so much to convey historical information (though, at some level, it does do so) as to transmit a vital past through time. Rather than simply recollecting the temporally distant event, sacred memory bridges time and draws one into the past event today. All elements of the Seder — drink, food, symbols, prayers, songs, stories, etc. — are "designed with one overall goal: to take each person at the Seder back to Egypt, to re-enact the dramatic Exodus story, to make each one of us feel as if she or he had actually been redeemed from Mitzrayim (Egypt)."[16] Sacred memory does not simply bring to mind (even the ordinary memory of wrongs suffered does more than that); it re-actualizes. In the words of the Talmud, "In each and every generation, each person can regard himself as though *he* has emerged from Egypt."[17]

The same holds true of Christian Holy Communion. When Christians celebrate it by reading Scripture, narrating the story of Christ, singing praise, praying, eating bread, and drinking wine, they do not simply recall the Passion of Christ — they ritually narrate the death and resurrection of Christ as events in which they themselves are most intimately implicated. In remembering Christ, they remember themselves as part of a community of people who have died and risen together with Christ and whose core identity consists in this spiritual union with Christ. They re-

15. Ibid., 44.
16. http://www.holidays.net/passover/seder.html.
17. As quoted by Yerushalmi, *Zakhor,* 45.

member Christ's story not just as his story but also as *their* story and, in a limited but significant sense, the story of every human being.

Sacred Memory: Community

Second, the sacred memories of Jews and Christians are essentially *communal* memories. As Maurice Halbwachs has argued in his seminal work *The Collective Memory, all* memories are communal. His main point is not that the community as a collective subject remembers, or that individuals are "not authentic subjects of attribution of memory";[18] rather, his point is that individuals do not remember alone but "as members of a group."[19] It is in society (or in a group, such as a family, or a community, such as a church) "that people normally acquire their memories. It is also in society that they recall, recognize, and localize their memories."[20] Imagine that you never told anyone about a particular occurrence in your life. Imagine also that your refraining from doing so was not the result of keeping a secret but rather because the event held no interest for anyone. Quite likely, the memory of that event would quickly wither like an unwatered plant.

If even such personal memories depend largely on community, *sacred* memories must depend on community all the more. One who has been personally wronged has experienced in flesh and soul the wrong she remembers; yet the memory of it is sustained *over time* within a group. In contrast, we receive the content of sacred memories from communities, rather than experiencing directly the events recalled therein, and these memories shape our identity not simply as individuals but as members of these communities. Religious communities sustain sacred memories and revitalize them in new contexts just as sacred memories

18. Paul Ricoeur, *Memory, History, Forgetting,* trans. Kathleen Blamey and David Pellauer (Chicago: University of Chicago Press, 2004), 122.

19. Maurice Halbwachs, *The Collective Memory* (New York: Harper-Colophon Books, 1950), 48.

20. Maurice Halbwachs, "The Social Frameworks of Memory," in his *On Collective Memory,* ed. and trans. Lewis A. Coser (Chicago: University of Chicago Press, 1992), 38.

define religious communities. Take the community away and sacred memory disappears; take the sacred memory away and the community disintegrates.

Sacred Memory: The Future

The third formal feature shared by memories of the Exodus and Passion is their concern with the *future*, not just the past. The idea of remembering the future may seem strange. Normally, we remember the past and hope for something in the future; but memory and hope are not disparate phenomena that never interact with each other. Indeed, memories shape hopes and hopes influence memories.[21] Though in our everyday usage it may at first seem odd to speak about remembering the future, note that we often speak of remembering to do something in the future ("Remember to turn out the lights when you leave!") or even of remembering what will happen in the future ("Remember, the sun will set at 6:25 p.m."). And in Chapter Four we observed that traumatic memories are in part so disturbing because they project themselves into the future in an unwelcome way; they become a "prememory" of what will happen. Careful consideration reveals that the same is often true of experiences of reliability and love; trustworthiness and love experienced are trustworthiness and love anticipated. We remember them not simply as virtues we have experienced but in the same act as virtues we will experience.

So it goes with the memories of the Exodus and Passion. We remember, and looking at the past we see the future. If the Exodus is our story, then we remember deliverance not only as the past deliverance of our community, but also as our and our community's future deliverance.[22] The story of the Exodus tells not just what happened "then and there," but also what *will* happen in our own future. Similarly, if Christ's story is our story, then in remembering Christ we remember not just his past but

21. See Reinhard Koselleck, *Futures Past: On the Semantics of Historical Time*, trans. Keith Tribe (Cambridge, Mass.: MIT Press, 2004), 287-88.

22. See Franz Rosenzweig, *The Star of Redemption*, trans. William W. Hallo (Boston: Beacon, 1972), 295.

also in a significant sense our future. In remembering Christ's death and resurrection, we remember what will happen to us, to our community, the world over. Memories of the Exodus and Passion are intrinsically memories of the future.[23] To use the terms coined by Reinhard Koselleck, for Jews and Christians sacred memory is not just a "space of experience" (the past made present in memory) but also a "horizon of expectation" (the future made present in that same memory).

Sacred Memory: God

Fourth and finally, the memories of the Exodus and Passion are most basically *memories of God.* In this way we add to the temporal repertoire of memory remembrance of the present, in which God manifestly exists. We can understand such remembrance by analogy: When lovers part they sometimes promise, "I'll always remember you," or plead "You won't forget me, will you?" When we remember in this way, we make a commitment to keep the object of our love present in our minds and hearts, to live in consideration of a relationship that matters to us.

At one level, the memories of the Exodus and Passion are memories of flesh-and-blood events in the history of Israel and the life of Jesus Christ. We remember a people eating the bread of affliction and passing through the Red Sea to reach the Land of Promise. We remember a person condemned, beaten, crucified, and then raised to new and immortal life with God. In all these events, however, God is remembered to have been at work in faithfulness to God's people. And it is on God that memory zeroes in. *God* heard the cries of the Hebrews suffering under the yoke of slavery in Egypt; *God* delivered them with his outstretched hand. The same holds true of the Passion. "In Christ *God* was reconciling the world to himself," writes the Apostle Paul (2 Corinthians 5:19), and it is *God* who raised Christ from the dead (Acts 2:24).

If in recounting the Exodus and Passion we forget God, we fail to re-

23. For the use of the phrase "memory of the future," see Letty M. Russell, *Human Liberation in a Feminist Perspective: A Theology* (Philadelphia: Westminster, 1979), 72.

member the Exodus and Passion no matter how many details of the story we line up in the correct order. We may tell a story of suffering and deliverance; and it may be a good story, a story of our people and our hero, a story that we find inspiring and that defines our identity. But we will have left out what matters most. For the memory of the Exodus and Passion is not primarily the memory of an exalted example of human victory over suffering and oppression. It is primarily the memory of God's intervention in behalf of humankind.

It is also the memory of God's promise. A promise does not describe what *was* or what *is;* it states what the one who is making the promise *will bring about.* As the people of Israel were delivered from the depths of affliction by the "One-Who-Is" (Exodus 3:14), so will the community that remembers the event be delivered. As Jesus Christ was raised from the dead by God, so will those who remember him be raised free from slavery to sin and the fear of death. Hence the memory of the Exodus and Passion is primarily the memory of God.

So the sacred memory of the Exodus and Passion shapes identity, is embraced and deployed in community, defines a horizon of expectations, and primarily concerns God. Whatever we do we always act in a framework comprised of at least four components: a sense of (1) who we are, (2) where we belong, (3) what we expect, and (4) what, or who, we ultimately trust. When the people of God remember wrongs suffered, they remember them out of a sense of identity and community, out of expectations and ultimate trust derived from the sacred memory of the Exodus and Passion. So how do these memories shape our everyday memories of wrongs suffered?

CHAPTER SIX

Memory, the Exodus, and the Passion

To learn the right lessons from memories of wrongs suffered, we need to place those memories into the framework of the sacred memory of the Exodus and Passion, I argued in the previous chapter. As the discerning reader will no doubt have noticed, that sacred memory, though first introduced in conjunction with the rule, "Remember so as to learn from the past," was at work from the very beginning of my exploration of what it means to remember rightly. The call to *truthfulness* in remembering was underwritten by God's final judgment of grace, which itself is an extension of the way in which God treated human sin as God delivered Israel from oppression and as Jesus Christ hung on the tree of shame. All three elements of the *healing* of memories — a new identity, new possibilities, and an integrated life-story — drew their basic content from the memory of the Passion understood as a new Exodus, a new deliverance.

The memory of the Passion even provided the initial heartbeat of my project as I formulated the original question that has guided the whole book, namely, "How does the one who loves the wrongdoer remember the wrongdoing?" That question is simply an echo of the conviction that God "proves his love for us in that while we still were sinners Christ died for us" (Romans 5:8). From the Christian standpoint, to remember *rightly* wrongs that we have suffered is to remember them through the lens of the memory of Christ's death and resurrection.

Let us now look at sacred memories in greater detail and examine what bearing they have on how to remember rightly. I will start by exploring the significance of the memory of the Exodus for remembering wrongs suffered and then expand how the memory of the Passion both reaffirms and readjusts the lessons drawn from the memory of the Exodus.

Lessons of the Exodus Memory

In Scripture the memory of the Exodus is put to several uses, of which I will examine only two principal ones: the lesson of deliverance of the oppressed and the lesson of punishment of the oppressors.

Consider first the texts that directly link the Exodus experiences of Israel with the nation's post-Exodus prescription for the treatment of slaves and aliens, whose servitude and "outsider" status ranked them among the most economically and socially vulnerable groups not only within Israel but also in ancient societies generally.[1] The helplessness of slaves and aliens within the Israelite community parallels Israel's helplessness in Egypt. So how are the post-Exodus Israelites, now free and comparatively powerful, to treat them? Regarding temporarily indentured fellow Israelites, Deuteronomy 15:12-15 instructs:

> If a fellow Hebrew, a man or a woman, sells himself to you and serves you six years, in the seventh year you must let him go free. And when you release him, do not send him away empty-handed. Supply him liberally from your flock, your treasure or your wine press. Give him as the Lord your God has blessed you. And then, remember that you were slaves in Egypt and the Lord your God redeemed you. This is why I give you this command today.

---

1. See Leo Baeck, *This People Israel: The Meaning of Jewish Existence*, trans. Albert H. Friedlander (New York: Holt, Rinehart and Winston, 1964), 46.

The benevolent treatment of *aliens* living among the Israelites is also motivated by an appeal to the memory of God's redemption of Israel from Egypt. In Deuteronomy 24:17-18 we read:

> Do not deprive the alien or the fatherless of justice, or take the cloak from the widow as a pledge. Remember that you were slaves in Egypt and the Lord your God redeemed you from there. This is why I give you this command.

For the Israelites, properly remembering their slavery and liberation involved treating their own slaves and aliens differently from the way they themselves were treated in Egypt. Their model was the redeeming God, not the oppressing Egyptians. Emulating the Egyptians was to return to Egypt even while dwelling in the Land of Promise. Emulating God was to enact the deliverance God had accomplished for them.

But the significance of emulating God went deeper than a relationship simply defined by example and imitation, for the Exodus was the founding story of Israel as a people. Acting toward slaves and aliens as God did toward Israel expressed what lay at the origin of Israel's national existence and the very heart of Israel's identity: their deliverance from slavery as an act of God's grace.[2] For the nation to fail to imitate God would not simply be to disregard wise counsel or disobey a moral command but, in a sense, to betray themselves, no less than the redeeming God, by living in contradiction to their true identity.

The temptation to such betrayal by emulating their former Egyptian overlords was never far from the people of Israel; thus the instructions in the sacred writings on the right way to treat slaves and aliens. These instructions incorporate concrete remembrance ("you were slaves in Egypt") and explicit commands ("you must let him go free . . . supply him liberally" and "do not deprive the alien or the fatherless of justice"). The two reinforce each other: memory grounds and illustrates the commands, and the commands specify the lessons of memory.

---

2. See Emmanuel Levinas, "Difficult Freedom," in *The Levinas Reader*, ed. Sean Hand (Oxford: Blackwell Publishers, 1989), 252.

The crucial link uniting the memory and the commands consists in God's redemptive activity in behalf of Israel. It is not enough for the Israelites to remember that they "were slaves in Egypt"; they must also remember that "the Lord God redeemed" them. The commands about the proper treatment of slaves and aliens are *not* summaries of lessons learned from wrongs suffered. Recall from Chapter Five that of themselves, memories of wrongs suffered teach close to nothing, except perhaps to avoid getting into similarly harmful situations. And the lessons we draw from suffered wrongs go in morally divergent directions. They might lead us to conclude, on the one hand, that we should empathize with those who suffer, or on the other hand, that we have the right to disregard their suffering; their lesson might be that we should treat others differently from the hurtful ways we ourselves have been treated, or that we should not hesitate to inflict suffering on others if that is the most effective way to avoid suffering ourselves.

Thus the commands that issue from the memory of the Exodus are lessons drawn not from Israel's oppression but from God's deliverance. It is not the memory *of* past suffering but the memory of *God's deliverance from* past suffering that underwrites the command to be just and generous toward the weak and needy. The memory of wrong suffered becomes exemplary when God's command to do justice and love mercy directs it and God's liberation of the downtrodden undergirds it.

Contradictory Lessons?

In the Old Testament, the same memory of the Exodus that bolsters the command to protect slaves and aliens also grounds the command to punish Israel's enemies. Here the story of Amalek, which is part of the Exodus memory, may be extreme, but it is characteristic:

> Remember what the Amalekites did to you along the way when you came out of Egypt. When you were weary and worn out, they met you on your journey and cut off all who were lagging behind; they had no fear of God. When the Lord your God gives you rest

from all the enemies around you in the land he is giving you to possess as an inheritance, you shall blot out the memory of Amalek from under heaven. Do not forget! (Deuteronomy 25:17-19)

The lesson of the Exodus with regard to Amalek seems different from that concerning aliens and slaves. Amalek, who had no regard for weak Israel, must be punished with the cruelest of punishments: the extermination of its people and the obliteration of all memory of them. The same lesson — and the same excess! — is inscribed in the deliverance from Egypt itself: plague follows after plague, and the violence culminates in the killing of the Egyptian firstborn. The memory of the Exodus teaches not only merciful protection of the weak and afflicted but also severe punishment of violent afflicters.

Are these two lessons from the memory of the Exodus contradictory, with one urging mercy and the other punishment, even revenge? In a sense they are. Amalek's punishment is horrifyingly excessive — it is out of proportion to their crime, and it falls on all Amalekites indiscriminately, whether or not they participated in the injustice committed against Israel and whether or not they even lived at the time injustice was committed. Yet purge the lesson of the Exodus memory of its vengeful excess — for purged it must be — and it becomes the flip side of the Exodus memory's lesson with regard to slaves and aliens. The single divine action of freeing oppressed slaves provides the impetus for both. Just as God freed all the Israelite slaves — aliens living under Egyptian oppression — so the Israelites must, in time, free their compatriot slaves and always treat kindly all aliens in their midst. Just as God afflicted the Egyptians with plagues and drowned their army in the Red Sea, so the Israelites must punish and kill those who maliciously hinder their liberation.

The memory of the Exodus contains two related lessons. The first is that of *deliverance:* Act in favor of the weak and oppressed just as God acted in your favor when you were weak and oppressed. The second is the lesson of unbending retributive *justice:* Oppose oppressors and punish them just as God opposed and punished those who have oppressed you. The two lessons are closely linked; the second is portrayed as the consequent obligation of the first. In an unjust and violent world, deliverance of the downtrodden requires uncompromising struggle against their oppressors — or so the memory of the Exodus suggests. As I will show shortly, the memory of the Passion will partly reaffirm and partly modify these two lessons of the memory of the Exodus.

Remembering the Exodus — Remembering Wrongs Suffered

What are the implications of the sacred memory of the Exodus for ordinary memories of wrongs suffered? The first implication is the imperative to *remember;* for if the afflicted are to be *delivered,* their suffering cannot be forgotten by them or swept under the rug by their oppressors or by callous, disinterested observers. It cannot be forgotten, at least not until justice has been done. No deliverance without memory.

The second implication is the imperative to remember *truthfully;* for if deliverance of the afflicted is to be an act of *justice,* rather than an act of violence that attempts to rectify one injustice by committing another, the wrongdoing will have to be remembered truthfully. No justice without truthfulness. All in all, no just deliverance without truthful memory.

Thirdly, the Exodus memory implies the imperative to remember so as to *help* those in need. Viewing ordinary memories of wrongs through the lens of remembering the Exodus leads to empathizing with those who suffer and coming to their rescue by struggling against their tormentors. As God heard the cries of the people of Israel and came to their rescue, so those whose lives have been shaped by the Exodus memory will hear the cries of the afflicted and come to their aid.

The fourth implication of the Exodus for ordinary memories concerns *God and the future.* If we claim the Exodus as our story, then we will be able to link the memory of wrongs suffered to a redeemed future. No matter how hopeless a situation might seem, God will ultimately vindicate the afflicted and judge the wrongdoers involved. Wrongdoing does not have the last word. If we remember a wrongdoing — no matter how horrendous — through the lens of remembering the Exodus, we will remember that wrongdoing as a moment in the history of those who are already on their way to deliverance.

The Exodus Memory and the Rules of Remembering

As presented here, the memory of the Exodus serves to reinforce the three rules of remembering set forth in the previous three chapters: "Remember truthfully!" "Remember therapeutically!" "Remember so as to learn from the past!" It also addresses at least some of the concerns about the potential misuse of these rules.

As to truthfulness in remembering, the memory of the Exodus provides a reason to be truthful even when doing so is not in one's own interest: The God we are called to emulate is a God of truth and justice. It also nullifies a primary motivation for being *un*truthful: Since our ultimate deliverance is in the hands of a faithful and omnipotent God, as illustrated by God's deliverance of Israel, we need not resort to deceit to achieve our purposes.

As to remembering therapeutically, the memory of the Exodus guards against the tendency to pursue healing at the expense of others. Even though God *is* the God of Israel, God is not a private deity to be placed at the service of particular interests; rather, God desires the flourishing of all peoples. For the God of Exodus is the God of Abraham, and the God of Abraham is the God who pronounced blessing not only on Abraham but on the whole of humanity. We cannot consistently worship the God of the Exodus while pursuing our own healing by oppressing or injuring others.[3]

3. Here we come up against the difficult issue of the destruction of the Canaanites, who, unlike the Amalekites, had not actively hindered the Hebrews' deliverance from Egypt. Theologically speaking, the view that would see their destruction as a necessary consequence of Israel's redemption is completely unacceptable. Even when the Old Testament texts speak about God as "driving out" the Canaanites before the children of Israel, the Canaanites' expulsion is a consequence of their own misdeeds, not simply a correlate of Israel's redemption. Whatever we may believe to be the reason they were driven out, it was not so that Israel *could* be redeemed.

True, it is also possible to read the account of Israel's conquest as misrepresenting the Canaanites' worship practices to quasi-legitimize their being driven out. If this ap-

As to learning from the past, the lesson of the Exodus is very clearly one of struggle for deliverance of the afflicted. Yet in its sanction of excessive and indiscriminate violence to accomplish deliverance, does the Exodus memory not also teach that the exertion of brute force is justified in a world dominated by lust for power? With regard to perpetrators, it seems to encourage rather than curtail excesses of vengeance. If the treatment of the Egyptians and Amalekites were to become paradigmatic, some lessons of the memory of the Exodus would be unjust. On its own, the Exodus memory is not a fully adequate framework for remembering rightly.

From the Exodus to the Passion

Even if retributive justice replaces indiscriminate vengeance as I have suggested earlier, the question of the adequacy of the Exodus memory remains. Should even legitimate retributive justice have the last word? For injustice permeates the behavior of every human being and qualifies all social relations. To live is to be unjust, observed Friedrich Nietzsche,[4] echoing Martin Luther's assessment of the human condition. The point of this observation is not that human beings are unjust through and through, but that the stains of injustice mar even the most just of our deeds. If this observation is correct, we are faced with two unacceptable options: We can simply disregard justice (as Nietzsche did) and abandon the world to the interplay of forces, thus plunging the unprotected weak into suffering; or we can insist on the relentless pursuit of justice and end up with a "rectified" world-in-ruins, a world completely torn apart by the unsparing hands of retributive justice.

---

proach is correct, then these texts are obviously a deeply problematic part of the Exodus memory, not simply because of the mandate to punish all the people because of the sin of some, but also because Israel's own redemption and possession of the land would have then been bought illegitimately at the expense of others.

4. Friedrich Nietzsche, "The Utility and Liability of History," in *The Complete Works of Friedrich Nietzsche*, trans. Richard T. Gray (Stanford: Stanford University Press, 1995), 2:107.

There is a third option, however. It is expressed in an old rabbinic idea: Before the dawn of creation God, having seen all the evil humankind would commit, had to forgive the world before creating it. Between the complete disregard of justice and the relentless pursuit of justice lies *forgiveness.* For Christians, forgiveness is paradigmatically enacted in Christ's death. In that event, God shouldered the sin of the unjust and ungodly world and reconciled it to its divine source and goal. In relation to sinful humanity, God acted as the One who is just but who at the same time justifies the ungodly, as the Apostle Paul puts it (Romans 3:26). Without disregarding justice, Christ's death pointed beyond the struggle for retributive justice for victims to the wonder of transforming grace for perpetrators and reconciliation of the two.

For those who see the world in simple moral terms — with clearly divided camps of the righteous, deserving vindication, and wrongdoers, deserving punishment — any talk of grace and reconciliation seems sentimental, even immoral. The death of Christ understood as an act of grace is an undeniable offense against dues-paying morality governed by a need to restore the balance disturbed by transgressions. For Christ's Passion embodies the core conviction that, under certain conditions, *the affirmed claims of justice should not count against the offender.* It is understandable that a person passionate about justice would reject the normative claims about how to relate to wrongdoers embodied in the memory of the Passion. And yet if the salvation of the world, not justice, matters the most, it is also understandable that a lover of humanity would embrace the grace of the Passion — and suffer under the scandal of justice both unmistakably affirmed and unequivocally transcended.

The Passion

Much as the memory of the Exodus is central to the identity of the Old Testament people of God, the memory of the death and resurrection of Jesus Christ is central to Christian identity. The defining salvific events of the two communities are related. The memory of the Passion is historically and theologically tied to the memory of the Exodus. The Last Supper celebrated by Jesus with his disciples was a Passover Seder, and the Holy Communion of the Christian church, which has its origin in the Last Supper, is a celebration of the new Exodus of the people of God, a new kind of deliverance. It is not surprising, then, to find the memory of the Passion adopting important dimensions of the memory of the Exodus and adapting others.

Before we examine the lessons of the Passion memory, let me note two differences between the Exodus and the Passion. First, the story of the Exodus is a story of a particular *people*, the people of Israel, chosen and liberated by God; the story of the Passion is a story of a single *person*, Jesus Christ, chosen by God for the salvation of *all humanity*. Christ, the new Adam, is representative of humanity as a whole (Romans 5:12-21). What happened to Christ happened for humanity and to humanity;[5] more precisely, it happened for humanity by *in him* happening to humanity.

Second, the relationship of the Exodus to the future is that of enacted promise.[6] As God has delivered the people of Israel in the past, so God will finally and definitively redeem Israel in the future. Christians, however, believe that the world to come has not merely been promised in the Passion; in fact, that new world has decisively *entered* this present world of sin and death. As a consequence, the future of humanity has, in a sense, already happened in Christ. The idea of the future's taking place *before* it takes place is obviously a difficult one, and here is not the place even to begin to explore it. But let me draw attention to one implication of this idea as it is embraced along with the conviction that what happened to Christ happened to humanity as a whole: When we remember the Passion, we remember the future of redeemed humanity in the world to come.

What lessons, then, does the memory of the Passion teach for the here and now? How are these lessons related to those of the Exodus

5. See Dietrich Bonhoeffer, *Ethics*, gen. ed. Wayne Whitson Floyd Jr. (Minneapolis: Fortress, 2005), 84-85.

6. For a treatment of liturgical enacting of ultimate redemption in Jewish tradition, see Lawrence A. Hoffman, "Does God Remember? A Liturgical Theology of Memory," in *Memory and History in Christianity and Judaism*, ed. Michael A. Singer (Notre Dame: University of Notre Dame Press, 2001), 41-72.

memory? In answer, let us begin by considering two interrelated sets of issues: oppression and liberation, and enmity and reconciliation.

Oppression and Liberation

In the 1960s and 1970s, German theologian Johann Baptist Metz placed the memory of Jesus Christ — especially of the Passion — at the center of his thought,[7] with the categories of oppression and liberation being the main lens for his reflections. Christ suffered in solidarity with those who suffer, and they can find solace in his company, Metz observed. In the memory of Christ's Passion, all suffering people are remembered. But, he continued, Christ's solace is not simply one of empathic companionship. If Christ were just a fellow sufferer who understands, he would be, as David Kelsey has put it, "well-intentioned but terminally ineffectual."[8] The solace Christ gives consists also in anticipated liberation. For when we remember Christ's Passion, we remember his vindication by God, not only his suffering at the hands of the evildoers. As Christ was raised, so also will those who suffer be raised with him. They are not forever imprisoned in their present suffering or their tormented past. Along with Christ they are on the path through death to resurrection — in this life and the next. What happened to him will also happen to them.

Metz described the memory of the Passion as "dangerous" — dangerous, that is, for all victimizers, who leave behind them a trail of blood and tears in search of unfair gain, technological mastery, or political power, and dangerous also for the systems that support such evildoers. The dangers of this memory reside in its orientation not just to the past but also to the future. "We remember the future of our freedom in the memory of his suffering," Metz writes.[9]

---

7. On memory in the thought of Johann Baptist Metz, see Bruce T. Morrill, S.J., *Anamnesis as Dangerous Memory: Political and Liturgical Theology in Dialogue* (Collegeville, Minn.: Liturgical, 2000), 19-72.

8. David Kesley, *Imagining Redemption* (Louisville: Westminster John Knox, 2005), 55.

9. Johann Baptist Metz, *Faith in History and Society: Toward a Practical Fundamental Theology*, trans. David Smith (New York: Seabury, 1980), 111.

The Christian memory of suffering is in its theological implications an anticipatory memory: it intends the anticipation of a particular future of man as a future for the suffering, the hopeless, the oppressed, the injured and the useless of this world. Hence this memory of suffering does not indifferently surrender the political life oriented by it to the play of social interests and forces. . . . The memory of suffering . . . brings a new moral imagination into political life, a new vision of others' suffering which should mature into a generous, uncalculating partisanship on behalf of the weak and underrepresented.[10]

The "anticipatory memory" of Christ's Passion enlists its bearers into the service of the Crucified for the good of suffering humanity. In their own way and in their own time and place, followers of Christ remember him by reenacting his solidarity with the victims of oppression.

Important as political liberation is on its own, however, it leaves forever in captivity the unvindicated oppressed who have died, with the possible consolation that their suffering has contributed to the well-being of future generations and that their story will live on in the memory of posterity. But this possibility offers meager hope. Faith in "progress" — a conviction that future generations will live more fulfilled and more humane lives than past generations — is no more than a modern superstition. As to posterity's memory it fades quickly, especially in the novelty-obsessed, entertainment-saturated cultures of late modernity. The teeth of time gnaw even at memorials made of stone, and eventually most of them forever disappear from view, notwithstanding the work of archeologists and historians. How will those who have died while under oppression see the dawn of freedom in new life? How will they be vindicated while their tormentors are brought to justice? Only if they are raised to new life in God's new world! This future new life too we remember in the memory of Christ's Passion.

In Metz's account, the memory of the Passion exemplifies the same redemptive pattern as the memory of the Exodus: *suffering and deliver-*

10. Ibid., 117-18.

ance. Israel suffered at the hands of the Egyptians, and God delivered them; people suffer at the hands of evildoers or evil systems, and Christ's victory over death lifts them to a new life of freedom. Correspondingly, the lessons from the sacred memory of the Passion for the ordinary memories of injustice are similar to the lessons from the memory of the Exodus: Remember wrongs so that you can protect sufferers from further injury, remember them truthfully so as to be able to act justly, and situate the memories of wrongs suffered into the narrative of God's redemption so that you can remember in hope rather than despair. So Metz's account of the Passion memory shares the strengths of the Exodus memory — a transcendent framework in which the faithful God promises redemption, and moral clarity in the service of the downtrodden. But it also shares the major weakness of the Exodus memory: How helpful can such memory be in a world permeated by ineradicable injustice?

Enmity and Reconciliation

Does Metz's understanding of Christ's death and resurrection go deep enough? No doubt, solidarity with those who suffer *is* an important aspect of Christ's work on the cross. The downtrodden and the needy through the ages have found comfort at the foot of the cross and hope in front of the empty tomb. But Christ did not die only in solidarity with sufferers but also as a *substitute for offenders.* He died for those who do wrong, who cause suffering — for the *enemies* of God, the Defender of the oppressed. Moreover, in the New Testament substitution is arguably the dominant dimension of Christ's work and solidarity a subordinate one. The sacred memory of the Passion will be flawed if it contains only the pair "suffering/deliverance." It must also include the more dominant couplet, "enmity/reconciliation."[11]

11. On the relation between the axes "suffering/deliverance" and "enmity/reconciliation," see Miroslav Volf, *Exclusion and Embrace: Theological Reflections on Identity, Otherness, and Reconciliation* (Nashville: Abingdon, 1996), 22ff.

Consider the Apostle Paul's explication of the significance of the Passion in Romans 5, the culmination of a long argument that started at the beginning of the epistle. In that chapter, he writes only of reconciliation with God, but his overarching purpose clearly has in view reconciliation among people, too. For later in the epistle he insists that God's embracing of humanity provides a model for human beings to emulate in their own, human way (Romans 15:7).

> You see, at just the right time, when we were still powerless, Christ died for the ungodly. Very rarely will anyone die for a righteous man, though for a good man someone might possibly dare to die, but God demonstrated his love for us in this. While we were still sinners, Christ died for us. Since we have now been justified by his blood, how much more shall we be saved from God's wrath through him? For if when we were God's enemies we were reconciled to him through the death of his son, how much more, having been reconciled, shall we be saved through his life? (Romans 5:6-10)

Love is at the heart of the Apostle Paul's account of Christ's death. But surprisingly, even scandalously, love not just for victims but also for perpetrators — for those who are "powerless" because they are caught in the snares of "ungodliness," those who are unrighteous, "sinners" deserving of God's wrath, "enemies." It is not, of course, that love for those who suffer is absent in Paul's writings. A quick look at his instructions about remembering Christ's death while celebrating the Lord's Supper, for instance, will reveal that he considers it a major failing when the arrogant wealthy "humiliate those who have nothing" (1 Corinthians 11:22). And yet at the heart of his gospel is a powerful conviction that God loves the ungodly — loves them so much that Christ died *for* them and *in place of* them. Ungodly — the kind of person Paul himself was before being called as an apostle. A very pious and yet deeply misguided person. A wrongdoer who persecuted people simply because they worshiped Jesus as the Messiah. And then the God of grace encountered this "foremost" of sinners on the road to Damascus (Acts 9:1-19; 1 Timothy 1:15).

But let us beware that some accounts of what it means for Christ to have died on behalf of the ungodly — what theologians sometimes call his "substitutionary" death — are deeply problematic. If we view Christ on the cross as a third party being punished for the sins of transgressors, we have widely missed the mark. For unlike a financial debt, moral liability is nontransferrable.[12] But Christ is not a third party. On account of his divinity, Christ is one with God, to whom the "debt" is owed. It is therefore *God* who through Christ's death shoulders the burden of our transgression against God and frees us from just retribution. But since on account of Christ's humanity he is also one with us, the debtors, it is *we* who die in Christ and are thus freed from guilt. Christ's oneness with both creditor and debtors leaves only two categories of "actors" and thus negates the notion of his involvement as a third party.

We also miss the mark if we believe that Christ's suffering somehow encourages the abused passively to accept their abuse. The message of the cross is not that it is legitimate to "force people to serve in functions that ordinarily would have been fulfilled by someone else," as Dolores Williams has stated.[13] Since no third party is involved, in Christ's Passion no one is forced to do anything for anyone else. Substitution is a gift initiated and willingly given to wrongdoers by the One who was wronged, not a burden of service placed on an outsider. And it is a gift that, far from signaling the passive acceptance of abuse, most radically calls into question such abuse. For it condemns the wrongdoing while at the same time freeing the wrongdoers, who receive forgiveness in repentance, not just from punishment and guilt but also from the hold of the evil deed on their lives.

The Promise of the Passion

If we embrace both ways of interpreting Christ's death — solidarity with sufferers of wrongs and substitution for wrongdoers — what does the

12. Immanuel Kant, *Religion within the Boundaries of Mere Reason*, trans. and ed. Allen Wood and George Di Giovanni (Cambridge: Cambridge University Press, 1998), 89.

13. See, for instance, Dolores Williams, *Sisters in the Wilderness* (Maryknoll, N.Y.: Orbis, 1993), 60.

Passion imply for those sufferers, for wrongdoers, and for their relationship with each other? What effect does remembering Christ's Passion have on how we as wronged people remember wrongdoers and our relationship to them?

First, the Passion of Christ requires us to recognize that the grace of God — as displayed in God's granting of divine favor to Israel via the Exodus irrespective of their worthiness or lack thereof — extends to every human being. As noted earlier, the universal relevance of the Passion constitutes one way in which it differs from the Exodus, which concerned a particular people. The difference may seem merely quantitative — "all" replaces "some." And yet it implies a change in the very character of the redemptive act. Since perpetrators are part of the "all" for whom Christ died, they also obtain emancipation — divine emancipation that frees them from the guilt of their evil deeds and the power of their evil desires. In the memory of the Passion, wrongdoers are remembered as forgiven and as freed from the hold of evil on their lives.

Second, in the memory of the Passion we honor victims even while extending grace to perpetrators. In shouldering the wrongdoing done to sufferers, God identifies it truthfully and condemns it justly. As a substitute, Christ may remove from wrongdoers the *guilt* of their sin, but he does not distort or disregard the sin itself. Even more, to victims Christ offers his own saving presence, as we have seen in Chapter Four. He shields the sufferer's self so that the wrongdoing can neither penetrate to the core of her identity nor determine her possibilities. He promises that her life will acquire wholeness, whether or not the wrongdoing she has suffered can be rendered meaningful. And Christ, who by the Spirit is present in sufferers, gives them the power to emulate God by both loving the wrongdoers and struggling against wrongdoing. The memory of the Passion is a memory of returning the wronged to themselves as cherished children of God empowered to emulate God in their own, human way.

Third, the memory of the Passion helps the wronged and the wrongdoer reconcile. For complete healing, victims need more than inner healing and judgment against those who have wronged them; they need more even than the power to love their victimizers notwithstanding their wrongdoing. Bound in a perverse bond with wrongdoers by having suffered at their hands, victims can be fully liberated and healed from the wounds of wrongdoing only if the perpetrators genuinely repent and the two parties are reconciled to each other. Through the cross, Christ also made possible such reconciliation, exemplified in the Old Testament in Isaiah's vision of peace between Israel, Egypt, and Assyria despite the horrendous violence that marked their history with each other (Isaiah 19:24-25). Christ has reconciled both the wronged and wrongdoers to God, to themselves, and to each other.

In sum, since Christ identified with the wronged as well as took on himself the burden of wrongdoing, the memory of the Passion anticipates the resurrection from death to new life for both the wronged and wrongdoers. But since he also reconciled them in his own flesh on the cross, the Passion memory anticipates as well the *formation of a reconciled community even out of deadly enemies.*

Such community is exactly what we commemorate in Holy Communion. Central to the rite is the solidarity of God with each human being and the reconciliation of each human being to God. Inseparable, however, from reconciliation to God is reconciliation to fellow human beings. As Alexander Schmemann puts it in *The Eucharist,* in this holy ritual, "we *create the memory of each other,* we identify each other as living *in* Christ and being united with each other in him."[14] In the eucharistic feast we remember each other as those who are reconciled to God and to each other. Our past, marked by enmity, has given way to a future marked by love. By remembering Christ's Passion, we remember ourselves as what we *shall be* — members of one communion of love, comprised of wrongdoers and the wronged. The Passion memory is a hopeful memory since it anticipates deliverance from wrong suffered, freedom from the power of evil, and reconciliation between the wronged and wrongdoers — for the most part, a reconciliation between people who have both suffered wrong and inflicted it. The midday darkness of Good Friday that is our sins, sufferings, and enmity will be over-

14. Alexander Schmemann, *The Eucharist: Sacrament of the Kingdom,* trans. Paul Kachur (Crestwood: St. Vladimir's Seminary Press, 1988), 130.

come by the new light of Easter morning that is our rejoicing in each other in the presence of God.

Just as liberation seen through the lens of Christ's death and resurrection is not only a political event but also, and most profoundly, an eschatological event, so too is reconciliation. If it were not, there would be no hope for those who have died in the grip of enmity. Dead victims would never find the complete healing made possible by the repentance and transformation of their victimizers. Dead wrongdoers would never be freed from their burden of guilt. And the two parties would be marked by unresolved enmity for eternity. As I will show in Chapter Nine, the Passion culminates in that grand reconciliation at the threshold of the world to come, in which former enemies will embrace each other as belonging to the same community of love — a reconciliation without which no truly new world would be possible.[15] That new world is what we remember when we remember Christ's death and resurrection.

Lessons of the Passion Memory

When we remember the Passion, we remember what God has done for the whole of humanity, both the wronged and wrongdoers. Just as with the memory of the Exodus, the memory of the Passion recalls God's acts as exemplary and demonstrates how God frees and empowers humanity to emulate them. Through the death of Christ God aims to liberate us from exclusive concern for ourselves and to empower us through the indwelling of the Holy Spirit to reach out in grace toward others, even those who have wronged us. Because the God who justifies the ungodly lives in us, when we imitate God we do not do so as people who simply observe and do likewise, but instead as human beings whose lives reverberate the life of God. What does such imitating of God's acts through Christ entail — imitating understood not strictly as replicating but as

15. See Miroslav Volf, "The Final Reconciliation: Reflections on a Social Dimension of the Eschatological Transition," *Modern Theology* 16 (2000): 91-113.

doing in our human way what God does in a divine way? What are the practical lessons of the Passion memory?

First, the Passion memory teaches us to extend *unconditional grace.* Since in Christ we ourselves were reconciled to God while still God's enemies, we in turn must seek to extend unconditional grace to (fellow!) wrongdoers, irrespective of any and all offenses committed. No offense imaginable in and of itself should cause us to withhold grace.

The second lesson of the Passion memory teaches that we must affirm as valid the claims of *justice.* That lesson, which partially overlaps the lesson from the memory of the Exodus, may seem to contradict the first lesson. But the extension of unconditional grace does not disregard the demands of justice; rather, grace recognizes those demands as valid and precisely as such sets them aside. This tension-filled verdict, which both honors and transcends the claims of justice, is only possible because the Lamb of God took on himself the sin of the world. In doing so, he sanctioned both the affirmation of justice and the extension of unconditional grace.

The two lessons together translate into the pursuit of forgiveness. Forgivers forgo the punishment of persons who deserve it and release them from the bonds of their guilt. Of course, to obtain this release wrongdoers must receive forgiveness of their misdeeds as just that — *forgiveness* — just as any person must accept a gift for the gift to be given, not simply offered. Wrongdoers must acknowledge their actions as wrongdoing, distance themselves from their misdeeds, and where possible restore to their victims what the original violation took away. Failure to do so would not result in the withdrawal of forgiveness; that gift is unconditional. But it *would* result in the suspension of forgiveness between its generous giver and the intended but untaking recipient.[16]

Thirdly, the Passion memory instructs us to aim for *communion.* It is possible to forgive and to elicit genuine repentance and restitution from the wrongdoer but still not want anything else to do with the offender. Forgiveness that reflects what Christ has done for sinful humanity hopes

16. Miroslav Volf, *Free of Charge: Giving and Forgiving in a Culture Stripped of Grace* (Grand Rapids: Zondervan, 2005), 181-86.

for more, however — it hopes for the repair of damaged relationships. We forgive out of God-like love for the wrongdoer; and by forgiving, we take one crucial step in a larger process whose final goal is the embrace of former enemies in a community of love.

The Memory of the Passion and the Memory of Wrongs

Now take the effect of the Passion memory on the wronged, wrongdoers, and their relationship, put it together with the lessons to be drawn from that sacred memory, and add the result to the framework for remembering ordinary wrongs being constructed in this chapter. So far, we have built this framework from the memory of the Exodus — God's deliverance of Israel and the consequent commands given to them. What does the Passion memory imply for the memory of the person who has been wronged, the remembered wrongdoing, and the relationship between the wrongdoer and the wronged?

First, when a victim remembers a suffered wrong at the foot of the cross, he does not remember it as a righteous person but as a person who has been embraced by God, his own unrighteousness notwithstanding. In my relationship with Captain G. in those military interrogations of some twenty years ago, I was certainly on the receiving end of most of the wrongdoing. But I, too, am a wrongdoer. I have wronged the Captain — not in any outward way, for that was nearly impossible and to the extent that it was possible it would have been counterproductive. But I've wronged him in my imagination, which, nourished by the feeling of humiliation and impotence, has, on occasion, given in to the desire for revenge. And then there is the mountain of my unrighteousness that has nothing to do with Captain G. I have "sinned against God and neighbor" and continue to do so. My having been unjustly interrogated by the Captain does not mean that I stand in the light and he enveloped in darkness. We stand together as sinners before the righteous God, and my sin, precisely to the extent that it is sin, is totally inexcusable. Granted, my being counted among sinners together with him takes nothing away from his wrongdoing. It simply places truthfully the story of my own sin alongside his.

Second, as seen through the lens of the Passion memory, any wrong-doing committed against me is, in a significant sense, already atoned for. Forgiven. Even hidden by God from God's own eyes. It is a wrongdoing for which Jesus Christ died on the cross. Has the wrongdoing then ceased to exist? No, it has not; but it owes any remaining potency only to the unwillingness of the wrongdoer to receive forgiveness, be transformed, and be reconciled to her victims and to God. Since Christ died for the salvation of all people, he atoned for the very sin Captain G. committed against me. If I remember that wrongdoing through the lens of the Passion, I will remember it as already forgiven. More precisely, I will remember that sin in its paradoxical existence as that which both *is* and, at the same time, *is overcome.*

It may seem that such remembering takes wrongdoing too lightly. But the "lightness" is only apparent. The terrible weight of the wrongdoing has, in fact, to be borne by God; because it was, I can — indeed, in some sense I must — treat it "lightly." If I remember Captain G.'s wrongdoing simply as wrongdoing, without further qualification, I do one of two things: I either fail to see the wrongdoing through the lens of the Passion, or I do not appreciate sufficiently the effect of the Passion on wrongdoing. I must admit, I do resist the idea that in the death of Christ God forgave this wrongdoing against me. I even rebel against it. The cross is a scandal for me, too — an affront to my sense of justice, without which life would hardly be possible. Yet against these inclinations, and as I recognize myself as a wrongdoer in need of forgiveness, I embrace the grace of the cross as God's strangely beautiful solution for the ill effects of human sin, the divine "lightening" of the load of wrongdoing both suffered and committed.

Last, since the memory of the Passion is an eschatological memory of the anticipated final reconciliation, I will remember every wrongdoing in the light of that hopeful horizon of future reconciliation with the wrongdoer. And here another scandal rivals that of already-forgiven sin: In Jesus Christ and apart from my own say in the matter, in an important sense God has made both Captain G. and me to belong to one community of love even if our relationship continues to be marked by enmity. That realization is the direct consequence of the conviction that humanity as a whole is united with Christ in his death and resurrection, that when Christ died, all died in him, as the Apostle Paul put it (2 Corinthians 5:14). When I remember my violation by Captain G. through the lens of the Passion memory, I remember it trusting that we already are, in a sense, reconciled, and I do so in the hope that we will one day be seated together at the eternal table of friendship, with Christ as our host.

The Passion Memory and the Framework for Remembering

How does the memory of the Passion affect the framework for remembering already sketched from the memory of the Exodus? The Passion does not set aside the implications of the Exodus memory for our ordinary memories, but it does reframe them.

As to the first implication — the commitment to truthfulness — the memory of the Passion reinforces it. Just like the Exodus memory, the memory of the Passion grounds truthfulness by insisting that God is the God of justice and therefore of truth. Thus the main motivation for untruthfulness and deceit is undercut by promised deliverance. But the Passion memory also helps *form* persons capable of being truthful in situations marked by wrongdoing. Through my memory of the Passion, God can "purify" my memory of wrongs suffered because my identity stems neither from the wrongdoing done to me, which would require the perpetual accusation of my wrongdoer, nor from my own (false) innocence, which would lead me to (illegitimate) self-justification. I am not merely beloved of God; I am beloved of God notwithstanding my sin. The same holds true of the person who wronged me. At the foot of the cross I can accept a differentiated view both of myself and of the wrongdoer — a view not schematized by the stark polarity of light on the one side and darkness on the other; so I can be truthful, whether I am thereby accused or justified.

Second, the Passion memory reaffirms the commitment to remember suffered wrongs in the service of opposing wrongdoing, whether it is directed against me or someone else. But that opposition now takes the form not of retribution, and certainly not of vengeance, but of grace. I will remember a wrongdoing committed against me so as to condemn it *and* so as to be able to work for just relations between the wrongdoer and the wronged. And I will remember the wrongdoing so as to release the offender from the guilt incurred and the retribution deserved on account of his wrongdoing. The memory of the Passion urges — indeed, obligates — me to place the memory of suffered wrong in the service of reconciliation.

Third, the commitment to remembering out of concern for protection and well-being is reinforced and recast by the memory of the Passion. Recall that seen through the lens of the Passion memory, violation endured is not an intrusion of darkness into the bright light of the victim's innocence, but a condemnable injustice committed against a person who, in his own way, is also condemnably unjust. For the wronged, the view through this lens crops out resentment (a temptation of the weak) and vindictiveness (a temptation of the strong) — the sour fruits that grow from the soil of memories wrongly polarized by presumptions of total innocence and total culpability. The Passion memory helps the wronged to use the shield of memory responsibly.

Finally, as to healing, by inserting wounding events and wounded selves into the story of divine judgment and vindication, the Passion memory wards off the dangerous tendency toward self-care at the expense of others. The memory of the Passion demonstrates that the ultimate goal of divine judgment and vindication is God's formation of the community of love, which includes both the wronged and their offenders. Personal healing is no longer one's private affair, no longer a process that takes place internally, without reference to the wrongdoer or to one's broader community. Remembering the Passion brings healing to victims, yes, but healing in community and *with* wrongdoers, not at their expense.

Memories of Wrongs, Communities of Memory

Let us assume that my argument so far has been persuasive: It is salutary to filter memories of suffered wrongs through the lens of the sacred memories of the Exodus and Passion. Memories of these redeeming events in the history of God's people help us redeem ordinary memories of wrongs suffered. Most of what I have written thus far has suggested what would be good for us to do, even what we *should* do. But simply to *know* what we should do in order to remember rightly is not yet *actually* to remember rightly. The question remains as to how we *can* do what we should do. Does what I have written here simply load onto the shoulders of victims the burden of remembering rightly — and pile it on top of their burden of having suffered wrong? Remembering rightly is work. It requires commitment and discipline. It is difficult even if those who have suffered wrong undertake it not simply for the sake of their wrongdoers, but also for their own sakes so that, with the help of Christ living in them, they can live in a way that resonates with what is best in our humanity by imitating the God who loves the ungodly.

Because it is so difficult for the wronged person to be "a Christ" to her neighbors by remembering rightly, it is vitally important to belong to a community that can, through its own practices, support her in remembering suffered wrongs through the lens of the Exodus and Passion. Building on the work of Maurice Halbwachs, I argued in Chapter Five that remembering is a communal activity. We don't remember as isolated individuals, even if the memories each of us has are very much our own — so much so that we would be hard-pressed to think of anything that is more particularly "our own" than our memories. And yet we remember as members of communities. We do so with ordinary memories (of, for example, summer vacations with family members), and we do so with sacred memories. The conclusion, then, is straightforward: To remember wrongs suffered through the lens of the sacred memories of the Exodus and Passion, we need to be members of sacred communities.

Christian churches are communities that keep themselves alive — more precisely, that God keeps alive — by keeping alive the memories of the Exodus and Passion. Their identity is wrapped up in the memory of the death and resurrection of Jesus Christ, which resound with the echoes of the Exodus redemption. Churches are, therefore, communities that can offer the memories of the Exodus and Passion as a lens through which to view memories of wrongs suffered.

Churches *can* offer the lens of sacred memory, I write advisedly. Often they do not. They do remember the death and resurrection of Christ as they celebrate Holy Communion; there is no avoiding that. But often they simply fail to incorporate right remembering of wrongs suffered into the celebration of Holy Communion. And even when they do incorporate such remembrance, they often keep it neatly sequestered from the memory of the Passion. That memory becomes simply the story of what God has done for us wrongdoers or for us sufferers, while remaining mute about how we ourselves should remember the wrongs. With such stopping short, suffered wrongs are remembered only for God to comfort us in our pain and lend religious legitimacy to whatever uses we want to put those memories. No wonder we sometimes find revenge celebrating its victory under the mantle of a religiously sanctioned struggle for the faith, for self protection, for national preservation, for our way of life — all in the name of God and accompanied by celebration of the self-sacrificial love of Christ! Thus does this dangerously one-sided memory of the Passion turn our memories of suffered wrongs into an abomination, to use again Elie Wiesel's term.

But imagine the alternative![17] Imagine what would happen if during Holy Communion I participated in the communal celebration of the Lamb of God, now seated at the right hand of the Holy One, who both suffered with all those who suffer and removed the guilt of their transgressors! Imagine what would happen if I celebrated the presence of *this* Christ in the life of the community and in my own life! In such a liturgical setting, both Captain G. and I would participate in the worship (I directly and he in my imagination) precisely in our capacities as the wronged and the wrongdoer. Equally importantly, the whole community would be celebrating my transformed memory of his wrongdoing — a memory that allows me to name the Captain's offenses as wrongdoing but that does not elicit in me only condemnation and disgust; a memory through which I, in receiving Christ in the sacrament of his body and blood, also receive myself as a new creature, made in the image of the God who loves

17. For a reflection on the transforming impact of the proper celebration of the Lord's Supper in the context of great disparity of wealth see Tammy R. Williams, "Proclaiming the Lord's Death Until He Comes: Toward a Theology of the Lord's Supper" (Ph.D. Dissertation, Fuller Theological Seminary, 2006).

the ungodly, with an identity that transcends anything anyone could ever do to me; a memory that frees me from the hold of my suffered wrong and motivates me to extend a reconciling hand to the Captain, whom Christ has already embraced with open arms on the cross; a memory that I ponder in the hope of the final reconciliation.

To remember in a reconciling way, I need to do more than participate in celebrations of Holy Communion crafted to foster reconciliation. Everyday practices must reflect what the community celebrates. In a community that nurses resentments so it can exact revenge, or that keeps score so just retribution will befall wrongdoers, the practice of remembering through the lens of the Passion falters. The whole endeavor seems implausible, even when grounded in good reasons; so, like a tropical plant in a desert climate, it fails to take root in people's lives. The immediacy of violations overwhelms desire and imagination and nourishes graceless memories that identify wrongdoers as offenders only, that legitimize their punishment, and that thrust them even farther away from us into the camp of those we consider our deadly enemies. To remember in a reconciling way, I need to observe the community struggle to remember through the lens of the Passion, to see that struggle both succeed and fail. My participation in a community of those who celebrate right remembering and struggle to practice it will make my own right remembering both intellectually plausible and practically possible.

Mediating Christ the Reconciler and embodying reconciliatory remembering is the double gift the community of sacred memory gives both to those who suffer wrong and to those who commit it. Communities of sacred memory are, at their best, schools of right remembering — remembering that is truthful and just, that heals individuals without injuring others, that allows the past to motivate a just struggle for justice and the grace-filled work of reconciliation.

PART THREE

How Long Should We Remember?

CHAPTER SEVEN

River of Memory, River of Forgetting

———⟤ᴏ/ᴏ/ᴏ⟥———

I began this book by noting the ubiquity of the injunction, "Remember!" in contemporary Western culture. Whatever misfortune befalls us or whatever wrongdoing we suffer as individuals or communities, we have one response that's always ready — a pledge that we will remember.

"Remember, yes; but *how?*" sums up the issue I pursued in the first part of the book. We rarely pause to reflect on this question, and yet it is a crucial one. Since memories of wrongs suffered are morally ambiguous — since they are as much a source of ill as they are of good — once we make the injunction our own, we have an obligation to help such memories to bring blessing rather than curse. To this end, I argued in Chapters Three and Four that we should remember truthfully and therapeutically. In Chapter Five I advocated that we should use memories to motivate and inform a just struggle in behalf of victims and reconciliation with wrongdoers. And in Chapter Six I suggested that we can remember for good rather than ill if we filter memories of suffered wrongs through the lens of the sacred memories of the Exodus and Passion.

"Remember, yes; but for *how long?*" sums up the issue I will pursue in the third part of this book. If today we rarely reflect on how we should remember wrongs suffered, we hardly ever permit ourselves even to imagine that at some point it may be good to let go of such memories. When someone has been wronged, we often seal our pledge to remember with the promise to remember *"always."* I have done so myself. On occasion as I looked into the eyes of my interrogators in the Yugoslavian military, I found myself swearing to God that I'd *"never* forget" — the same pledge, put in the negative. Mine was an almost instinctive response to a moderately severe wrongdoing. Increase the severity of the wrongdoing, and any response other than remembering forever seems unthinkable. Moreover, the cultural forces of which I wrote in Chapter Three that press upon us to remember suffered wrongs also demand that we never stop remembering them. By pledging to remember always, we seek to counter the fast-paced culture of quick forgetting and honor all those who suffer as we have come to believe we should honor the victims of the great social catastrophes of the past century — two world wars and many attempts at genocide. To cease to remember in the future is as unacceptable as failing to remember now, and it is unacceptable roughly for the same reasons.

Forgive and Forget

But is it right to insist on the everlasting memory of suffered wrongs? Might it be salutary not just to remember but also, after a while and under certain conditions, to allow these memories to slip out of our minds? Might there be a season to remember suffered wrongs and then, when remembering has served its purpose, to let go of such memories? Might good remembering in some situations even *aim* at proper "forgetting"? Just to entertain these questions sounds strange, even dangerous, to our ears as twenty-first-century Westerners — strange and dangerous in a similar way as claiming that high self-esteem could be more harmful than beneficial for oneself and one's neighbors or suggesting that Western-styled democracy might not be the best form of government for all times and places. Yet for centuries the Christian tradition has claimed that to forgive rightly and fully means to be willing to let go of memories of wrongs.

Let me offer a sampling from what that tradition has had to say about the relationship between forgiving and "forgetting" — some thoughts on the matter by a few seminal and representative thinkers. Then I will delve deeper into the idea by examining what the great medieval statesman and poet Dante Alighieri has to say about memory of sins in *The Divine Comedy,* a text that in more ways than one stands in the middle of the centuries-long Christian tradition.

Gregory of Nyssa, a fourth-century Eastern church father, in his *Commentary on Song of Songs* counted "forgiveness of trespasses," "forgetfulness of evil deeds," and "the cleansing of sins" among divine gifts.[1] The idea was part of his larger vision, in which the soul forgets what is behind and moves ever deeper into the mystery of the infinite God.[2] Similarly, the fifth-century Western church father Augustine envisaged at the end of his *City of God* a heavenly city "freed from all evil and filled with all good, enjoying unfailingly the delight of eternal joys, forgetting all offences, forgetting all punishments."[3] In the heavenly city, the injured will neither remember offenses nor ponder punishing them. According to the sixteenth-century Protestant reformer John Calvin, in the here and now to forgive is not only "willingly to cast from the mind wrath, hatred, desire for revenge" but also "willingly to banish to oblivion the remembrance of injustice."[4]

A positive attitude toward "forgetting" of forgiven wrongdoing is not a feature of pre-modern theologies only. Two major twentieth-century theologians think along similar lines, though they relate "forgetting" explicitly to the guilt of wrongdoers rather than to the suffering of the wronged. Explicating a fundamental feature of Christian salvation, the great Catholic theologian Karl Rahner writes,

1. Gregory of Nyssa, *Commentary on the Song of Songs,* ed. N. M. Vaporis, trans. Casimir McCambley (Brookline, Mass.: Hellenic College Press, 1987), 47.

2. See Gregory of Nyssa, *On the Soul and Resurrection,* trans. Catharine P. Roth (Crestwood: St. Vladimir's Seminary Press, 1993), 78-79; Gregory of Nyssa, *Song of Songs,* sermon 6, 888A.

3. Augustine, *City of God,* trans. Henry Bettenson (Harmondsworth: Penguin, 1976), XXII.30.

4. John Calvin, *Institutes of the Christian Religion,* ed. John T. McNeill, trans. Ford Lewis Battles (Philadelphia: Westminster, 1977), 912.

We are really allowed to forget our guilt, even though we do not understand how it is possible for us to forget and how it is that our guilt does not eternally remain before us. The incomprehensibility of this ability to forget is ultimately identical with God's forgiving love.[5]

Karl Barth, who has acquired the status of twentieth-century Protestant church father, thinks similarly. "And we are enabled [by God] to [forget]. If it were otherwise, we should be in a terrible plight. We should never be able to bear the sight of our whole being in time."[6] As I will note in Chapter Nine, today we worry that if we were to forget wrongs committed and suffered, we would lose a sense of identity and may not even be able to recognize ourselves. Barth's worry is different: if we were to remember the wrongs we have committed, we may not be able to live with ourselves, especially if we remembered them not as perceived by our own vision occluded by self-exculpations but with the clarity of divine sight.

As these five representative figures attest, the close association of forgiving and "forgetting" was part of the Christian tradition for centuries. It is not a Christian invention, however; Christians learned it from the Hebrew Bible — the Old Testament — where it is even better attested than in the New Testament. In the book of the prophet Jeremiah, God announces a new covenant and makes a promise: ". . . I will forgive their iniquity and remember their sin no more" (31:34). Hope engendered by such a promise can be expressed in the form of a penitent's petition. The psalmist, oppressed by the weight of his sin, prays for God not only to wash him of sin so that he will be clean, but also "to blot out all my iniquities" (51:9). As Avishai Margalit points out, forgiveness in this full-blown Old Testament sense is "overcoming all traces and scars of the act to be forgiven."[7] Through "forgetting," forgiveness enacts a return of a person to the state prior to committing the forgiven wrongdoing.

5. Karl Rahner, *Theological Investigations,* trans. Lionel Swain (New York: Crossroad, 1982), XV.78.

6. Karl Barth, *Church Dogmatics,* III/2 (Edinburgh: T. & T. Clark, 1960), 540.

7. Avishai Margalit, *Ethics of Memory* (Cambridge, Mass.: Harvard University Press, 2002), 206. Margalit himself, however, rejects this idea of forgiveness.

In the early Jewish traditions complete forgiveness involves "forgetting." As to the Christian tradition, so far as I can tell, the classic writers, academic theologians, popular preachers, and lay folk all thought so too — until recently. Using Dante as my guide, I will expound this idea by looking at God's forgiveness as it relates to the memory of wrongdoing not in the midstream of our lives but at the threshold of the world to come — the ultimate model, even if important adjustments need to be made when applying the model to human forgiveness in the here and now. After we have finished examining Dante's vision of God's forgiveness, we will be only one short step away from my main topic in these last chapters of the book: *human* forgiveness in the world to come as it relates to memory of wrongs suffered. Enter with me briefly the world of Dante's *Divine Comedy* at two key stages of this masterpiece, first at the end of *Purgatorio* and then at the end of *Paradiso.*

Two Rivers

In *The Divine Comedy,* Dante the writer is also a pilgrim on a voyage through the regions of the afterlife, "from the deepest hollow in the universe, up to the . . . height" of the tenth heaven.[8] The ancient poet Virgil is his guide through hell and purgatory until they come to the garden of earthly pleasures, the site of original innocence, from which Adam and Eve would have been transposed into the heavenly paradise had they not sinned. At the threshold of that place of never-ending spring and perfect beauty and with purgatory behind him, Dante was left for a moment without a guide, only to follow his will, made "free, erect, and whole."[9] As he entered the garden, he came upon two streams. A lady from the other side — most likely Lady Wisdom — explained their significance to perplexed Dante:

> The water that you see does not spring from
> a vein that vapor — cold-condensed — restores,

8. Dante Alighieri, *Paradiso,* Canto XXXIII, in *The Divine Comedy,* trans. and ed. Allen Mandelbaum (New York: Alfred A. Knopf, 1986), 22-23.

9. Dante, *Purgatorio,* Canto XXVII, line 140.

like rivers that acquire or lose their force;
   it issues from a pure and changeless fountain,
which by the will of God regains as much
as, on two sides, it pours and it divides.
   On this side it descends with power to end
one's memory of sin; on the other,
it can restore recall of each good deed.
   To one side, it is Lethe; on the other,
Eunoe; neither stream is efficacious
unless the other's waters have been tasted:
   their savor is above all other sweetness.[10]

At the end of her explanation the lady reminds Dante that "those ancients who in poetry presented the golden age" sang of the incomparable "nectar" of the streams.[11] So the earthly paradise, in which sins are forgotten and good deeds remembered, is the fulfillment not only of Christian promises but also of ancient pagan aspirations.

To bring more clearly into focus Dante's conception of the departed soul's memory, compare it with that of Plato at the end of *The Republic*, his classic tale about the other world. For Plato, when human souls leave their bodies, they first face the judges of the dead to receive their sentences: either severe "penalties and tribulations"[12] — "for every wrong they had done to anyone they suffered tenfold"[13] — or "blessings as great." After enjoying blessings or undergoing penalties, "a new cycle of life and mortality" begins for each soul.[14] The souls must choose a life for themselves: "The responsibility is with the chooser," wrote Plato and added, "God is justified."[15]

Before they can enter a new cycle, however, the departed souls must

---

10. Ibid., Canto XXVIII, lines 121-33.

11. Ibid., Canto XXVIII, lines 142-44.

12. Plato, *The Republic*, Book X, in *The Dialogues of Plato*, trans. B. Jowett (Oxford: Clarendon, 1990), 616.

13. Ibid., 615.

14. Ibid., 617.

15. Ibid.

forget the previous life. With the future life of their choice before them, the souls "marched on in a scorching heat to the plain of Forgetfulness,"[16] which, in marked contrast to Dante's earthly paradise, was "a barren waste destitute of trees and verdure."[17] As each soul drank from the "river of Unmindfulness," it "forgot all things." "Now after they had gone to rest," writes Plato, describing the rebirth to new life, "about the middle of the night there was a thunderstorm and earthquake, and then in an instant they were driven upwards in all manner of ways to their birth, like stars shooting."[18]

Bitter Savor, Sweet Draught

Note a rough parallel between Dante's and Plato's accounts and two important differences. According to Plato, the souls drink from the river of unmindfulness only *after* they have passed through judgment. For Dante, too, before one's "sad memories" can be "obliterated,"[19] one must discharge the debt incurred by sin and be purged. Memories of sin can end only *after* the sins have been named and condemned and the sinners transformed. Dante writes,

> The deep design of God would have been broken
> if Lethe had been crossed and he had drunk
> such waters but had not discharged the debt
> of penitence that's paid when tears are shed.[20]

Whereas in Dante's hell and purgatory the soul remembers evil — in hell so as to know why it is suffering and in purgatory so as to be purified — it can release the memories of evil after the guilt has been removed. To underscore the importance of remembering sins before their memory

16. Ibid., 621.
17. Ibid.
18. Ibid.
19. Dante, *Purgatorio,* Canto XXXI, lines 11-12.
20. Ibid., Canto XXX, lines 142-45.

can be effaced, Dante describes how he saw himself reflected in the river before drinking of it and was unable to bear the sight of his shameful image — so much so that he cried to God for help. As Dante was plunged into the river — a "supernatural" river, whose waters are not supplied by natural processes but come directly from God — he heard the singing of Psalm 51:7: "You will sprinkle me with hyssop, and I shall be cleansed; you will wash me, and I shall be whiter than snow."[21] The river of forgetting does its work in two steps: it exposes sin and then it makes it disappear from memory. For Dante, there can be no forgetting of sin without its clear acknowledgment, followed by genuine repentance and profound transformation.

Plato's and Dante's accounts are parallel in that the loss of memory follows the final *judgment*. But the parallel is very rough, for their understandings of judgment differ markedly. Plato's judgment is according to works, with a tenfold repayment both for bad and good. In contrast, grace is an essential element in Dante's judgment. True, his tears pay the debt of his sins, as he puts it, but he is not punished for them; rather, he is forgiven of them.

The differences deepen when it comes to the consequence of forgetting. For Plato, the river of unmindfulness makes possible a new earthly life that is essentially unrelated to the old. After death, a new cycle of life and mortality begins for souls; hence they must shed all of their memories. For Dante, in contrast, Lethe does not erase all memories but instead washes away what otherwise would be a permanent stain left on the soul if the forgiven sin continued to be remembered. It is not enough for souls' "repented guilt . . . [to be] set aside"; after forgiveness, the souls still need "to cleanse themselves," insists Dante.[22] The river of forgetfulness is then the water of divine purification, a means of the most radical release from sin's grip on the soul.

Absent from Plato's account is the other river, the river of mindfulness of all good deeds. This absence is the second important difference between Plato's and Dante's conceptions. For Plato, one story of the soul

21. Ibid., Canto XXXI, lines 97-98.
22. Ibid., *Inferno*, Canto XIV, lines 136-38.

ends with death, and a completely new story begins after it; hence all memories must be erased. For Dante, the soul's single life-story continues after death; hence some memories must be preserved. Plato knows only of Lethe, the river of forgetfulness. Dante adds Eunoe, the river of remembering the good, and clearly privileges it.

Somewhat against our expectations, Dante finds Lethe deeply unpleasant. Would it not be desirable for sinners to receive the gift of their sins' non-remembrance? It would, were it not that before they forget their sins they must remember them in their full horror. Dante complains about the "bitter . . . savor" of the river's "stern pity," which allows one to forget sins only after being reminded of his guilt and being "weighed by shame."[23] Full of "remorse" and "self-indictment," which make him physically collapse, he must be plunged into the river and his head must be thrust under "to that point where I had to swallow water," as he puts it.[24] The redeemed can forget their sins only *after* they have faced their sins' reality unadorned. In contrast, there is nothing unpleasant about being bathed in Eunoe and drinking of it. In fact his "thirst was limitless" for its "sweet draught."[25]

Dante's account of the two rivers concludes by describing how the pilgrim was finally made ready to arrive at his destination and enter the heavenly paradise:

> From that most holy wave I now returned
> to Beatrice; remade, as new trees are
> renewed when they bring forth new boughs, I was
>   pure and prepared to climb unto the stars.[26]

As a world of love, the heavenly paradise can begin only after sins have disappeared from memory and all encountered and practiced goodness has been restored to it.

---

23. Ibid., *Purgatorio,* Canto XXX, lines 78-81.
24. Ibid., Canto XXXI, lines 88-96.
25. Ibid., Canto XXXIII, line 138.
26. Ibid., Canto XXXIII, lines 142-45.

Gathered Good

The theme of memory dominates the transition from the world of sin to the world of love at the end of *Purgatorio*. It resurfaces at the end of *Paradiso* when Dante finally gets to see God as "the Eternal Light." In the heavenly paradise, too, both remembering and forgetting are part of the memory of the blessed.

Dante notes first the irresistible draw of the divine Light, and both remembering and forgetting in the heavenly paradise are a direct consequence of the attraction the divine Light exerts on the blessed:

> So was my mind — completely rapt, intent,
> steadfast, and motionless — gazing; and it
> grew ever more enkindled as it watched.[27]

But why are the blessed so irresistibly drawn to the Eternal Light? Why is it that "whoever sees that Light is soon made such that it would be impossible for him to set that Light aside for other sight?"[28] Why is it that the Light brings the forgetfulness of everything except the Light? Dante explains,

> because the good, the object of the will,
> is fully gathered in that Light; outside
> that Light, what there is perfect is defective.[29]

The blessed see the divine Light, and in seeing it they *at once* see and remember *everything* they want to see and remember. They want to cling to the good, and in God all goodness is present.

Have all specific memories now disappeared — memories of good as well as memories of sin — so that the blessed see nothing and know nothing but the divine being? Would not then Eunoe, the river of mind-

---

27. Ibid., Canto XXXIII, lines 97-99.
28. Ibid., Canto XXXIII, lines 100-102.
29. Ibid., Canto XXXIII, lines 103-4.

fulness of all good, have been superfluous at the end of *Purgatorio?* But how could it have been, given that its "savor is beyond all other sweetness" and that Dante's thirst for it was "limitless"?[30] The thought of "the good" as being "fully gathered in that Light" gives us a clue how the end of *Purgatorio* and *Paradiso* fit together. In God all the good that has happened in the world is "ingathered and bound by love into one single volume."[31] Rapt in the vision of God, the blessed see; and by seeing, they remember all goodness — "each good deed."[32] *So precisely by seeing the God of infinite goodness, who makes one forget everything except God, one remembers — gets back, in a sense — all earthly goodness and forgets all sin.*

In *Purgatorio* and *Paradiso,* forgetting and remembering are stages on the journey of the soul toward the God of love. The soul drinks of Lethe and Eunoe in order to enter the world of love. Once in that world, it is rapt by love for God — a soul unwilling and "unable" to gaze at anything but Infinite Goodness. Forgetting is not a flight from the defective or the unbearable. It is a byproduct of the attachment to the perfectly Good, more precisely, a byproduct of being attached to the Good by the Good's own action upon the soul. The forgetting of evil is in the service of remembering the good, and remembering the good is the consequence of being engrossed in God, "the end of all desires."[33]

The Gift of Innocence

So goes Dante's vision: sins will not be remembered in the world of perfect love because the soul will be rapt in God, who is nothing but Goodness and in whom all past earthly good is not discarded but preserved and fulfilled. Building on the long tradition of Christian thinking about the memory of wrongs, in this and the following three chapters I will develop and defend a version of Dante's vision. I will argue that such memory of wrongs suffered — a particular example of the memory of sin —

30. Ibid., Canto XXVIII, line 133, and Canto XXXIII, line 138.
31. Ibid., *Paradiso,* Canto XXXIII, lines 85-86.
32. Ibid., *Purgatorio,* Canto XXVIII, line 129.
33. Ibid., *Paradiso,* Canto XXXIII, line 47.

will not come to the minds of the citizens of the world to come because they will be fully immersed in the love that God is and that God will create among them. Non-remembrance of wrongs suffered is the gift God will give to those who have been wronged. It is also a gift they will gladly share with those who have wronged them.[34]

At the outset, notice four important features of this admittedly strange gift. First, wrongdoers do not deserve it! They deserve punishment! Most of those who have been abused react the way I would react if Captain G. were to demand the gift of non-remembrance regarding his treatment of me twenty years ago. I would swell with anger. In fact, the more I grasp what he did to me, the less I am willing to let his violation slip out of my memory. It isn't easy to give *any* gift to those who have wronged you, let alone the gift of innocence by not remembering their transgression. Inner resistance to giving such a gift can be overwhelming.

Second, we do not give the gift of non-remembrance because we "must." We give it to imitate God, who loves wrongdoers despite their wrongdoing. And more: we give it to echo in our own way God's forgiveness of us — wrongdoers all! We give it because "God is at work" in us, enabling us "both to will and to work for his good pleasure" (Philippians 2:13). And so I often hear myself praying, not just in regard to Captain G.: "Oh merciful God, forgive my unwillingness even as I say that I want to align myself with you! Repair this cracked and untuned instrument that I am and make it resound with your love!"

---

34. In this last part of the book, I am engaging in what from one angle might be described as a "thought experiment" — not a straightforward argument for a position but an argumentative exploration of a *possibility* that is very much in sync with what Christian tradition claims about redemption, both now and in the future. But "thought experiments" are normally undertaken in the hard sciences, whose main goal is to explain phenomena and which, as far as the consequences of such experiments are concerned, simply let the chips fall where they may. Theology is different. It does not simply explain. It proposes a way of life — and one that sometimes crosses our expectations. Thus my theological thought experiment attempts to imagine one aspect of a Christian way of life. In theoretical terms, I argue that memories of wrongs will not come to the minds of those who perfectly enjoy God and one another in God. In practical terms, the question I am pursuing is this: What would it mean to give a wrongdoer the ultimate gift — the gift of innocence?

Third, though non-remembrance of wrongs suffered is a gift, it presupposes both that the one who suffered wrong has forgiven and that the wrongdoer has repented, received forgiveness, and mended his ways. Accordingly, I ought *not* give Captain G. the gift of non-remembrance yet, for though I have forgiven him, he has not accepted forgiveness as such — at least he has not accepted it from me.

Fourth, the gift can be given irrevocably only in God's new world, where the wronged are secure, wrongdoers transformed, and both unalterably reconciled. Here and now, if we give the gift of non-remembrance at all, we give it only tentatively, haltingly, provisionally, and often with a great deal of pain. As evidenced by the record of his interrogations in this book, I have not yet given the gift to Captain G., and this published account of his violation makes it likely that he will have to wait till the end of the ages to get it from me!

I write of non-remembrance of wrongs suffered as though it were a beautiful and good gift. But today the association of forgiveness with the letting go of memories of wrongs strikes us as immoral, unhealthy, dangerous — to top it off, impossible. The association seems immoral because giving up on such memories breaks faith with victims and whitewashes perpetrators; unhealthy because memories of evils suffered and committed are deemed essential to our identity, and it is claimed that their disappearance would wreak even greater havoc on our psyches than their painful presence; dangerous because the absence of the memory of misdeeds leaves no deterrent for future perpetrators and seduces potential victims to let down their guard; and finally, impossible because major events in our lives remain indelibly inscribed in our memories and continue to be operative in subconscious memory even if they disappear from conscious memory.[35] In due course I will respond to most of these concerns, and I will do so partly by suggesting that, though they are on

---

35. According to Freud, it is an error to suppose that "the forgetting we are familiar with signifies a destruction of the memory-trace — that is, its annihilation" (Sigmund Freud, *Civilization and Its Discontents* [New York: Norton, 1962], 16). He goes on to qualify that judgment, however, by stating that "perhaps we ought to content ourselves with asserting that what is past in mental life *may* be preserved and is not *necessarily* destroyed" (18).

the whole warranted in the here and now, they do not apply in the world of perfect love — my primary concern in this last part of the book.[36]

But before I respond by delving into the substance of my argument in the following chapters, let me offer some explanatory remarks in the rest of this one. These remarks address three questions I am often asked when speaking about this topic: (1) What does "forgetting" as I use it here really mean?; (2) By arguing for "forgetting," am I not devaluing remem-

---

36. Even if my responses turn out to be plausible (which I believe they are), they may still not dissuade doubters completely. For that to happen would require both a defense of the importance of "forgetting" for full-blown forgiving and a genetic accounting for the change in cultural sensibilities that makes suspect any talk about "forgetting." I cannot give such an accounting here. I would venture a guess, however, that the more contractual relations predominate in our individualistic culture, and the more interactions between individuals are regulated by a logic of desert (i.e., you get what you deserve), the more *suspect* will be the thesis advocating the non-remembrance of evil. Conversely, the more covenantal relations predominate between persons who are understood from the start as being in relation to one another, and the more their interactions are regulated by a logic of grace (i.e., generosity irrespective of what one deserves), the more *compelling* will be that thesis.

This suggestion about the reasons for suspicion of "forgetting" may or may not be correct. Even if it is correct, it will not suffice as an explanation for the change in modern cultural sensibilities. Clearly, other important factors have also figured prominently. Freud's psychoanalysis (or rather, its more superficial cultural reception), with its stress on the retrieval of memories as a prerequisite for healing, has contributed in part. The Holocaust and the way it has come to be remembered from the 1960s on, under the influence of such important and powerful cultural prophets as Elie Wiesel, have certainly played a major role. So has the increasing tendency to construe identity in narrative terms. These are, of course, only gestures toward an explanation of the change in cultural sensibilities, and all of them, except the predominance of the strict logic of desert, are ultimately compatible, if not with the traditional notions of "forgive and forget," certainly with the much more nuanced thesis I advocate here.

In the absence of a full-blown genetic accounting for this change, I want to note two phenomena: first, the occurrence of a shift away from "forgetting," so that what used to be accepted without question has become deeply suspect; and second, the impossibility of explaining such a shift simply in terms of an increase in "objective" knowledge about memory and its functions. What is at stake in the debate about "forgetting" (or, in more precise terms, "not-coming-to-mind" or "non-remembrance" — phrases I will explicate below and use interchangeably) are alternative visions of how we ought to relate to ourselves and to our neighbors in the context of wrongdoing and enmity, and how concerns for justice and love figure into these visions.

bering?; and (3) What is the point of talking about memory in the world to come when we obviously live in a very different world?

On Not-Coming-to-Mind

As the reader will notice, in the remainder of this book I will use "forgetting" only when thinkers with whom I am in conversation use the word. Otherwise, I will use "non-remembrance" or, more precisely, "not-coming-to-mind." What do I mean in claiming that memories of evil will *not come to mind* for the citizens of the world of love? Well, exactly what the phrase says. I do *not* mean that certain memories will be erased from each person's cerebral "hard-drive" so as to make all retrieval impossible.[37] Complete erasure would go against the way we remember and forget now; though important memories may completely fade, they never really get erased. I propose instead that memories of wrongs, rather than being deleted, will simply fail to surface in one's consciousness — they will *not come to mind*. If I were to withdraw to some remote corner of the world to come and determine to remember a wrong suffered, I could presumably remember it. But there I would have neither the need nor the desire to do so.

"Not coming to mind" is therefore *not* best described as *forgetting*, unless we use the term in a carefully defined sense. In the minds of philosophers and theologians over the centuries, "forgetting" has had a rather broad range of meanings — all the way from unconscious "failure to notice" something to intentionally and completely deleting what we once knew — and it has carried both negative and positive connotations. In common parlance, however, we generally understand forgetting as an

37. Something like that *might* happen, of course; strange happenings may occur in the world to come, though a degree of continuity is reasonably to be expected if that world is to be a consummation of this one, as the biblical sources and main representatives of the Bible's eschatological tradition claim. See John Polkinghorne, "Eschatology: Some Questions and Some Insights from Science," in *The End of the World and the Ends of God*, ed. John Polkinghorne and Michael Welker (Harrisburg, Pa.: Trinity International, 2000), 38-41.

undesirable inability to recall what we need or want to recall (as in, "I just forgot what I was going to say!"). That is clearly *not* what I mean by not-coming-to-mind.

Repression does not work as an equivalent for "not-coming-to-mind" either. For repression is, in Freud's terms, highly "motivated forgetting" and is motivated essentially by a negative experience.[38] We cannot bear to remember; therefore, we push an experience out of our conscious memory and into unconscious memory.

Freud's *effacement,* or the *fading* of memories so that they are no longer "affectively operative," comes closest to capturing the idea of non-remembrance or not-coming-to-mind.[39] But even *effacement* misses an essential point: The eschatological "non-remembrance" of wrongs suffered will not be a result of "affective entropy." As for Dante so also for me, such non-remembrance is a consequence of the world's having been ultimately set aright, as well as of people's being rapt in the enjoyment of God and of each other. The prophet Isaiah used the phrase in precisely that way. Speaking of the new and glorious creation, the God of Isaiah says,

> For I am about to create new heavens and a new earth; the former things shall not be remembered or come to mind. But be glad and rejoice forever in what I am creating; for I am about to create Jerusalem as a joy, and its people as a delight. (Isaiah 65:17-18)

The not-coming-to-mind of memories of wrongs suffered is a divine gift — not a direct gift, but an indirect one that follows from the creation of the world of love. Consequently, one should never *demand* of those who have suffered wrong that they "forget" and move on. This *impossible* advice would be also the *wrong* advice. The "forgetting" of wrongs must happen as a consequence of the gift of a new "world." Any forgetting other than that which grows out of a healed relationship between the

38. Sigmund Freud, *The Psychopathology of Everyday Life,* in *The Standard Edition of the Complete Works of Sigmund Freud,* vol. 6 (London: Hogarth, 1960), 147.

39. Sigmund Freud, *Studies on Hysteria,* in *The Standard Edition of the Complete Works of Sigmund Freud,* vol. 2 (London: Hogarth, 1955), 9.

wrongdoer and the wronged in a transformed social environment should be mistrusted. The term "not-coming-to-mind" underscores the passivity of the agent. It also fits well with my claim that "forgetting" is a consequence of God's gift to the transformed self enjoying reconciled relationships in a redeemed world.

On the Importance of Memory

Lest one should still wonder, my topic here, as in the first part of the book, is not memory in general. As my leaning on Dante's comments at the end of *Purgatorio* and *Paradiso* makes plain, I am not arguing against memory and for amnesia. Memory is so fundamental to our being human that we would not be able to function without it. Without memory, I could not write, and you could not read what I have written, let alone read it with understanding, for example. Friedrich Nietzsche, in his meditation on the utility and liability of history (which, as we will see, contains a powerful defense of "forgetting"), contrasts human remembering (often accompanied by regret) with animal forgetfulness (which seems like serene bliss). He imagines a human being asking an animal, "Why do you look at me like that instead of telling me about your happiness?" In response, the animal "wanted to answer, 'Because I always immediately forget what I wanted to say' — but it had already forgotten this answer and said nothing. . . ."[40] To be a speaker, which is to say, to be a human being, is to be a rememberer.

More broadly, memory is fundamental not only to human functioning but also to our sense of identity. Without memory, you could not be you and I could not be I, for we could not recognize ourselves or each other as temporally continuous beings moving along the axis of time. To be human is to be able to remember. It is as simple as that: no memory, no human identity.

---

40. Friedrich Nietzsche, *Unfashionable Observations,* in *The Complete Works of Friedrich Nietzsche,* vol. 2, ed. Ernst Behler (Stanford: Stanford University Press, 1995), 87.

My thesis about memories of wrongs suffered not coming to mind in the world of love in no way implies that I generally disfavor remembering. Not only am I in favor of remembering, I also *dis*favor ascribing equal importance to remembering and non-remembering, as though their supposed parity meant that we should strive to maintain a happy balance between them. As Paul Ricoeur puts it in a somewhat different context in *Memory, History, Forgetting,* memory is an event; forgetting is not an event but an absence.[41] Hence forgetting can never even approximate remembering in significance; obviously, remembering does much more work for us as humans than forgetting does.

One may grant all these observations but still worry that I believe that, when it comes to significant events from our past, it is on the whole better to be a "forgetter" than a "rememberer." I don't.[42] In point of fact, I believe that such a worry is a misguided way to put the issue in the first place. Given how central memory is to human identity, the question cannot be whether we *should* remember our past or forget it. The interesting questions are rather: *What* should we remember? *How* should we go about remembering? Should wrongs be remembered *eternally?* My argument is not that memory is bad and amnesia good, or that forgetters have a comparative advantage over rememberers, but rather that *under certain conditions the absence of the memory of wrongs suffered is desirable.*

Memory in the World to Come

Finally then, my primary concern is the same as Dante's: memory of wrongs suffered after crossing the threshold of paradise and entering the

---

41. Paul Ricoeur, *Memory, History, Forgetting,* trans. Kathleen Blamey and David Pellauer (Chicago: University of Chicago Press, 2004), 502.

42. David Gross pursues this question in *Lost Time: On Remembering and Forgetting in Late Modern Culture* (Amherst, Mass.: University of Massachusetts Press, 2000), 139. Though he is interested in asking the "how" and "what" questions with respect to memory, he, unlike I, also believes that it is worthy of serious investigation to determine "whether it would be better *as a rule* to remember one's personal past or to forget it."

world of perfect love. Obviously, we don't live in that paradise now. We live in a world in which loves are at best imperfect and even the closest relationships are threatened by dissolution and violence, as ubiquitous family feuds amply illustrate. Ours is a world in which Cain envies and spills the blood of his brother Abel. We remember wrongs suffered to make sure that justice is served and to protect ourselves from violence in the future. But by definition, in the world to come the questions of justice will have been settled, and there will be no dark corners in which dangers could possibly lurk. Does the way we will remember there and then have anything to say about the way we should remember here and now?

It does. But the connection between memories in the world to come and memories in the present world is not straightforward. Though connected, they are not identical, and we should *not* argue: "Since memories of evil will not come to mind in the world to come, we can responsibly give up on such memories now." This conclusion might be accurate with respect to memories of trivial wrongs, but it is certainly not true with respect to more horrendous ones. And it is not true primarily because in this morally imperfect world the question of justice remains open, and the danger of similar wrongs being perpetrated persists. But neither should we argue: "Since we must remember now, we have to remember forever." Even if one believes that the conclusion of such an argument is correct — i.e., that one should remember wrongs forever — the argument itself is faulty. It disregards the existence of fundamental differences between this world and the world to come.

So how does the future non-remembrance of wrongs suffered inform the way in which we should live in the here and now? By showing how reconciliation reaches completion: a wrongdoing is both condemned and forgiven; the wrongdoer's guilt is canceled; through the gift of non-remembrance, the wrongdoer is transposed to a state untainted by the wrongdoing; and bound in a communion of love, both the wronged and the wrongdoer rejoice in their renewed relationship. In the here and now this rarely happens — and for the most part should not happen. In a world marred by evil, the memory of wrongdoing is needed mainly as an instrument of justice and as a shield against injustice. Yet every act of reconciliation, incomplete as it mostly is in this world, stretches itself toward completion in that world of love. Similarly, remembering wrongdoing now lives in the hope of its own superfluity then. Even more, only those willing to let the memory of wrongdoing slip ultimately out of their minds will be able to remember wrongdoing rightly now. For we remember wrongs rightly when memory serves reconciliation.[43]

But is there not tension, perhaps even contradiction, between the struggle to remember rightly now (the second part of the book) and the promise of non-remembrance then (the third part of the book)? Only if we fail to recognize the *difference* between this world and the next and

---

43. As my thesis about the non-remembrance of wrongs in the world to come stands, it presupposes a quasi-realistic account of the life of the world to come — realistic because I assume that conscious human beings will enjoy God and one another in God in a world of love, but *quasi*-realistic because I expect significant discontinuities between life as it is now and life in the world to come. Not all will share my expectations; but I hope that even for those who do not, the question I am pursuing will be relevant, at least with some adjustments.

Among Christian theologians in recent years, the major alternative to the idea of everlasting life I am advocating here consists in the idea of the rising of the lived life. According to this view, it is not so much the person as a self-conscious being who acquires immortality, but rather the narrative of the life she has lived that acquires eternal preservation, possibly in divine memory. (See, for instance, Eberhard Jüngel, *Death: The Riddle and the Mystery,* trans. Ian and Ute Nicol [Philadelphia: Westminster, 1974]; Jürgen Moltmann, *The Coming of God: Christian Eschatology,* trans. Margaret Kohl [Minneapolis: Fortress, 1996], 71ff.; Wolfhart Pannenberg, *Systematic Theology,* vol. 3, trans. Geoffrey W. Bromiley [Grand Rapids: Eerdmans, 1998], 555ff. On all three of these thinkers in relation to their conception of the life after death, see Miroslav Volf, "Enter into Joy! Sin, Death, and the Life of the World to Come," in *The End of the World and the Ends of God: Science and Theology on Eschatology,* ed. John Polkinghorne and Michael Welker [Harrisburg, Pa.: Trinity International, 2000], 256-78). But even here the question of *what* will be preserved or remembered remains; indeed, in this "narrative" view of "life" in the world to come, the importance of this question is actually heightened.

My comments about memories of evil in the world to come may even be of some relevance to those who do not believe in any sort of life after death. Since I describe the world to come as a world of perfect love, it is possible to translate my reflections from a quasi-realistic eschatological register to an earthly utopian register. The procedure would then no longer be to narrate "heaven" with the view of the significance of that narration for the here and now, but to imagine an ideal human future and inquire about its impact on life as we live it. From my perspective, much would be lost with such a utopian use of my thesis; nonetheless, it is compatible with what I am offering here.

disregard the fact that a *journey* from here to there must be undertaken. As to the *difference,* in the here and now justice is hardly ever attained and threats persist; hence we remember wrongs suffered. In the world to come justice will have been done, and threats will no longer present themselves; therefore, we will be able to let go of memories of wrongs suffered.

As to the *journey,* it follows the path that starts with remembering truthfully, condemning wrong deeds, healing inner wounds, releasing wrongdoers from punishment and guilt, repentance by and transformation of wrongdoers, and reconciliation between the wronged and their wrongdoers; and it ends with the letting go of the memory of wrongdoing. We take this journey partially and provisionally here and now when we forgive and reconcile — and on rare occasions release the memory of wrong suffered. We undertake it once again, definitively and finally, at the threshold of the world to come.

Or so goes the argument I will build in the following three chapters. My first task will be to lay the groundwork and bring some construction materials to the site for the building I will erect by mining the thought of three prominent defenders of "forgetting" — Søren Kierkegaard, Friedrich Nietzsche, and Sigmund Freud.

CHAPTER EIGHT

Defenders of Forgetting

T he idea that there might be something good about not remembering suffered wrongs after they have been appropriately dealt with
was readily embraced by many great minds throughout the history of
Christianity. Dante, whose thoughts on the matter I examined in the previous chapter, is a typical example. But as I also noted there, traditional
Christians are not the only ones who extolled the virtues of (a certain
kind of) "forgetting." After all, they inherited the idea from the Hebrew
Bible, their Old Testament, in which the Hebrew prophets speak repeatedly about the God who forgives the sins of God's people and does not remember them any longer.

The modern period boasts three great and influential thinkers who
defend "forgetting" — Søren Kierkegaard, Friedrich Nietzsche, and
Sigmund Freud. For all three, and especially for Nietzsche and
Kierkegaard, "forgetting" was not some strange psychological quirk for
which they felt a curious proclivity; rather, forgetting constituted an essential part of their broader picture of being human and of their conceptions of "health" and "redemption." Though none of the three consistently uses forgetting in the sense of "not-coming-to-mind" as I will, and
though they never posit it for the world to come (though Kierkegaard
does affirm that *perfect* love hides sins), their ideas nonetheless set the

stage for my thesis. I will start with Freud and work my way backward in time to Kierkegaard, the only one of the three who can be described as "Christian."

Disposing of Pathological Memories

That Freud's name should be among the defenders of "forgetting" may come as a surprise to many. Was he not the great proponent of psychological healing through bringing subconscious memories to consciousness? Was not part of his legacy — as the person who invented, so to speak, "repression" — the awakening in contemporary culture of an attitude toward "forgetting" as personally and socially deleterious? And yet his position on the matter is clear, especially in his early writings. At a minimum, Freud, the most influential psychiatrist of the twentieth century, is a strong witness in favor of the thesis that "forgetting" need not have an adverse impact on mental health. *Nothing* in his account of psychoanalysis requires that *unrepressed* memories of wrongs suffered be kept alive instead of being allowed to sink into oblivion — or so I will argue.

How does the psychotherapeutic procedure cure? This is the main question that Freud and Joseph Breuer (whom Freud credits for bringing psychoanalysis into being)[1] pose in their co-authored *Studies on Hysteria*. They sum up the answer in words that are precise but more complicated than they need to be:

> It brings to an end the operative force of the idea which was not abreacted in the first instance, by allowing its strangulated affect to find a way out through speech; and it subjects it to associative correction by introducing it into normal consciousness (under light hypnosis) or by removing it through the physician's suggestion, as done in somnambulism accompanied by amnesia.[2]

1. Sigmund Freud, *Five Lectures on Psycho-Analysis*, vol. 11 of *The Standard Edition of the Complete Works of Sigmund Freud* (London: Hogarth, 1957), 9.
2. Sigmund Freud, *Studies on Hysteria*, vol. 2 of *The Standard Edition of the Complete Works of Sigmund Freud* (London: Hogarth, 1955), 17.

In plainer English, if traumatic experiences have not been abreacted (i.e., if the tension they have generated has not been released) either through action or speech, the memories of them are suppressed from conscious memory. Then, lodged in the subconscious memory, they continue to plague the person "like a foreign body which long after its entry must continue to be regarded as an agent that is still at work."[3] Cure takes place by allowing this "strangulated affect" to be discharged through recollection of the event. Once the memory is brought to consciousness, the opportunity arises "for the normal discharge of the process of excitation."[4]

Psychological cure by bringing memories "into normal consciousness" is what we expect from Freud. But Breuer and Freud also propose an alternative way of healing, namely, through *removing* memories. This is not simply an idea of Freud's co-author with which Freud may have disagreed or which may have stood in tension with his own approach. Freud gave a long account of his own practice of removing patients' memories. In the discussion of the case of Frau Emmy von N., he repeatedly speaks about "wiping out,"[5] "taking away,"[6] "removing,"[7] "disposing of,"[8] "getting rid of" tormenting recollections until "the accessible stock of her pathological memories seemed to be exhausted."[9] He describes the process thus:

> ... and I made it impossible for her to see any of these melancholy things again, and not only by wiping out her memories of them in their *plastic* form but by removing her whole recollection of them, as though they have never been present in her mind.[10]

---

3. Ibid., 6.
4. Freud, *Five Lectures*, 19.
5. Freud, *Studies on Hysteria*, 59.
6. Ibid., 79.
7. Ibid., 65.
8. Ibid., 80.
9. Ibid., 90.
10. Ibid., 61.

Freud could, of course, remove such memories only after the patient had expressed them. But the expression of memories did more than just give the therapist access to them. It served to discharge "the strangulated affect," a key step in therapy. Freud reported that after he removed *expressed* memories, patients' general conditions improved and particular symptoms (such as a stammer) disappeared.

Fading of Memories

Freud's removal of memories was tied in with the hypnotic method. It was under hypnosis that patients could remember experiences they could not recall in a normal psychical state, and it was under hypnosis that the therapist could use suggestion to remove these memories. Freud later abandoned the hypnotic method in favor of the psychoanalytic method,[11] in which bringing subconscious memories to an awake rather than a hypnotized consciousness is essential. Could there be any place for removing pathological memories in the new procedure? Clearly their removal could not be an *element of cure,* for the analytic method operates at the level of normal consciousness, and it is impossible for the therapist to wipe out the memories of a patient who is in a state of normal consciousness. Furthermore, patients themselves cannot dispose of memories for the same reason that human beings in general cannot *make* themselves forget anything: By definition, an attempt requires mental concentration on the attempted task, so making oneself forget a particular memory by concentrating on it is inherently impossible. The psychoanalytic cure, therefore, has to take place through means other than the removal of memories. But could such removal be a *desirable result* of a successful or partially successful cure? That issue is important quite apart from the question of whether, according to Freud, cure ever *can* be fully achieved.

11. For an account see the beginning of the twenty-eighth lecture of Sigmund Freud, *A General Introduction to Psychoanalysis,* trans. Joan Riviere (New York: Washington Square, 1960), 456ff.

Freud makes an important distinction between "motivated forget-ting" and "fading of memories." In *The Psychology of Everyday Life*, he speaks of "an elementary endeavour . . . to fend off ideas that can arouse feelings of unpleasure — an endeavour which can only be compared with the flight-reflex in the presence of painful stimuli."[12] Here forgetting is motivated by the defensive desire to banish emotionally distressing im-pulses. If a patient cannot make such experiences conscious, Freud calls such forgetting "repression." Erased from conscious memory, events get transcribed onto subconscious memory, where they lead a subversive underground life and damage the psyche.

But Freud also knows of a different type of forgetting that has noth-ing to do with repression. It is a "general effacement of impressions, the fading of memories which we name 'forgetting' and which wears away those ideas in particular that are no longer affectively operative."[13] Nega-tive affective reactions — "feelings of unpleasure" — can push memories into subconsciousness (though, according to Freud, negative affective reactions can also keep memories alive);[14] the absence of affective reac-tion lets memories *slip* out of consciousness; for without affective rejuve-nation, memories are subject to "normal wearing-away processes."[15] Oc-casionally Freud can sound as though he believes that no memory can ever get lost, no trace of memory ever be destroyed. But his more consid-ered opinion is rather close to conventional wisdom: We "ought to con-tent ourselves with asserting that what is past in mental life *may* be pre-served and not *necessarily* destroyed."[16] But destroyed or not, starved of affective food memories are sapped of strength and lie dormant.

Given the distinction between motivated forgetting and the fading of memories, consider the fact that the psychoanalytic healing process consists precisely in releasing the strangulated affect and therefore in re-moving the affective force of memories. When the reasons for motivated

12. Freud, *The Psychopathology of Everyday Life*, in *The Standard Edition of the Com-plete Works of Sigmund Freud*, vol. 6 (London: Hogarth, 1960), 147.

13. Freud, *Studies on Hysteria*, 9.

14. See the fourth lecture of Freud, *A General Introduction to Psychoanalysis*, 80.

15. Freud, *Studies on Hysteria*, 11.

16. Freud, *Civilization and Its Discontents* (New York: Norton, 1962), 18.

forgetting have been removed, the fading of memories can set in. For Freud, cure does not *require* the fading away of pathological memories; rather, it requires that people no longer "cling to them emotionally."[17] A healthy person will not behave like "a Londoner who paused today in deep melancholy before the memorial of Queen Eleanor's funeral . . . instead of feeling joy over the youthful queen of his own heart."[18]

So one can be psychically cured yet remember the injury. But *must* one remember to be psychically healthy? There is no reason to believe that a person freed from the "fixation of mental life to pathogenic traumas" could not remain healthy if he or she let memories of those traumas be effaced. Nothing in Freud's psychoanalytic method demands that memories of traumas be kept alive, and much speaks in favor of the thesis that such memories, if properly treated, will eventually fade away without loss to psychic health.

There may be, however, reasons to cling to memories of traumas other than people's psychic health, such as their sense of identity, the requirements of justice, or the need to prevent future injuries. I will attend to these issues in Chapter Nine, but Freud himself does not address them. Equally significantly, more may be needed for "cure" than Freud suggests if it is to lead to the letting go of memories. A major limitation of Freud's work on memory is the lack of a robust sense that *relationships between people* as well as *broader social relations* need to be healed, not just individuals. In Freud's account, a person who has caused a trauma does not figure in its healing, because healing takes place primarily through the traumatized individual's "reconciliation with the repressed material which is coming to expression in his symptoms."[19] Freud — and a good deal of trauma literature in recent years — concentrates on the individual's freedom from symptoms so as to be able to function normally in wider society. That goal, while important, is clearly limited. It leaves unaddressed the social and moral dimensions of traumatic experiences.

17. Freud, *Five Lectures on Psycho-Analysis,* 17.

18. Ibid., 16-17.

19. Sigmund Freud, "Remembering, Repeating, and Working Through," in vol. 12 of *The Standard Edition of the Complete Works of Sigmund Freud* (London: Hogarth, 1958), 152.

My primary purpose for engaging Freud — one of the strongest advocates of the *retrieval* of memories — has been not so much to draw positively on his approach to the healing of traumatic memories, though much can be learned from him in this respect. Instead, I wanted to protect my "thought experiment" against a possible counter argument that the "not-coming-to-mind" of memories of wrongdoing would be either impossible or psychologically unhealthy. The early Freud practiced the hypnotic removal of pathological memories as a key element of cure. The later Freud left the door wide open for their effacement after the wound caused by trauma has been psychoanalytically cured.

Being Human and . . . Forgetting

Friedrich Nietzsche, that *enfant terrible* of late nineteenth-century philosophy and a precursor of contemporary postmodernism, is likely the most famous defender of "forgetting." He uses the term in at least four interrelated senses, and all four come closer to my "non-remembrance" than to a more colloquial sense of forgetting as an inability to recall. A paradigmatic example of what he means by forgetting is "a man seized and carried away by a vehement passion for a woman or for a great idea"[20] — a man who "forgets" because his energies and attention are turned away from the past and centered on an object in the present.

Yet unlike my "not-coming-to-mind," which emerges in the wake of a divine gift of a new world, all four of Nietzsche's forms of forgetting are, in Freud's terms, highly motivated; they are more a flight from the negative than the fruit of attachment to the positive. Freud praised Nietzsche for being attuned to the influence of emotional factors on memory, to "the contribution towards forgetting made by the endeavour to fend off unpleasure."[21] He was particularly impressed with Nietzsche's famous aphorism in *Beyond Good and Evil* quoted earlier: "'I have done that,' says

20. Friedrich Nietzsche, *Unfashionable Observations*, in *The Complete Works of Friedrich Nietzsche*, vol. 2, ed. Ernst Behler (Stanford: Stanford University Press, 1995), 91.

21. Freud, *The Psychopathology of Everyday Life*, 146-47, n. 2.

my memory. 'I cannot have done that,' says my pride, and remains inexorable. Eventually — memory yields."[22]

I will explicate Nietzsche's four senses of forgetting by focusing on one of his famous *Unfashionable Observations,* titled "On the Utility and Liability of History for Life."[23] "Utility" and "Liability," or more generally "use," are the key words. The main thrust of Nietzsche's argument is that the study of history should *serve* life rather than be pursued simply for the sake of gathering factual information. A historian might take exception to this claim by arguing that the task of history is to find out, in Leopold von Ranke's famous phrase, "wie es eigentlich gewesen ist" — how things actually happened. And since the opposition between *being* truthful and *using* memories is a false one, as I argued in Chapters Three and Four, discovering historical truth *is* already and by itself a form of using history. Nonetheless, Nietzsche's approach is at least partly right for the very reason that as a rule we *do* something with memories of the past. To a greater extent than anyone who preceded him, Nietzsche underscored the *uses* of remembering — and of forgetting.

Nietzsche develops the first sense of forgetting — which I will call *historical* — in the context of this broader argument about the use of history. Human beings are interested in history because they act in the world, because they desire to venerate, and because they suffer and long for liberation.[24] In this way history serves life. But these interests cannot be satisfied by "knowledge-hungry individuals who can be satisfied by knowledge alone and for whom the increase of knowledge is an end in itself."[25] If knowledge of the past is to serve life, "absolute veracity" will not be the goal. Instead, the "historian" will see the past from the vantage point of the present and zoom in on what seems relevant; evaluate the past against the yardstick of present-day values; and artificially create similarities between events in the past and the present that are unmis-

22. Friedrich Nietzsche, *Beyond Good and Evil: Prelude to a Philosophy of Future,* in *Basic Writings of Nietzsche,* trans. and ed. Walter Kaufmann (New York: Modern Library, 1968), #68.

23. Nietzsche, *Unfashionable Observations,* 85-167.

24. Ibid., 96.

25. Ibid., 108.

takably *dis*similar. As a consequence, "the past itself suffers as long as history serves life and is governed by the impulses of life."[26] To pursue history for the sake of life requires an "ability to *forget* and to enclose oneself in a limited *horizon*."[27]

Nietzsche's approach here seems (wrongly) to uphold the false opposition between being truthful and using memories — at least using them to serve life for constructive ends. But the more modest point he is making is well taken: All use of memories by finite beings — indeed, all remembering — requires forgetting, even if it is guided by the most conscientious desire to do justice to the past. We approach the darkness of the past with the light of our own interests, we search for what we need, we take what we find useful (even if it proves not to be exactly what we were looking for); and in taking it we adapt it to our purposes and leave the rest behind. At every stage of this process — not just at the last one — "forgetting" is involved.

"Historical forgetting," which inhabits all useful memories, is a special case of a more fundamental forgetting, one that constitutes an inescapable feature of human life in general. I will call this second kind of forgetting *anthropological*. "It is possible to live almost without memory, indeed, to live happily, as the animals show us,"[28] Nietzsche writes, "but without forgetting, it is utterly impossible to live at all."[29] This comment comes *after* he has noted that human beings, unlike animals, are inescapably rememberers. A child, "which, not yet having a past to disown, plays in blissful blindness between the fences of the past and the future" may move us "as though it were the vision of a lost paradise. And yet," he continues, "the child's play must be disturbed,"[30] for every child must enter the world of remembering.

---

26. Ibid., 104.

27. Ibid., 163.

28. For Nietzsche, memory is *conscious* memory, otherwise he could not have drawn the contrast with animals as sharply as he does. For an argument that "brutes have memory" in philosophical literature before Nietzsche, see John Locke, *An Essay Concerning Human Understanding*, ed. P. H. Nidditch (Oxford: Clarendon, 1975), II.10.10.

29. Nietzsche, *Unfashionable Observations*, 89.

30. Ibid., 88.

But remembering as a *human* capacity requires forgetting. To live and be able to remember (what, by default, is past), one must forget (both what was and what is immediately present). In that sense, forgetting is for Nietzsche even more fundamental to life than remembering (which is not to say that we can be human without remembering).

> Imagine the most extreme example, a human being who does not possess the power to forget, who is damned to see becoming everywhere; such a human being ... would see everything flow apart in turbulent particles, and would lose himself in this stream of becoming.[31]

Just as a person could not be herself if she did not remember at all, so she could not be herself if she did not forget at all. Just as a person could not act purposefully without remembering, so she could not act purposefully without forgetting. If not partly forgotten, the past becomes "the gravedigger of the present."[32] For Nietzsche, that is an anthropological given. And he is not far off the mark.

Happiness and the Ability to Forget

There is yet a third sense of forgetting in Nietzsche's thought. I will call it *eudaemonic*. Here forgetting is a condition of happiness, both of the ability to feel happy and to make others feel happy. Nietzsche writes,

> But in the case of the smallest and the greatest happiness, it is always just one thing alone that makes happiness happiness: the ability to forget, or, expressed in a more scholarly fashion, the capacity to feel ahistorically over the entire course of its duration. Anyone who cannot forget the past entirely and set himself down on the threshold of the moment, anyone who cannot stand, with-

31. Ibid., 89.
32. Ibid.

out dizziness or fear, on one single point like a victory goddess, will never know what happiness is; worse, he will never do anything that makes others happy.[33]

Nietzsche is not simply reiterating a well-known psychological fact that the experience of happiness requires immersion in the present, and that those who are unhappy tend to dwell in the past by recollecting or in the future by hoping.[34] Those who are happy want to hold the present as their captive.

Beyond this psychological observation, eudaemonic forgetting rests on two fundamental anthropological persuasions. The first is that any activity, especially activity directed toward the happiness of others, requires forgetfulness. Direct yourself toward making a person happy, and you'll need to forget — at least temporarily — a great deal that lies outside the field of vision required to pursue that activity. Dwell on your past, and you'll be incapable of attending to the needs of others.

The second persuasion is that memory always brings with it the pain of the irreversible *"it was."* Recall Nietzsche's child blissfully playing between the fences of the past and the future. As the child leaves the land of oblivion and enters the land of memory, he steps into the space of inescapable sadness. For with memory comes the realization of the irreversibility of time. "It was" is a watchword that "brings the human being strife, suffering, and boredom, so that he is reminded what his existence basically is — a never to be perfected imperfect."[35] Reprieve from the grief over the imperfection of the past can be found only in the present. Happiness requires forgetting, a suspension of the immediate relation to the past and an immersion in the present.

33. Ibid., 88-89.

34. See Søren Kierkegaard's discussion of temporal modes in relation to happiness in *Either/Or*, ed. and trans. Howard V. Hong and Edna H. Hong (Princeton: Princeton University Press, 1987), 1:222-25, and in *Repetition: An Essay in Experimental Psychology*, trans. Walter Lowrie (New York: Harper & Row, 1964), 132.

35. Nietzsche, *Unfashionable Observations*, 88.

Forgetting Against Forgiving

Building on the distinction between aristocratic and slave morality in Nietzsche's *The Genealogy of Morals,* I will adopt his language and call the final sense of forgetting *aristocratic.* Nietzsche related aristocratic forgetting explicitly to "life's most savage and devastating disasters" and people's "own malicious actions,"[36] in other words, to the kinds of events that interest me in this book — wrongs suffered. A strong nature, argued Nietzsche, is able to "appropriate and incorporate into itself all that is past, what is its own as well as what is alien, transforming it, as it were, into its own blood. Such a nature knows how to forget whatever it has not subdued; these things no longer exist."[37] In *The Genealogy of Morals,* an exemplar of such aristocratic forgetting is the celebrated French Revolutionary statesman and writer, the Comte de Mirabeau, "who lacked all memory for insults and meannesses done him, and who was unable to forgive because he had forgotten." Nietzsche continues, "such a man simply shakes off vermin which would get beneath another's skin — and only here, if anywhere on earth, is it possible to speak of 'loving one's enemy.'"[38]

Aristocratic forgetting is Nietzsche's alternative to Christian forgiveness. One could interpret aristocratic forgetting as an expression of moral callousness and of a radical unconcern for the claims of justice. This interpretation is basically correct, provided one does not take it flatly. For Nietzsche's undoubted callousness is a consequence of a posture that is its very opposite — an exceptional moral sensitivity and the strictest possible reading of the demands of justice. If it were otherwise, how could he have claimed, in a way reminiscent of that almost singularly morally sensitive German by the name of Martin Luther,[39] that "living and being unjust are one and the same thing"?[40] For Nietzsche, it is because life is ines-

---

36. Friedrich Nietzsche, *On the Genealogy of Morals,* I.10, in *Basic Writings of Nietzsche,* trans. and ed. Walter Kaufmann (New York: Modern Library, 1968), 90.

37. Ibid.

38. Ibid.

39. To affirm Luther's extraordinary moral sensitivity is *not* to deny his indisputable dark sides.

40. Nietzsche, *Unfashionable Observations,* 107.

capably permeated by injustice that all pursuit of justice is doomed to failure. This insight has repercussions for forgiveness. Since I can forgive only if someone has transgressed against me, forgiveness requires a good deal of clarity about justice. I must be able to identify injustice, have a sense of its extent, and apportion an appropriate amount of blame before I can adequately forgive. But achieving clarity about justice is impossible, argued Nietzsche. So forgiving is impossible, too.

Nietzsche's response to the impossibility of identifying what is just and achieving justice is radical but consistent: Situate the relation between the offender and the offended outside the pursuit of justice. This is the function of aristocratic forgetting. Absorb as much injury as you can, and forget the rest. At one level, disregard for justice is not meant to drag a person's behavior below the requirements of justice, but rather to elevate it above justice. It takes "absorbing" and "forgetting" truly to "love one's enemies," Nietzsche claims. By practicing aristocratic forgetting a person does what, according to *The Anti-Christ,* a Christian ought to do: "Neither by words nor in his heart does he resist the man who does him evil."[41] Such an attitude is part of what he calls the "psychology of redemption," or an aspect of the way one would have to live "in order to feel oneself 'in Heaven.'"[42]

And yet there is another, much harsher side to Nietzsche's aristocratic forgetting. In *Thus Spoke Zarathustra,* he imagines the metamorphosis of a camel (who obeys) into a lion (who creates freedom for himself), and of the lion into a child. "Why must the preying lion still become a child?" he asks and then explains,

> The child is innocence and forgetting, a new beginning, a game, a self-propelled wheel, a first movement, a sacred "Yes." For the game of creation, my brothers, a sacred "Yes" is needed: the spirit now wills his own will, and he who had been lost to the world now conquers his own world.[43]

41. Friedrich Nietzsche, *The Anti-Christ,* trans. R. J. Hollingdale (London: Penguin, 1990), #33.

42. Ibid.

43. Friedrich Nietzsche, *Thus Spoke Zarathustra,* in *The Portable Nietzsche,* trans. Gordon Kaufmann (New York: Penguin, 1976), 139.

"Child," "innocence," "game," "a sacred 'Yes'" — all sound quite pleasant. So where is the harshness? It lies precisely in the innocence of the playful creation of new worlds of value and in the innocence of willing one's own will. Under the condition of impossible justice, no other rightness is recognized but the rightness of one's own action. True, this innocence is of the kind that will be unaffected by an offense; but it is also of the kind that will offend without a second thought. Nietzsche's "child" will forget both that it *was* offended and that it *has* offended.[44]

Nietzsche's reflections on forgetting aim at a heaven of sorts — not a heaven that one can inhabit, but a heaven in which one can *feel* oneself *as being;* not a heaven in which love between people reigns, but one in which the individual is untouched by suffering and offenses endured and is unconcerned about the consequences of his or her actions. Nietzsche's heaven exists as the psychological state of a towering individual endowed with creative force. Like Freud, but with much more "seriousness," Nietzsche is concerned with individuals — with their forgetting so as to be able to use history in the service of life, to be able to act, feel happy like goddesses of victory, and play the game of creation, each on her own terms.

To engage at all meaningfully in forgetting of wrongs suffered, must we be concerned only with ourselves, given that forgetting serves the *individual* for personal "healing" (Freud) or for "redemption" (Nietzsche)? Echoing a tradition that goes at least as far back as the Old Testament prophets, Søren Kierkegaard will answer an emphatic "No." Love of the other, not just concern for oneself, has its own reasons for letting go the memory of wrongs suffered.

---

44. A famous incident with a horse suggests that Nietzsche himself was not prepared to practice the harsher side of aristocratic forgetting. At the very end of his productive phase and just before he became incapacitated by insanity, Nietzsche saw a cab driver beat his horse one morning and was deeply troubled. He approached the horse, flung his arms around the animal's neck — and fell irretrievably insane. See Ronald Hayman, *Nietzsche: A Critical Life* (London: Weidenfeld and Nicolson, 1980), 334-35. This event I take to be one more testimony to Nietzsche's extreme moral sensibility.

Love Hides a Multitude of Sins

At one stage at least, Søren Kierkegaard offered something like a general theory of recollecting and forgetting. All human life "moves in these two currents,"[45] he argued in *Either/Or.* He believed, therefore, that humans need to learn both "the art of forgetting" and "the art of recollecting."[46] He suggested that "no part of life ought to have so much meaning for a person that he cannot forget it any moment he wants to; on the other hand, every single part of life ought to have so much meaning for a person that he can remember it at any moment."[47] Further, he advised counter-intuitively that one should apply the art of forgetting to the pleasant experiences no less than to the unpleasant ones.[48]

Unfortunately, it is not clear what precisely he meant by "recollecting" and "forgetting" in this sense. Various metaphors he employed to express the idea remain obscure,[49] but the fog that envelops forgetting in *Either/Or* is later lifted when it comes to one particular type of forgetting — the forgiving and forgetting of offenses by the one who loves. In *Works of Love*[50] (which, along with *Eighteen Upbuilding Discourses,*[51] is the most

---

45. Kierkegaard, *Either/Or,* 1:292. As is well known, Kierkegaard used pseudonyms extensively, and the books he composed do not always give expression to stances he himself advocates.

46. Ibid., 294.

47. Ibid., 293.

48. Ibid., 294.

49. "Forgetting is the scissors with which one snips away what cannot be used, but, please note, under the maximal supervision of recollection," he wrote in *Either/Or* (294). "Forgetfulness is the silk curtain which is drawn in front of the stage, and recollection the vestal virgin which retires behind the curtain," he observed in *Stages on Life's Way* (Søren Kierkegaard, *Stages on Life's Way: Studies by Various Persons,* ed. and trans. Howard V. Hong and Edna H. Hong [Princeton: Princeton University Press, 1988], 27). The forgotten is both obliterated and somehow preserved, and remembering controls the process. But precisely what gets obliterated and what preserved, and how is what gets obliterated preserved? Furthermore, how does remembering control the forgetting? Kierkegaard did not say.

50. Søren Kierkegaard, *Works of Love: Some Christian Reflections in the Form of Discourses,* trans. Howard and Edna Hong (New York: Harper & Row, 1964).

51. Søren Kierkegaard, *Eighteen Upbuilding Discourses,* ed. and trans. Howard V.

significant text for my purposes) he employs the metaphor of "hiding." There he discusses what love does with sins in a chapter titled "Love Hides a Multitude of Sins," inspired by 1 Peter 4:8 ("Above all, maintain constant love for one another, for love covers a multitude of sins").

Love hides sins in three basic ways. The first way is by not seeing them — by being, in a sense, "blind" to them; the eyes of love are charitable and hesitant to see sin even where sin is present. Second, those sins that love does see, it hides either behind silence, with a mitigating explanation, or with the help of forgiveness. Third, love hides sins by preventing them from coming into existence. Commenting on the second way, Kierkegaard writes:

> Keeping silent does not actually take away anything from the generally known multitude of sins. The mitigating explanation wrests something away from the multitude by showing that this and that were not sin. Forgiveness removes what cannot be denied to be sin. Thus love strives in every way to hide a multitude of sins; but forgiveness is the most notable way.[52]

Forgetting Sins

And just why is forgiveness the most notable way? Because it *takes away sins*. Here is a longer text in which Kierkegaard describes the process and in which forgetting is a central concept:

> It is blotted out, it is forgiven and forgotten, or, as Scripture says of what God forgives, it is hidden behind his back. But of course one is not ignorant of what is forgotten, since one is ignorant only of

---

Hong and Edna H. Hong (Princeton: Princeton University Press, 1990). Again, Kierkegaardian scholars ascribe *Eighteen Upbuilding Discourses* and *Works of Love* to two distinct though related stages, religiousness A and religiousness B. But since, according to those same scholars, A is retained in B, the distinction can be disregarded for my purposes here.

52. Kierkegaard, *Works of Love*, 294.

what one does not and never has known; what one has forgotten, one has known. Forgetting in this highest sense is therefore not the opposite of recollecting but of hoping. To hope is in thinking to give being; to forget is in thinking to take away being from that which nevertheless exists, to blot it out. . . . Forgetting, when God does it in relation to sin, is the opposite of creating, since to create is to bring forth from nothing, and to forget is to take back into nothing. What is hidden from my eyes, that I have never seen; but what is hidden behind my back, that I have seen. The one who loves forgives in this way: he forgives, he forgets, he blots out the sin, in love he turns toward the one he forgives; but when he turns toward him, he of course cannot see what is lying behind his back. It is easy to understand that it is impossible to see what lies behind one's back, hence also that this metaphor has appropriately been invented by love; but on the other hand it is perhaps very difficult to become the loving one who with the help of forgiveness puts another's guilt behind his back. Ordinarily people find it easy to place a guilt, even if it is a murder, upon the conscience of another; but by way of forgiveness to place another's guilt behind one's back — that is difficult. But not for the one who loves, because he hides a multitude of sins.[53]

What does Kierkegaard mean by "forgetting" in relation to sins? If we take as the key the claim that "one *is not ignorant* of what is forgotten," then forgetting might mean something like not letting the offense committed count against the offender. Strictly speaking, we would remember the offense but would not reckon it to the offender. Or as Luther put it, commenting on 1 Peter 4:8, we would "pretend not to see it."[54] So Kierkegaard, in using the metaphor of "hiding," would be expressing no more than treating offenders as though they were not offenders. But he seems to be after more.

53. Ibid., 295-96.
54. Martin Luther, *Luther's Works,* ed. Jaroslav Pelikan, vol. 30 (St. Louis: Concordia, 1986), 123.

"Forgetting . . . is the opposite of creating," he writes; regarding offenses, it entails taking them "back into nothing." Here forgetting comes close to undoing. But since time is irreversible, no deed can be undone. So how can the one who forgets "take away being" from sin? One does it "in thinking," says Kierkegaard. The forgiver has known the offense — and forgiveness presupposes knowledge of the offense *as* offense, otherwise there would be nothing to forgive — but it no longer comes to mind; therefore, in a pragmatically relevant sense it no longer exists. Kierkegaard is describing something more than just forgetting but less than undoing. He is describing the absence from consciousness of what was placed "behind one's back," or what I have called "not-coming-to-mind."

Comparing *Works of Love* with *Eighteen Upbuilding Discourses* (which includes two discourses titled "Love Will Hide a Multitude of Sins") confirms this interpretation. Consider how Kierkegaard treats three Gospel stories of forgiveness. He says that the father of the Prodigal Son (Luke 15:11-32) "stands with open arms and waits for the delinquent, has forgotten everything and brings the delinquent himself to forget everything."[55] About Jesus' writing on the ground in the story of the woman caught in adultery (John 7:53–8:11) he notes, "it [i.e., personified love] wrote with its finger in order to erase what it itself knew."[56] Finally, of the sinful woman who washed Jesus' feet with her tears (Luke 7:36-50) Kierkegaard says, "as she wept, she finally forgot what she had wept over at the beginning; the tears of repentance became the tears of adoration."[57]

Love and Forgetting

Kierkegaard associated forgiveness with the forgetting of offenses partly because he read in the Scriptures that God blots out sins, sweeps them away like mist, and does not remember them. In the text quoted above, he appeals directly to divine forgiving as a model for human forgiving. As

---

55. Kierkegaard, *Eighteen Upbuilding Discourses,* 63.
56. Ibid., 67.
57. Ibid., 75-76.

God is said in the Old Testament to hide the sins of people, so Christians are encouraged in the New Testament to do the same. But Kierkegaard could have taken these references to divine forgetting as metaphors; so his reading of the Bible cannot suffice to explain fully his account of the relationship between forgiveness and forgetting.

Kierkegaard associated forgiveness and forgetting mainly because his larger account of love — which God *is* — led him to that position. In the chapter of *Works of Love* that precedes the discussion of forgetting, he argued that love, rather than seeking its own, not only gives but even "gives in such a way that the gift looks as if it were the recipient's property."[58] To remember the forgiven sin is to know the forgiven one as receiver and to know the forgiver as giver. But true love makes the rendered help go unnoticed; therefore it dissolves the relationship of dependence implied in forgiveness by forgetting both the sin and the act of forgiveness.

Similarly, true love dissolves the "humiliating feeling" evoked by being forgiven.[59] In Kierkegaard's account, love both overcomes sin through forgiveness and seeks to win the sinner over. Why does love need to win the sinner over? Because the more deeply the wrongdoer feels his wrong "and in that way his defeat, the more he of course must feel repelled from the one who lovingly deals him this merciful blow."[60] So how can love accomplish the difficult task of winning the sinner over? Here, too, forgetting can come to love's aid.[61] Because the offense and the forgiveness are forgotten, the humiliation of forgiveness is taken away.

Forgetting may be a loving act, but how does one do it? The advice, "You must try to forget!" is "nothing but empty mockery," writes Kierkegaard.[62] If one tries to brush the unpleasant away, "one will soon see

58. Kierkegaard, *Works of Love*, 274.

59. Ibid., 338.

60. Ibid.

61. Kierkegaard himself does not mention forgetting in this context but seeks to remove humiliation by noting that it is not actually the forgiver who overcomes the forgiven, but love as "the third." Moreover, the difference between the offender and the offended notwithstanding, "the presence of God makes the two essentially equal" (ibid., 342).

62. Søren Kierkegaard, *Practice in Christianity*, ed. and trans. Howard V. Hong and Edna H. Hong (Princeton: Princeton University Press, 1991), 152.

what good that is. In an unguarded moment, it often surprises a person with the full force of the sudden."[63] In *Practice in Christianity* he recommends a different approach. "If there is something you want to forget, then try to find something else to remember; then you will certainly succeed."[64] The way to forget wrong endured is to remember Christ — every day and in every undertaking. With memory zeroed in on Christ, we forget "everything that ought to be forgotten" like an "absentminded person."[65] Why? Because we are drawn out of ourselves and resituated in Christ.

Christ is more than just a model and enabler of forgetting, however. In fact, such forgetting makes sense only in the context of the worship of Christ as God, suggests Kierkegaard. Love hides sins and therefore forgets. But not all forgetting is the work of love, and even when love is in play it may not be love as it ought to be. Consider Kierkegaard's portrayal in *Either/Or* of three women abandoned by their lovers — Marie Beaumarchais, Dona Elvira, and Margarete.[66] They seem to be doing exactly what in *Works of Love* Kierkegaard says that love does: they remain blind to the transgression, they hide it behind a mitigating explanation, and they would even be willing to forget it if only their lover would return.

But something is amiss, because they can find no rest and no redemption. The only solace Kierkegaard imagines for them is in the womb of the dark night, which in "eternal oblivion" shortens everything, "day and time and life and the irksomeness of recollection."[67] Why? Not because these women have failed to love themselves or because they have loved another being, but because Dona Elvira has loved Don Giovani "more than her soul's salvation" and Margarete related to Faust as "my all, my god."[68] The bond between the lover and the beloved is "an

---

63. Kierkegaard, *Either/Or*, 1:294.

64. Kierkegaard, *Practice in Christianity*, 152.

65. Ibid., 153.

66. I owe this way of juxtaposing "Love Hides a Multitude of Sins," from *Works of Love*, with "Silhouettes," from *Either/Or*, to conversations with Amy Laura Hall. See Amy Laura Hall, "Treacherous Intimacy: Fallen and Faithful Engagements in Kierkegaard's Works of Love and Other Writings" (Ph.D. diss., Yale University).

67. Kierkegaard, *Either/Or*, 1:168.

68. Ibid., 1:196 and 1:213.

alliance of self-love that shuts God out."[69] As a result of this selfish idolatry, the self of each woman is left unprotected and subject to the mercy of her fickle lover.

The self that loves can be protected only if love is "redoubled" — only if we receive what we give. But we cannot count on love's being redoubled if it is directed primarily to changeable objects in this world; instead, it must be attached above all to the One who *is* Love and who will, therefore, give love back to the giver of love.

> No, the one who in love forgets himself, forgets his suffering, in order to think of someone else's . . . truly such a person is not forgotten. There is one who is thinking about him: God in heaven, or love is thinking about him. God is Love, and when a person out of love forgets himself, how then would God forget him![70]

Protected in divine love, one can forget a piece of oneself by forgetting another person's transgression.

In Freud and Nietzsche, forgetting is a "narcissistic relation of the self to itself,"[71] notwithstanding the fact that the self's injury might have been a result of a social interchange. By forgetting, the self relates to itself in order to cure itself (Freud) or "conquer its own world" (Nietzsche).[72] In Kierkegaard, however, forgetting is a loving relation of the self to another — precisely the one who has caused the injury. Yet that loving relation is carefully circumscribed. Just as only the injured party can forgive, so also only the injured party can forget the injury and allow the injurer to forget his own guilt too. Forgetting cannot be commanded either by oneself or by another, least of all by the injurer; and it cannot be accomplished by a third party. For Kierkegaard, a human being can legitimately forgive and forget only if she is protected by God from the loss of self and if her activity echoes the divine hiding of sins.

69. See earlier drafts of Kierkegaard, *Works of Love,* 439.

70. Kierkegaard, *Works of Love,* 281.

71. So Paul Ricoeur, "Memory, Forgetfulness, and History," *The Jerusalem Philosophical Quarterly* 45 (1996): 23, though not in relation to Freud and Nietzsche.

72. Nietzsche, *Thus Spoke Zarathustra,* 139.

Is Forgetting Unjust?

But what about justice? Kierkegaard seems to dismiss any need for human justice. God, of course, is engaged in judging the world, but Christians are to dispense with it, he asserts. Judgment in the here and now should be placed into the hands of worldly judges. "Let the judge appointed by the state, let the servant of justice work at discovering guilt and crime; the rest of us are called to be neither judges nor servants of justice, but on the contrary are called by God to love, that is . . . to hide a multitude of sins."[73] But what is the relation between serving justice and serving love? And if one is to hide sin, does one not need to know it as sin and therefore at least to that extent serve justice?

A byproduct of Kierkegaard's exclusion of justice when talking about love is a jarring disjunction between forgiveness and repentance. In *Purity of Heart Is to Will One Thing,* he reflects on what the offender should do and warns him against wanting to "get away from guilt," wanting to "banish all recollection of it."[74] That is good as far as it goes. The offender should not get the gift of non-remembrance without having done anything to deserve it, without repentance and transformation. But in this text justice seems so much to have taken the upper hand that he suggests eternal guilt and therefore eternal repentance in the form of the sinner's remembering what he "had been." Why eternal guilt? Because guilt is not changed by the passage of time, argues Kierkegaard.[75] And yet, Kierkegaard has gotten the relation between memory and guilt wrong here.

He is right, of course, about one thing: the passage of time has no effect on guilt. But that does not mean that guilt must remain. Forgiveness has effect on guilt, as Kierkegaard knows well. And if forgiveness can blot out guilt, would it not be appropriate for the wrongdoer — and the wronged! — *not to remember* the guilt that was blotted out? In fact, Kierkegaard echoes this very thought in *Eighteen Upbuilding Discourses* when he notes the effect of forgiveness on the Prodigal Son — the fa-

73. Kierkegaard, *Works of Love,* 293.

74. Søren Kierkegaard, *Purity of Heart Is to Will One Thing: Spiritual Preparation for the Office of Confession,* trans. Douglas Steere (New York: Harper, 1948), 44.

75. Ibid., 45.

ther's embrace has brought "the delinquent himself to forget everything."[76] Moreover, in *Works of Love,* "eternity" does not preserve guilt but removes it. "Get rid of the past," he advises, "drown it in the oblivion of eternity by abiding in love."[77]

So what effect does eternity have on sin? Does it preserve guilt? Swallow it up? Both? Kierkegaard seems unclear. If one banishes from love the concern for justice as he does, then forgiveness and repentance will remain at odds — the one, following the dictates of love, releases from guilt and allows guilt to slip from memory, and the other, following the dictates of justice, holds onto guilt.

Kierkegaard has gotten the relation between love and justice wrong, however. Love includes a concern for justice and is not opposed to it. The two, love and justice, come together in forgiveness. Because forgiveness presupposes that the claims of justice are valid (blame being prerequisite to forgiveness), repentance is an appropriate way for the wrongdoer to receive the gift of forgiveness and then cease to be remembered as guilty.

There is at least one more problem with the idea that love leaves justice behind: the place of the third party who heeds God's call to love. Imagine, writes Kierkegaard, that the loving one who hides sins committed against him "had a wife who loved him."

> See, just because she loved him she would discover how he had been sinned against in a multitude of ways. Injured and with bitterness in her soul, she would discover every mocking glance; with broken heart she would hear every derision — while he, the one who loves, discovered nothing.[78]

Now apply this to forgetting — which, along with being blind to sins, is a mode of hiding sins — and extend it to all life's relationships. What is a lover to do when an offender has injured her beloved? She will pursue

76. Kierkegaard, *Eighteen Upbuilding Discourses,* 63.
77. Kierkegaard, *Works of Love,* 307.
78. Ibid., 288.

justice out of love. But then she won't be able to hide sins in any of the ways suggested by Kierkegaard, at least not until the sins have been exposed and in some way dealt with. Again, love and justice seem incompatible, the one requiring blindness and hiding and the other demanding acknowledgment and exposure.

So What Now?

In conclusion, let me retrace my steps in this chapter. I engaged three great modern defenders of "forgetting." Freud, my most unlikely ally, helped show that non-remembrance need not be seen as repressive and that it may in fact be a consequence of successful psychic healing. Nietzsche, my ambiguous helper, underscored that non-remembrance is basic to our lives, to our very being as humans (from the way we perceive to the way we construe our identity), to uses to which we put the past, to our ability to be happy and to make others happy. His thought also embodies rather starkly a potential misuse of non-remembrance: a narcissistic preoccupation with oneself and a "playful" creation of one's own worlds of value in sovereign disregard of others. Kierkegaard, the most helpful of the three, showed how the non-remembrance of offenses endured is a gift the lover gives to the beloved — indeed, a gift profoundly in sync with the nature of love.

The strong tie between love and the non-remembrance of offenses established by Kierkegaard has, in a sense, taken me back to Chapter Seven, to Dante. He grounded in love the "forgetting" of sins as well as the remembering of what is good — in being taken by Love out of oneself and placed into Love's own pure Goodness, untainted by sin or evil. But integral to Dante's vision was something lacking in Kierkegaard's thought, namely, a concern for justice. Dante's spirits can "cleanse themselves" by bathing in and drinking of Lethe (the river of forgetfulness) only "when their repented guilt is set aside."[79] Lethe, along with Eunoe

79. Dante, *Inferno*, in *The Divine Comedy*, trans. and ed. Allen Mandelbaum (New York: Alfred A. Knopf, 1986), Canto XIV, lines 136-38.

(the river of remembering the good), is therefore situated at the boundary between purgatory and paradise, at the transition from the world as it is to the world to come. With the help lent by Freud, Nietzsche, and especially Kierkegaard, as well as many lesser-known minds, I will defend and develop in the next chapter a vision close to Dante's of what will happen with the memory of wrongs in the world to come.

CHAPTER NINE

Redemption: Harmonizing
and Driving Out

My thesis in the third part of this book has been simple: memories of suffered wrongs will not come to the minds of the citizens of the world to come, for in it they will perfectly enjoy God and one another in God. I will not address memories of what may be described as "natural" evils — awful sicknesses, devastating earthquakes, and the like. Here my topic focuses specifically on the ultimate fate of memories of wrongs suffered at the hands of fellow human beings — a limited topic with immense ramifications.

For many my thesis will touch a raw nerve — as it does for me! Let go of the memory of suffered wrong, and the ground on which you stand as a victim seems to disappear from underneath your feet! The offense no longer sticks to the offender! The food that nourishes your righteous anger gets cleared from the table! The accusing finger pointed at the offender — so that others can see what he has done and what you have suffered — loses its target! No longer do you have any reason for keeping the offender at bay! Indeed, the offender ceases to be an offender, for non-remembrance has taken away the very being of the offense, as Kierkegaard put it.[1] The victim

---

1. See Søren Kierkegaard, *Works of Love: Some Christian Reflections in the Form of Discourses*, trans. Howard and Edna Hong (New York: Harper & Row, 1964), 295-96.

screams in protest: A done deed cannot be undone, and the wrongdoer is guilty — forever guilty — before God, in the judgment of humanity, before his own conscience. An indelible tattoo inked by our memory onto his forehead and reading "Wrongdoer!" is the least of the punishments he deserves!

And yet. . . . We human beings — wronged and wrongdoers alike — are finite, fallible, fragile. We fall so easily into the snare of evil. Can we bear the weight of eternal memory? Would it be right for one horrible deed to mark us eternally, as some people believe that a single sin deserves the punishment of everlasting torment in hell? Even if such marking were fair, would love do that — the kind of love that wishes well and does good even to the enemy? Would we not wish to let go of the pain inflicted both by the wrong we have suffered and by our own guilt through letting go their memory, if somehow we could do so without detriment to ourselves or to our loved ones?

"Oh, Captain G., *bad* Captain G., terror of my unforgettable days and fear of my well-remembered nights! The strange God of utterly beautiful goodness whom I serve wants to give you a gift — and wants to give it through me! Yes, first the divine lover of wayward humanity will give a gift to me. A new self in a new world will help me let go of the memories of abuse I've suffered. That's the easy part, even if now I sometimes cling to those memories as though the salvation of my soul depended on them. The hard part will be passing that gift on to you! Yes, if the faith that I embrace has it right, you too will be given a new self in a new world — or so I hope, even if I can't be quite sure. But still, a wrongdoing is a wrongdoing, so I am reluctant. To help myself entertain the possibility of future innocence for the likes of you and the prospect of my full freedom from the wrong done to me (and by me!), to water the seed of hope that God's love has planted, I'm writing this book. And especially these last chapters. . . ."

So here is what I intend to do. In the present chapter, I will look at the transition from the world as it is to the world of perfect love and then examine how the idea that memories of wrongs will not come to the minds of the citizens of the world to come fits with a plausible Christian account of redemption. The examination will continue in Chapter Ten by addressing three more key issues: human identity, moral obligation toward victims, and the final consummation.

Transition via the Final Reconciliation

The Christian tradition has spoken of the transition from the world as it is to the world to come under two main rubrics: resurrection of the dead and final judgment. The two are intimately related yet distinct. The former deals, very roughly, with the physical side of the transition (with the fate of body and embodiment); the latter deals, again roughly, with what might be broadly described as the cultural side (the fate of the individual and social relations).[2] I will leave the question of resurrection aside here. True, to the extent that memories of wrongs are inscribed in the bodies of those who suffered them, the re-creation of a new body from the ruins of the old one is clearly relevant to my topic in that it makes non-remembrance possible. But we are in no way actively involved in our own resurrection; God raises us to a new life. We *are* actively involved in the cultural side of the eschatological transition, even though God is the primary agent of our salvation. So I will concentrate my remarks on that cultural side; and in a partial departure from tradition, I will introduce the category of *Final Reconciliation* to designate it. The Last Judgment, the primary preoccupation of many Christian thinkers throughout the centuries, is in my account one crucial aspect of that reconciliatory transition; the other aspect is *mutual embrace* by those who were formerly at odds with one another.[3]

But let us start with the Last Judgment. As a passageway from the world deeply marred by offense and debt to the world of perfect love, the Last Judgment has three important characteristics. First, it is a judgment of *grace*, for it is a judgment executed by the same Christ who died for the world's salvation. For grace to be enacted in judgment, two elements are essential: people's sins against God and neighbor must be brought to light in their full magnitude, and sinners must be freed from

2. See Miroslav Volf, "Enter into Joy! Sin, Death, and the Life of the World to Come," in *The End of the World and the Ends of God*, ed. John Polkinghorne and Michael Welker (Harrisburg, Pa.: Trinity International, 2000), 25ff.

3. On the Last Judgment and the Final Reconciliation, see Miroslav Volf, "The Final Reconciliation: Reflections on a Social Dimension of the Eschatological Transition," *Modern Theology* 16, no. 1 (2000): 102-5.

their guilt and transformed. Great debates rage in theology about who will be the recipient of God's judgment of grace — all people, or only some, with the rest being consigned to eternal damnation? I will leave this question open-ended here[4] and simply observe that God's is a judgment that both exposes sin and transforms the sinner.

Second, the Last Judgment is a *social* event; it happens not simply to individuals but between people. Human beings are linked by many ties to neighbors near and far, both in space and in time. We wrong each other and rightfully have cases against each other. At the Last Judgment God will settle all these "cases" — which all involve offenses against God, too, since any wrongdoing against a neighbor is also an offense against God. Ultimately, God will right all wrongs.

Finally, if the Last Judgment, understood as social event, is to succeed as a transition to the world of love, each person will joyfully *appropriate* the results of the judgment. The Last Judgment will reach its goal when all the wronged standing at the threshold of the world to come receive their rightful vindication, and when wrongdoers eschew attempts at misplaced self-justification, acknowledge their wrongdoing, and are freed from the hold of evil on their lives. In standing before Christ, the wronged and wrongdoers will see themselves and each other as does Christ, the just Judge who is full of mercy. Indeed, they will see each other and themselves *with the eyes of* Christ, for union with Christ begun in this life will be completed at the threshold of the world to come.

As noted earlier, the judgment of grace is one essential aspect of the Final Reconciliation understood as a transition from the world as it is to the world of perfect love. The other element I will call the *final mutual embrace*. The judgment of grace — effective forgiveness — affirmed by offender and offended alike, takes us out of the world of offenses. But it does not yet bring us into the world of perfect mutual love. For forgiveness may well leave the forgiven one humiliated on account of having been forgiven and therefore also repelled from the forgiver; and it may

4. For an excellent treatment of the issue, see Hans Urs von Balthasar, *Dare We Hope "That All Men Be Saved?": With a Short Discourse on Hell* (San Francisco: Ignatius Press, 1988).

leave the forgiver proud on account of having forgiven and therefore disdainful of the forgiven one.[5] If nothing more than forgiveness happened, each party could still go her own way, the one denigrated and repulsed and the other proud and contemptuous.

So even after the question of "right and wrong" has been settled by the judgment of grace, it is still necessary to move through the door of mutual embrace to enter the world of perfect love. And through that door the inhabitants of the world to come will move enabled by the indwelling Christ, who spread out his arms on the cross to embrace all wrongdoers. When former enemies have embraced, and embraced as belonging to the same community of love in the fellowship of the Triune God, then and *only* then will they have stepped into a world in which each enjoys all and therefore all take part in the dance of love.

Imagine that Captain G. and I find ourselves together in the forecourt of the world to come, both of us ready to enter it. If for *us* this world is to be a world of perfect love, neither of us can simply look aside pretending the other one is absent or that nothing wrong has happened between us. For then we would not love each other. We must reconcile — we must name the wrongdoings that were committed, we must agree about their nature, we must forgive and receive forgiveness, and we must affirm to each other the goodness of our being there together. If this does not happen, neither of us will enter the world of perfect love. After this does happen, after Christ has completed the eschatological transition through us, both he and I will be able to let the memory of wrongdoing slip into oblivion — a memory whose help as my guardian and a servant of justice will no longer be needed.

Such is my understanding of God's new world — a dance of love in the embrace of the Triune God, with love freely given, freely received, and never exhausted. For this new world to come about, not only must the dead be resurrected, but also the Final Judgment must expose sins and redeem persons, and the redeemed must receive each other in love in the final mutual embrace. And my hope is that wrongs suffered will not come to mind in *such* a world that has come about in *this sort of* way.

---

5. For this concept, see the chapter, "The Victory of the Conciliatory Spirit," in Kierkegaard's *Works of Love*, 331-44.

An Indestructible World

One more characteristic of the world to come needs to be noted to make plausible the proposal of the non-remembrance of wrongs suffered. It is the permanence of that world. Suppose you've entered the world of perfect love, but you suddenly think to yourself, "This isn't going to last very long. Sooner or later somebody is going to spoil the party. If we don't watch out, we'll have a brawl on our hands. We'd better remember who did what to whom and why, because we may be sorry if we don't!"

There *are* voices in the Christian tradition — notably, of the seminal third-century theologian Origen — who thought it possible, even likely, that the eschatological world of love could be undone. On the whole, however, tradition has affirmed the *permanence* of that world and argued for it in a variety of ways — for instance, by positing that it will be an atemporal world; that the object of love will generate desire for itself (as per Dante); that the soul's forgetting of what is past, even the past delights of divine love, will obviate its satiation and spur it to press on toward divine infinity (as per Gregory of Nyssa[6]). In whatever way its permanence is secured, the coming the world of love will be indestructible. Much like the communist society in Marx's vision,[7] the eschatological world of love cannot *have been.* If it were to pass out of existence (or even change character), its very pastness would make manifest the falseness of its claims to reality. So the worry about the eschatological party's getting spoiled is misplaced, at least in the Christian account of it. Then and there, no one will ever even be tempted to wrong others, just love them.

After Christ has completed the work of salvation and the eschatological transition has taken place, *after* the wrongdoers and the wronged have entered that world which cannot be undone — *after* the Last Judgment, *after* wrong committed and suffered has come to public light in God's judgment of grace, *after* the perpetrators have been accused and the victims vindicated, *after* they have embraced each other and recog-

6. See Gregory of Nyssa, *On the Soul and the Resurrection,* trans. Catharine P. Roth (Crestwood: St. Vladimir's Seminary Press, 1993), 77-81.

7. Karl Marx, *Economic and Philosophical Manuscripts of 1844,* ed. Dirk J. Struik, trans. Martin Milligan (New York: International, 1964).

nized each other as belonging to the same community of perfect love, *after all of these occurrences* — the memories of wrongs suffered will be released. They will no longer come to mind to diminish the joy that each person will know in the presence of others and all will know in the presence of God. *If* we believe in the world to come as a world of complete felicity in perfect love in the presence of God who blots out human transgression and takes humanity up into God's own joy, it would seem that we would need to believe something along these lines.

But *can* we? Some major questions need to be addressed before such belief will be possible. The first concerns the nature of salvation, and specifically the issue of redemption as it relates to the past.

Giving Meaning

What does salvation involve, if wrongs suffered will not come to mind in the world to come? Consider first the opposite — what would salvation involve if all memories of wrongs were eternally preserved? Whatever else salvation might include — such as the transformation of individuals, both victims and perpetrators, or the transformation of the world as envisioned above — it seems that it would need to entail rendering remembered wrongs in some way *meaningful*. If we are to remember them in a redeeming way — the way that, by definition, we would remember them in the world to come — the memories of these events would not be able to lead brute existences as mere mental monuments of our lives gone awry. They would have to be integrated into a narrative, given "significance as elements in a moral drama," to use a phrase from Hayden White.[8]

But why does meaning matter to us so much? The shift from traditional to modern societies in the West pushed the question of meaning into the foreground. As Charles Taylor argued in *Sources of the Self*, we moderns are less trying to meet the imperious demands of an unchal-

---

8. Hayden White, "Narrativity in the Representation of Reality," in his *The Content of the Form: Narrative Discourse and Historical Representation* (Baltimore: Johns Hopkins University Press, 1987), 21.

lengeable framework (as, for example, Martin Luther famously did) than to make sense of our lives. A basic condition for doing so is that we grasp our lives in a coherent narrative. He writes,

> We want our lives to have meaning, or weight, or substance, or to grow towards some fullness. . . . But this means our *whole* lives. If necessary, we want the future to "redeem" the past, to make it part of a life story which has sense or purpose, to take it up in a meaningful unity.[9]

Only that which is "recovered in its unity with the life yet to live" has meaning. Each event then becomes a preparation for what is to come and a fitting contribution to the whole.

It is not only historians of culture who note our yearning to integrate our whole past into a meaningful unity — a good deal of trauma literature echoes the same idea. In *Traumatic Stress,* Bessel A. Van der Kolk and Alexander C. McFarlane make a similar point. Since patients cannot change their past, they must place traumatic memories "in their proper context" and reconstruct them "in a personally meaningful way." In other words, "giving meaning is a central goal of therapy."[10] From this angle, to have segments of life containing significant experiences lost to memory and therefore not integrated into the whole of life is to sin against meaning and fail to heal what is broken.

Impossible Harmony

But is this true? Must our *whole* past be rendered meaningful to be redeemed? Might there not be experiences that stubbornly refuse to be integrated into a meaningful whole? Consider Lawrence Langer's much acclaimed *Holocaust Testimonies: The Ruins of Memory,* which is based on

9. Charles Taylor, *Sources of the Self: The Making of Modern Identity* (Cambridge, Mass.: Harvard University Press, 1989), 50-51.

10. Bessel A. Van der Kolk, Alexander C. McFarlane, and Lars Weisaeth, eds., *Traumatic Stress: The Effects of Overwhelming Experience on Mind, Body, and Society* (New York: Guilford, 1996), 19.

videotaped testimonies of Holocaust survivors. According to Langer, *written* accounts of life in the Nazi concentration camps often seek to integrate the Holocaust experience into a larger structure of meaning. The Holocaust then becomes a testimony to the "indomitable human spirit," an example of growing through suffering, a proof that moral integrity is possible even under extreme duress, a source of a more informed sense of ourselves as human beings, and more. In contrast, *oral* testimonies show that in the living memories of survivors, the Holocaust experience resists being tamed by the imposition of meaning; for the most part, the experience appears impossible to integrate into a larger narrative of meaningful life.

Consider the dilemma of Abraham P. He and his family arrived at Auschwitz from Hungary. His parents were sent to the left, which was to their death, while he, two older brothers, and a younger brother were sent to the right. Abraham P. recalls:

> I told my little kid brother, I said to him, "Solly, go to poppa and momma." And like a little kid, he followed — he did. Little did I know that I sent him to the crematorium. I am ... I feel like I killed him. My [older] brother, who lives in New York ... every time when we see each other he talks about him. And he says, "No, I am responsible, because I said that same thing to you. And it's been bothering me too." I've been thinking whether he reached my mother and father, and that he *did* reach my mother and father. He probably told them, he said, "Abraham said I should go with you." I wonder what my mother and father were thinking, especially when they were all ... when they all went into the crematorium [that is, the gas chamber]. I can't get it out of my head. It hurts me, it bothers me, and I don't know what to do.[11]

Can one give meaning to such experiences? As we listen to the "mutilated music" of such lives,[12] we *want* the dissonance to release itself into harmony so we can hear the whole as music rather than parts of it as

---

11. In Lawrence Langer, *Holocaust Testimonies: The Ruins of Memory* (New Haven: Yale University Press, 1991), 185-86.

12. The phrase is that of Nelly Sachs.

horrifying noise. But the dissonance remains unintegrable into anything that came before and will come after. "Harmony and integration," argues Langer, rightly referring to this and many similar stories, "are not only impossible — they are not desirable."[13]

Is, then, redemption possible for people such as Abraham P.? Langer seeks to offer some consolation. When "the self functions on the brink of extinction," we are left "with a series of personal histories beyond judgment and evaluation."[14] He seeks to relieve victims of the pressure of shame and guilt and between the lines tells them, "You should not expect to have acted differently in a situation of utter need and total loss of control." This counsel does not pretend to bring redemption, but it does at least offer a consoling explanation.

And yet the explanation itself simply confirms the dehumanization experienced. Insuppressible feelings of shame and guilt on the part of precisely the people who were at the edge of extinction and acted out of fear, out of confusion, or in ways that under normal circumstances they would not have acted are a form of rebellion against such dehumanization. Even while acknowledging their impossible circumstances, such victims cannot let go of their humanity, and therefore they instinctively reject explanations of their behavior and search for redemption. No effort to help them live with their deeply wounding or guilt-producing experiences by giving meaning to them ultimately satisfies.

Driving Out

So how can people whose experiences resist being rendered meaningful be redeemed? Locked in on meaning as we are, the only way we can imagine the redemption of anyone is through the redemption of *all* of his past experiences. If we were less concerned with meaning, as our pre-modern ancestors were and as many of our non-Western contemporaries are, we could entertain an alternative. A good deal of Christian tradition under-

13. Langer, *Holocaust Testimonies,* 83.
14. Ibid., 183.

stands redemption as the redemption of *people* without insisting on the redemption of all of their experiences. Below is a sampling of somewhat divergent ways of thinking about redemption, none of which has much to do with giving meaning.

Consider healings and the casting out of demons — two crucial aspects of Jesus' ministry. In the Gospels there is not even a hint that Jesus tried to give meaning to illnesses — especially not negative meaning as punishment for sin (see Luke 13:2-5). Illness is not integrated into a whole; it is healed, removed. It presents an occasion for God's glory to be revealed through deliverance (see John 9:1-3), not for some theoretical lesson that life has meaning notwithstanding negative experiences.

Or consider Gregory of Nyssa's vision of the eschatological movement of the soul — a soul that, like the Apostle Paul in Philippians 3, forgets what lies behind and stretches itself out toward and into that infinite ocean which is God. Such a soul, says Gregory of Nyssa in *On the Soul and the Resurrection*, "no longer gives any place in itself either to hope or to memory. It has what it was hoping for, and it drives out memory from its mind in its occupation with the enjoyment of good things."[15]

Think also of Martin Luther's account of redemption as a "wonderful exchange" between Christ the bridegroom and Christian the bride in *The Freedom of a Christian*. "By the wedding ring of faith," writes Luther, Christ makes his own the sins, death, and pains of hell that are properly his bride's.

> He suffered, died, and descended into hell that he might overcome them all. Now since it was such a one who did all this, and death and hell could not swallow him up, these were necessarily swallowed up by him in a mighty duel; for his righteousness is greater than the sins of all men, his life stronger than death, his salvation more invincible than hell. Thus the believing soul by means of the pledge of its faith is free in Christ, its bridegroom, free from all sins, secure against death and hell, and is endowed with the eternal righteousness, life, and salvation of Christ its bridegroom.[16]

15. Gregory of Nyssa, *On the Soul and the Resurrection*, 79.
16. Martin Luther, "The Freedom of a Christian," in vol. 31 of *Luther's Works*, 352.

Narrative integration into a larger framework of meaning? Nothing of the sort! Sin, along with death and hell, is not taken up into a meaningful unity but swallowed up by Christ in Luther's account. Memory of the past is not given meaning but driven from the mind in Gregory of Nyssa's vision of salvation. And in the Gospels, illness is not given meaning but healed. If deeply wounded and sinful people are to find redemption, they will need to experience this kind of salvation — one in which "driving out" and "overcoming" play at least as important a role as "integrating" and "harmonizing." The not-coming-to-mind of evils suffered is one aspect of salvation understood as the driving out of sin and the pains of hell. True, except for Gregory of Nyssa's, the conceptions of salvation mentioned do not make positive arguments for non-remembrance. They merely illustrate that there are plausible accounts of salvation that can dispense with the eternal memory of wrongs suffered.

Though my interrogations by the Yugoslavian military didn't even come close to the pains of hell, they were terrifying. Can I render those experiences meaningful? I could impose meaning on them — I could find some good that has come out of them. If I am honest, however, I doubt that they were meaningful (unless paradoxically their meaning lies in tuning me in to people's frequent suffering of meaningless wrongs). I seem to have gained from them nothing that I could not have gained by other means, and what I have gained does not seem worth the price. The memory of my negative experiences seems to me now a good candidate for consignment to oblivion (*after* Captain G. and I have been reconciled, of course). It may turn out that the experiences will prove meaningful when I survey my life from the vantage point of its end. If so, I will rejoice. But if not, I trust that I will still be fully redeemed by being freed from its incursions into my present through the gate of memory.

A Truncated Salvation?

Is not the price for entertaining such a notion of salvation too high, however? Does it not amount to denial, a flight from history? Our modern sense of the historicity of existence — of the fact that we are, essentially, part of a larger story and that in a deep sense we *are* our stories — makes us hesitate to take the step. The soul imagined by Gregory of Nyssa, which stretches itself into the divine while forgetting all that is behind, does seem to live ahistorically. Gregory of Nyssa stands in the great Platonic tradition, with its fundamental dialectic of remembering and forgetting. As Plato puts it in *Phaedrus,* it is only by "clinging in recollection to those things in which God abides, and in beholding which He is what he is" that the soul "becomes truly perfect." If the soul diverts its eyes from "the vision of truth" through "forgetfulness and vice," it decreases in perfection and drops to earth. Correspondingly, if it recollects rightly things it "saw while following God" it will "forget earthly interests" and be "rapt in the divine."[17] The earthly is significant only as the mnemonic device for attending to the divine; when a wise soul "sees the beauty of earth, [he] is transported with the recollection of the true beauty; he would like to fly away, but he cannot; he is like a bird fluttering and looking upward and careless of the world below."[18]

But such radical ahistoricity is not the only option for those who refuse to tie redemption too closely to conferring meaning on the whole of the lived life. Dante, it will be recalled, does not take this route. He asserts that what was good during this earthly existence will be remembered; the good is "ingathered and bound by love into a single volume" in the Eternal Light, which is God.[19] And gathering that comes after first being plunged and made to drink from the river of forgetting and then from the river of remembering can only be, to borrow a phrase of David Tracy, a "gathering of fragments,"[20] not integration of the *whole* of the lived life into a framework of meaning.

17. Plato, *Phaedrus,* in *The Dialogues of Plato,* 2nd ed., trans. J. Harward (Chicago: Encyclopaedia Britannica, Inc., 1990), 249.

18. Ibid., 249.

19. Dante, *Paradiso,* in *The Divine Comedy,* trans. and ed. Allen Mandelbaum (New York: Alfred A. Knopf, 1986), Canto XXXIII, 85-86.

20. See David Tracy, "Fragments and Forms: Universality and Particularity Today," in *The Church in Fragments: Towards What Kind of Unity?* ed. Giuseppe Ruggieri and Miklos Tomka (London: SCM, 1997), 122-29; and "Fragments: The Spiritual Situation of Our Times," in *God, the Gift, and Postmodernism,* ed. John D. Caputo and Michael J. Scanlon (Bloomington: Indiana University Press, 1999), 181-84.

In addition to the objection of radical ahistoricity, there is another important objection to the refusal to integrate all past events into the redeemed future. It concerns the death of Christ. Was it not meaningful, all the horror of an assault on the only truly innocent victim notwithstanding? It most certainly was! *Not all wrongs suffered are meaningless.* Above all, suffering that we take upon ourselves for the sake of others is not meaningless; by definition, it is laden with positive meaning (see John 15:13: "No one has greater love than this, to lay down one's life for one's friends"). But its meaning often consists precisely in relieving others of pain and guilt that *cannot* be rendered meaningful. Attempts to give meaning to wrongs from which we are redeemed by pointing to the greatness of the redeeming acts they required — *O, felix culpa!* — are, I believe, misdirected.

If we couple the refusal to integrate all experiences into a larger framework of meaning with eschatological non-remembrance (as I am suggesting here that we do), another worry may arise in relation to Christ's death. If wrongs suffered will not come to mind in the world of perfect love, does it mean that the death of Christ will not come to mind either? Wouldn't non-remembrance amount to "uncrucifying Christ"? Today many argue that the cross is an eternal event in God. I do not think that it is. The New Testament claim that Christ was the "Lamb slain from the creation of the world" (Revelation 13:8) means that he was *destined* from eternity to be crucified in time, not that he was crucified from eternity. If Christ was not the Crucified One before creation, why would he have to continue to be "the Crucified One" after redemption has been completed and unassailably secured in the world to come? Because the Resurrected One bears the marks of crucifixion? Against such an assumption, many great theologians believed that after the ascension (Martin Luther and John Calvin) or after the Second Coming (apparently Cyril of Alexandria) Christ's body no longer bore the marks of his wounds.[21]

21. See Peter Widdicombe, "The Wounds and the Ascended Body: The Marks of Crucifixion in the Glorified Christ from Justin Martyr to John Calvin," *Laval theologique et philosophique* 59 (February 2003): 137-54 (although Widdicombe himself advocates, along with such theologians as Bede and Aquinas, the eternal presence and significance of Christ's wounds).

Moreover, is it true that if we do not relate to Christ *as* the Crucified One we are not relating to Christ at all, or we are relating to another Christ? I see no reason why we should think so — unless sin-bearing exhausts the identity of Christ. Does Christ eternally bear our sins and sufferings? Has he not died once and for all — and by doing so taken away our sin and suffering for eternity? Will we not relate to him in eternity as *new* creatures, which is to say as *former* sinners and sufferers? True, our being new creatures in eternity will have been achieved in part through Christ's death. But it does not necessarily follow that life as a new creature is predicated on the eternal display of the means by which such life was achieved. We relate to the crucified Christ as long as we are being redeemed. Once we *have been* unalterably redeemed, his death along with our sin can be swallowed in his own divine life as one of the Holy Three who are the Holy One.

Think of the immensity of the cosmos and the even greater immensity of God! To believe that Christ is forever the Crucified One because he died on Golgotha would be to take not only ourselves too seriously, living as we do on a tiny speck of a planet, but above all to take the sin and evil of humanity and their effects on God too seriously! The cross of Christ is, rather, a stage on the road to resurrection and exaltation, and finally to that "liberation" of God from the pain of human waywardness which will occur with God's complete and irrevocable redemption of humanity[22] — a stage that can be left in the past even if its effects last for eternity.[23] Then we, partakers of God's glory, will love God for who God is and not for what God has done for us, sinners and sufferers.

22. Jürgen Moltmann, *The Coming of God: Christian Eschatology,* trans. Margaret Kohl (Minneapolis: Fortress, 1996), 336-39.

23. Elsewhere I have offered an alternative proposal to the problem posed by Christ's suffering (*Exclusion and Embrace: Theological Reflections of Identity, Otherness, and Reconciliation* [Nashville: Abingdon, 1996], 139-40), a proposal that, unlike the present one, presumes that the cross will be eternally remembered. I have come to believe that the proposal offered here is more plausible.

CHAPTER TEN

Rapt in Goodness

We do not need for all of our lived life to be gathered and rendered meaningful in order to be truly and finally redeemed, I argued in the previous chapter — no need to take all of our experiences, distinct in time, and bind them together in a single volume so that each experience draws meaning *from* the whole as well as contributes meaning *to* the whole. It suffices to leave some experiences untouched (say, that daily walk I took to school in the second grade), treat others with the care of a healing hand and then abandon them to the darkness of non-remembrance (say, the interrogations by Captain G.), and gather and reframe the rest (say, the joy and the struggle of writing this book).

The way in which we are redeemed must fit the way we are made up as human beings, and both our redemption and our human makeup must fit the moral obligations we bear; otherwise, our redemption would (at least partly) undo our identity as human beings — as redeemed persons who acted in a morally responsible manner, we would work against our own humanity and well-being. So it matters whether the ways we think about redemption, humanity, and moral obligations fit. But do they in fact fit in my explorations of memory in the world of perfect love? If we take non-remembrance of wrongs suffered to be part of the experience of final redemption, will we somehow transgress against our sense of identity, our moral obligations, or both? In the present chapter I will take up these issues and conclude by suggesting that the eternal memory of evil sits uncomfortably with an eternity characterized by joyous mutual love.

Identity and Non-Remembrance

What does it mean for me to be who I am, and how do my memories of wrongs that I have suffered figure in my being who I am? I have already argued that we can be healed without harmonizing all the aspects of our past life into a meaningful unity. Now I will shift the attention away from healing to personal identity and explore whether we can be ourselves without *remembering* our whole past life. Notice what I am *not* asking, namely, whether we would be *objectively* the same person as we are now without these specific wrongs having happened to us. We manifestly would not. Experiences, especially painful ones, inevitably leave marks and change us. What I *am* exploring is whether we could be *subjectively* who we are — whether we could have a feeling that we are ourselves rather than sensing a gaping hole at the core of our being — if we *did not remember* all that had happened to us. If wrongs suffered did not come to our mind, could we avoid the sense that we were missing an important part of ourselves? If we could not avoid that sense, non-remembrance would distort and truncate us. But we can — or so I will argue.

Consider first how the memory of any given personal experience relates to our identity. I submit that not only *could* we be who we are if we did not remember all that has happened to us — in fact, we *are* who we are *because* we don't remember all that has happened to us. As I noted in Chapter Eight, Nietzsche plausibly argued that forgetting is implicated already in the way we perceive the world. Among many other attributes, forgetfulness marks how we human beings are different from God. God sees and does not forget, except in a metaphorical sense in which God is said to "forget" our sins, for instance (and if God dwells in eternity, then strictly speaking God does not remember either). In contrast, if *we* did not forget, we would have a hard time perceiving anything. To perceive the clock on my desk, I need to block out most of what is in the field of my vision as I cast my eye on it. To hear a specific instrument while an orchestra is playing, I must tune out many instruments in favor of one. I perceive by partly "forgetting" what surrounds the object of perception. Of course, remembering is also part of human perception, but remembering is not at issue here. If forgetting is part and parcel of perceiving objects in our world, it will certainly be part of our sense of identity, for this sense is formed partly through what we perceive in ourselves and in the world around us, including what we have suffered at the hands of others.

But not only is forgetting a condition of perceiving and therefore of identity; we also inescapably forget a good deal of what we have clearly perceived. And yet, such forgetting notwithstanding, our identity remains intact. In *A Treatise of Human Nature,* David Hume asks rhetorically,

> For how few of our past actions are there, of which we have any memory? Who can tell me, for instance, what were his thoughts and actions on the first of January 1715, the eleventh of March 1719, and the third of August 1733? Or will he affirm, because he has entirely forgot the incidents of these days, that the present self is not the same person with the self of that time; and by that means overturn all the most established notions of personal identity?[1]

Insist on total recall of personal history to establish personal identity, and you will get fragmentation of personal identity, not its unity; for given how faulty human memory is, you won't be able to connect the islands of remembered events floating in the sea of forgotten ones. Our actual sense of personal identity is a result of both remembering and forgetting. Against all the evidence, assume now that we *can* remember everything about our life. If we did so, we will experience ourselves as very different from who we sense that we are; in fact, we will hardly be able to recognize ourselves.

1. David Hume, *A Treatise of Human Nature* 1.4.6 (Glasgow: Collins, 1962), 311.

Indeed, it is possible to show that forgetting is inseparable from personal identity even if we operate with a *strong* sense of *narrative* identity, the belief that in a profound sense we are our stories. I will question such a notion of identity shortly, but for now let it stand as a test of my argument about the identity-constituting role of forgetting. As Paul Ricoeur has argued, every narration inscribes forgetting into the activity of remembering. Given that we are finite beings with particular interests, if we tell a story, we must leave out events and episodes that, from the perspective of the narrator, seem unimportant. The possibility of telling a story differently is grounded on this selectivity, which makes active forgetting part of remembering itself.[2] The same is true of the stories of our lives. Because narrative identities are always conferred *a posteriori* — after the events have happened — and from a particular vantage point, forgetting is an essential aspect of the work of identity-shaping recollection.[3]

Identity and the Memory of Suffering

For my purposes it is not enough, however, to show that forgetting is part of every remembering and of every construction of the self's identity. For the question is not whether we could be ourselves while failing to remember random events from the past, but whether we could be our-

2. I am using "forgetting" here in the technical sense of "not coming to mind." The possibility of telling a story differently presupposes that one can access memories other than the ones used in the construction of one's story. Aleida Assmann has correctly differentiated between a *functional* memory, which is identity shaping, and *recorded* memory, which is an amorphous mass of unused and unamalgamated memories surrounding functional memory. New configurations of functional memory make selective use of materials from recorded memory. For the sake of the flexibility of functional memory, it is essential to keep recorded memory from erasure (*Erinnerungsraeume: Formen und Wandlungen des kulturellen Gedaechnises* [Munich: C. H. Beck, 1999], 130-42). The role assigned to recorded memory does not touch my point, however. Functional memory is identity shaping, and functional memory is predicated on selectivity and therefore on "forgetting."

3. Paul Ricoeur, *Das Raetsel der Vergangenheit: Erinnern — Vergessen — Verziehen*, trans. Andris Breitling and Henrik Richard Lesaar (Essen: Wallstein, 1998), 111, 141-42.

selves without remembering specifically wrongs that we have suffered. The more egregious the wrongs, the more they seem to insinuate themselves into our identities to such an extent that we cannot think of ourselves apart from having suffered them.

Note that the issue here is not our emotional and physical capacity or incapacity. There are situations in which most of us lack the power to think of ourselves without thinking of the wrongs we have suffered. Many people, after all, want desperately to forget a disturbing episode of their lives but are unable to do so. The issue is, rather, the possibility of *being* and *feeling* ourselves if we did not remember such experiences, on the assumption that in the world to come we *will* have the power not to remember them.

So could we still be ourselves — could we experience ourselves as ourselves without a sense of loss — if we did not remember wrongs committed against us? We certainly could, and we do. Even now we do not remember some of the wrongs committed against us. For instance, who among us remembers that two-year-old playmate who repeatedly snatched a favorite toy out of our toddler-sized hands, or pulled our hair, or bit us out of what seemed like sheer meanness? We tend to remember nothing of the events from our early childhood that have, arguably, shaped us more than any single event in adulthood, and we are still manifestly ourselves. Or, according to psychologists who advocate the idea of repression, we may not remember a severely traumatic experience — trauma, in the technical sense, being defined as experience that is so unbearable that it *must* be repressed — and yet are manifestly ourselves. Of course, traumatic experiences may leave people severely incapacitated without their knowing quite why, but that is a question of memory and healing, not of memory and identity.

Moreover, as both experiments and at least some cases of "resurrected" childhood memories attest, we can have *false* memories of major traumas and invent *false* autobiographies while preserving our sense of identity.[4] In-

4. Jean-Pierre Changeux and Paul Ricoeur, *What Makes Us Think? A Neuroscientist and a Philosopher Argue about Ethics, Human Nature, and the Brain*, trans. M. B. DeBevoise (Princeton: Princeton University Press, 2000), 148.

deed, those who have such false memories must feel more themselves *with* those memories than without them — otherwise they would not invent the so-called memories! Similarly, it is possible for us to have false memories of *pleasant* experiences — experiences of exploits ("fish stories"!) or enjoyments — redraw our autobiographies correspondingly, and still be ourselves. My point is not that we should go about reinventing ourselves as we please by fabricating memories. There are *moral* constraints on our memories — such as the obligation to truthfulness — that should deter us from remembering falsely. I outlined some of these constraints earlier in the book, and I will return to the issue shortly. But the phenomenon of false memories underscores that our sense of identity — our ability to think and feel ourselves *as* ourselves — can and does accommodate a good deal of non-remembering of some rather formative experiences.

One more example illustrating that we can preserve identity without remembering certain events from our lives — this time of experiences we can recall if we try to, but about which we think only sporadically. To revisit my own experiences in the military, I can go for days, even for months, without thinking about Captain G. Am I somehow alienated from my true self during those periods? I am not. What would then prevent me from being myself if I *never again* thought about Captain G. or his mistreatment of me? The fact that this experience was important for me and that it has shaped me for ill or good does not mean that I am not fully myself without recalling it.

So we are able to maintain a sense of identity with a rather unruly memory — a memory that remembers some important events but not others, that remembers them for a time but not permanently, that plays tricks on us and "remembers" when there is nothing to remember and does not remember when there is something to remember, a memory that skips over vast neighborhoods of lived space but dances persistently in some small alley spinning a web of truths, half-truths, lies, deletions, additions, and embellishments. Many of us live happily without trying to give our memories narrative coherence. And even when we seek to tell our lives as a story, the story still ends up being more like a "gathering of fragments," a process in which snippets of the past are construed and the gathering undertaken from ever-changing vantage points.

Our selves are not unlike what post-modern thinkers describe them to be: dispersed in all centeredness, discontinuous in all continuities, fractured notwithstanding all attempts to render ourselves coherent, and ever changing while manifestly always being self-same. And memory is at the heart of all these pulsating tensions of our vital selves.

Life Hidden in God

If our identity is made and remade of gathered fragments, the non-remembrance of suffered wrongs will not violate our sense of identity. Superimpose on this account of personal identity a theologically informed notion of the self, and in fact the way is opened wide for such non-remembrance. Martin Luther's famous little treatise *The Freedom of the Christian* reaches its peak when he concludes,

> a Christian lives not in himself, but in Christ and in his neighbor. Otherwise he is not a Christian. He lives in Christ through faith, in his neighbor through love. By faith he is caught up beyond himself into God. By love he descends beneath himself into his neighbor. Yet he always remains in God and in his love.[5]

To be a Christian means, in a sense, to be displaced. A Christian does not live within herself; she lives outside herself — in God and in her neighbor. Reflect for a moment about the first and more fundamental displacement, on living by faith "in God" or being "caught beyond" and placed "into God." It is significant for Luther in two ways. First, it releases people from the pressure of having to gain favor with God by what they do. This idea lies at the heart of Luther's account of salvation. His point is not that what people do does not matter; it matters profoundly — to God, to their neighbors, to themselves. Yet nothing they do changes the fact that God loves them and, if they trust in God, will remake them into new creatures, freed from guilt and capable of loving others.

5. Martin Luther, *The Freedom of a Christian,* in vol. 31 of *Luther's Works,* 371.

Being "caught beyond" ourselves and placed "into God" is significant for Luther in yet another way. Behind his account of how God saves human beings lies his account of who human beings are. We are neither made nor unmade by what we do or by what others do to us. The heart of our identity lies not in our hands, but in God's hands. We are most properly ourselves because God is in us and we are in God. No doubt, what we or others have inscribed onto our souls and bodies marks us and helps shape who we are. Yet it has no power to define us. God's love for us, indeed God's presence in us and our being "caught up beyond" ourselves and being placed "into God" most fundamentally defines us as human beings and as individuals.

Now apply this defining character of God's presence in us to the whole of our lived lives, not simply to any given point in them. It follows that, in terms of identity, *we are not fundamentally the sum of our past experiences* (as we are also not fundamentally our present experiences or our future hopes added to our past experiences). Our memories, experiences, and hopes still matter; but they qualify rather then define who we are. If this is correct, the grip of the past on our identity has been broken.

A Shrunken Self?

The "grip" of the past, I wrote. But this is not how we think of it today. We think of the self as so much shaped by the past that the loss of some portion of it feels as though the self has shrunk. The difference between these two perspectives — Luther's and our own — is part of a major shift from pre-modern to modern anthropology. The shift can be observed already in the thinking of the seventeenth-century philosopher John Locke. Instead of construing identity either through the position of a person with respect to God, or a particular group, or even a stable social role, Locke construes it with the help of consciousness, self-reflection, and memory.[6] He writes:

6. See Assmann, *Erninnerungsraeume,* 95-98.

It is plain, consciousness, as far as ever it can be extended — should it be ages past — unites existences and actions very remote in time into the same person, as well as it does the existences and actions of the immediately preceding moment: so that whatever has the consciousness of present and past actions, is the same person to whom they both belong.[7]

In other words, we are ourselves because, with the help of memory, we connect our past with our present.

This Lockean understanding of identity is consonant with the experience of many of our contemporaries. In our novelty-obsessed (rather than tradition-shaped) cultures there is no ready-made, pre-shaped identity into which we can slip during transitional stages, such as when we take up a vocation, get married, or become parents. To answer the question, "Who are you?" as inhabitants of late modernity we must reach to significant experiences from our personal past. Such "reflexive mobilizing of self-identity" through the recourse to memory, writes Anthony Giddens in somewhat tortured sociological speak, is a "general feature of modern social activity in relation to psychic organization."[8] Put plainly and somewhat roughly: I am what I remember that I have experienced. The more that happens to me and the more of it I remember, the richer my identity. Inversely, the less that happens to me and the less of it I remember, the poorer my identity. From this perspective, not to remember something that happened to me is to lose a chunk of myself.

---

7. John Locke, *An Essay Concerning Human Understanding*, ed. P. H. Nidditch (Oxford: Clarendon, 1975), II.27.16. There are, of course, significant problems with such a close tying of identity with memory. The earlier quotation from David Hume was written in criticism of Locke's account of identity. Commenting on Locke, Charles Taylor correctly objects: "I would be the same person as the teenager who graduated from high school, because I still remember my graduation; and he would be the same as the five-year-old who had a birthday party, because he remembered the birthday party; but I would not be the same as the five-year-old, because over the years I've forgotten the party" (Taylor, *Sources of the Self: The Making of Modern Identity* [Cambridge, Mass.: Harvard University Press, 1989], 543n.17).

8. Anthony Giddens, *Modernity and Self-Identity: Self and Society in Late Modern Age* (Stanford: Stanford University Press, 1991), 33.

From Luther's perspective, however, things look almost the opposite. A self that defines itself primarily with respect to its past has shrunk virtually beyond recognition: From being the dwelling place of the Creator of the universe and a sojourner into the infinite mystery of God's life, it shriveled up to a mere receptacle of its own past experiences. Moreover, such a self always remains enclosed in itself — either dutifully bearing the whole burden of the past, with its highs and lows, or playfully reinventing itself by recombining selected portions from the past. What it lacks is precisely what, from Luther's perspective, is most fundamental to the self: drawing its identity from being rapt in God by faith.

Fulfilled, protected, and delighted in the divine life, the self can let go of itself and its memories of injustice suffered and guilt incurred. Yet the self does not remain simply with its God. If it is truly in God by faith, it will be in its neighbor by love, argues Luther, because God *is* love. Such a self acts as "Christ" in relation to the neighbor — it forgives transgressions and embraces the neighbor in love.

Is something lost to the self by being in God and neighbor and therefore not glued to its past? Nothing except that which such a self will rightly consider expendable — a willing "loss," to use the terminology the Apostle Paul employs in Philippians (3:7). Much would be lost if the self simply discarded its past and abandoned it in favor of "being in God." Our lived lives would then not matter at all. But being in God is not an alternative to living in time, so that we would have to choose one or the other. Rather, being in God frees our lives from the tyranny the unalterable past exercises with the iron fist of time's irreversibility. God does not take away our past; God gives it back to us — fragments gathered, stories reconfigured, selves truly redeemed, people forever reconciled.

Margarete's Cry

What light does this Christian notion of identity shed on the possibility or impossibility of the ultimate non-remembrance of wrongs suffered? Kierkegaard's handling of Margarete from Goethe's *Faust* in *Either/Or* provides a good example for the answer I will offer. Seduced by Faust,

Margarete had loved him, a human being, more than "God in heaven." In fact, she loved him so much that she had "completely disappeared in Faust."[9] But then Faust abandoned her and she was devastated, left not only with an open wound but also with an unbearable contradiction in her very identity. "Can I forget him?" she asks rhetorically, and everything in her rebels against the possibility.

> Can the brook, however long it keeps on running, forget the spring, forget its source, sever itself from it? If so, it would just have to stop flowing! Can the arrow, however swiftly it flies, forget the bowstring? If so flight would just have to come to an end! . . . Can I forget him? Then I would just have to cease to be![10]

Margarete's predicament is understandable. She has given her total self to Faust in love, and she can now hold onto herself only if she holds onto Faust, who has abandoned her. But her difficulty rests on a deep offense — not only the one Faust has undeniably committed against her, but even more basically the one Margarete has been seduced to commit against herself. She has allowed Faust to take the place of God by occupying her, and now she cannot disentangle her identity from her history with him.

Faust is expendable. Faust must be dethroned. Margarete is Margarete not on account of her relation to Faust but on account of God's unbreakable commitment to her and presence in her. Trusting in God as the source of our being and identity frees us from excessive attachments to any person, worldly good, or event. Placed by faith in God, we *can* forget any past event without "ceasing to be." Why? Because the spring of our brook and the bow of our arrow is nothing from our past, but instead the eternal God. Our identity consists in the fact that in faith we receive ourselves from God's hand. I expressed this thought earlier in terms of God's defining presence in our souls and of our being "in God." We can

9. Kierkegaard, *Either/Or,* ed. and trans. Howard V. Hong and Edna H. Hong (Princeton: Princeton University Press, 1987), 1:210, 213.

10. Ibid., 1:212.

also express it in terms of God's defining knowledge of us. As Eberhard Jüngel put it in relation to the Last Judgment, as we shall be known by God, "this is how we shall have been."[11] Either way, our identity is fundamentally in God's hands, not ours, and certainly not in the hands of those who have wronged us. So we can let go of the memory of wrong suffered without in any sense "ceasing to be."

The Obligation to Remember

We *can* let go of memories of wrongs suffered, I have argued. Neither our salvation nor our identity depends on it. But *should* we? Might there be moral reasons that speak against such non-remembrance? There are, but we must examine carefully to what extent they apply to the kind of non-remembrance for which I am arguing here: the not-coming-to-mind of wrongs suffered *after* justice has been served and *after* entrance into a secure world of perfect love.

Let us first consider the memory of any given event. It would be strange to say that we have a duty to remember our past in general. I do neither my family nor myself any wrong if I have forgotten some detail of a particular trip — one of many such trips — we took together some years ago. They, or I myself, may be disappointed that my memory is so leaky or that the detail meant so little to me that I have forgotten it. But that non-remembrance would be more like forgetting what the capital of Mauritania is, rather than like forgetting that I've promised to take my son on an outing. By not remembering, I would not be failing in an obligation — not unless there was a special investment of time and energy on their part to make that detail of the trip special to me.

If I claim to remember that trip, however, *then* I have a duty to remember it truthfully. That my memory will always involve a construction of events from a particular vantage point and therefore entail "forgetting" changes nothing in regard to this duty. As I have argued in

---

11. Eberhard Jüngel, *Death: The Riddle and the Mystery,* trans. Ian and Ute Nicol (Philadelphia: Westminster, 1974), 121.

Chapter Three, if I do not remember truthfully, I fail to give due credit to the past and to the actors from the past. But our concern here is not with the memory of any given event; it is, rather, with the memory of wrongs suffered. In their case, the same argument applies: if we remember them, then we have an obligation to remember them truthfully. We wrong others, and possibly also ourselves, if we remember wrongs untruthfully.

Assuming my argument is correct, the question is now whether we have an obligation to remember in the first place. Consider the case of Avraham Troy, a Lithuanian Jew whose meticulous diary chronicled three years of murderous Nazi rule. He had his notebooks buried underground in crates as soon as they were filled. In each crate he included the note: "I am hiding in this crate what I have written, noted, and collected with thrill and anxiety, so that it may serve as material evidence — 'corpus delicti' — accusing testimony when the Day of Judgment comes."[12]

When it comes to offenses against others, the obligation to remember is an extension of the obligation to attend to the wrongs committed. Sometimes no more will be possible than to offer victims "the most elementary compensation," which is "to give them a voice, the voice that was denied to them."[13] At other times vindication of victims and condemnation of perpetrators will be possible. Remembering is then part of the pursuit of justice for the victims. As long as the evildoers remain evildoers and have not been brought before the ultimate Judge, the wrongs they have committed will have to be remembered. Memory *is* judgment in the absence of more public judgment, including the Last Judgment. In fulfilling these obligations, Christians who take their faith seriously will aim at forgiveness and reconciliation. We remember so that we can forgive and reconcile, and since we have an obligation to forgive and reconcile, we have an obligation to remember. But forgiveness and reconciliation are also tied to the letting go of memories, I have argued earlier. So which is it? Do we remember so that we can forgive and reconcile, or do we forgive and reconcile so that we can let go of memories? It is both, and it is so in

12. *The New York Times,* March 18, 2002, A23.

13. Paul Ricoeur, "The Memory of Suffering," in his *Figuring the Sacred: Religion, Narrative, and Imagination,* trans. David Pellauer, ed. Mark I. Wallace (Minneapolis: Fortress, 1995), 290.

an unalterable sequence: in deliberate and often difficult steps, we remember, we forgive and reconcile, we let go of memories. The letting go of memories, as I advocate it, is not a unilateral act, one that persons who have been wronged do on their own. Even forgiveness is not a unilateral act. Though given unconditionally, it is a gift that has to be received, not just extended, for it to be truly given; I must receive forgiveness to be forgiven.[14] And the letting go of memories — non-remembrance of an offense — is even less a unilateral act. It makes sense only after the victim has been redeemed and the perpetrator transformed and after a relationship between them has been redefined through reconciliation. As long as reconciliation has not taken place, the obligation to remember wrongs stands. For not only does memory serve justice; memory *and* justice serve reconciliation.

A Difficult Obligation

Remembering wrongs is not an easy obligation to fulfill, however. In addition to the difficulties associated with remembering truthfully and to our proclivity to use memories to harm others, which I noted in Chapters Three and Four, the sheer scope of the obligation to remember wrongs suffered, if taken seriously, represents an almost unbearable burden. So we tend to think that only egregious offenses must be remembered, say, crimes against humanity.[15] The position is understandable because entire communities and even humanity as a whole has a stake in remembering such offenses. But it rests on a prejudice born of our limited capacity to remember and represents an injustice on top of it.

A non-utilitarian ethical standpoint such as my own dictates that if we have a moral duty to remember, then that duty must extend to *every* offense, however great or small. Not to remember small offenses while remembering great ones is to be unfair; for letting small offenders off the

14. For this account of forgiveness see Miroslav Volf, *Free of Charge: Giving and Forgiving in a Culture Stripped of Grace* (Grand Rapids: Zondervan, 2005), 181-83.

15. See Avishai Margalit, *Ethics of Memory* (Cambridge, Mass.: Harvard University Press, 2002), 78-83.

hook implicitly portrays great offenders as worse than they actually are. They appear in the grip of moral darkness, whereas the rest of us dwell in the splendor of moral light, which situation is manifestly not the case. But how could we remember every offense, great *and* small, if, as Nietzsche rightly noted and as Christian tradition uniformly affirms, to live is to be unjust, and inescapably though not totally so?

That memory is inescapably caught in the injustice of life is not sufficient reason to discard the obligation to remember, however. We must do as well as we can — and trust that full truth and justice will be revealed at the Day of Judgment. In the Christian account of life as it now is, we remember in hope for that day. So the obligation remains, but it ought to be fulfilled with the keen awareness that all of our remembering is partial and in that sense also partly unjust.

Where then does the obligation to remember wrongs suffered leave the thesis that *after* the Final Reconciliation, wrongs suffered will fade from our memory? For after that eschatological event, we will presumably be able to remember justly. *Would we be morally justified* to let go of memories of wrongs right at the point when we *can* remember as we ought to? Is the not-coming-to-mind of memories of wrongs in the world to come inescapably immoral, or at least morally deficient?

An Obligation to Remember Eternally?

It is easy to see why people who believe that the human story ends with death and who do not hope for the Last Judgment or the Final Reconciliation would want to remember forever — or at least as long as humanity lasts. The sentiment Elie Wiesel expressed in his testimony at the Barbie trial (1987) is argument enough for such a stance: "Justice without memory is incomplete justice, false and unjust. To forget would be an absolute injustice in the same way that Auschwitz was the absolute crime. To forget would be the enemy's final triumph."[16] Even if full justice could be achieved, it would not be enough, states Wiesel. For though justice vin-

16. Ibid., 187.

dicates, it is unable to bring the dead back to life. Memory does that, in a sense — it gives back life to those who are dead because it refuses to let them be effaced from memory as they have been torn from the land of the living. To remember is to deny the perpetrator ultimate triumph. Hence the obligation to remember "always."

If I did not hope in the world to come, I would embrace the "eternal" remembering of wrongs suffered. But I do hope in the world to come. I believe that we will be living with those who have died, not as with the dead but as with the living, looking into their eyes and not just remembering their past. Given this conviction, what moral obligation would there be to remember wrongs suffered eternally? After full justice has been done and final reconciliation accomplished, and after the dead are raised, will we need memory to keep victims "alive" and attend to their suffered wrongs? Will not they themselves be masters of the memory of their sufferings? Will they somehow transgress against themselves and others if they no longer remember there, *in that permanent world of perfect love*, which has come about after the Final Reconciliation? I do not think so.

Let me press the point a bit further. Would it not be right to ask those who in that world *wanted* to hold onto memories of evil suffered and committed why they wanted to do so (note: not those who *could not let go* of these memories but who *wanted to hold onto* them)? What function would those memories serve in a secure world of perfect love? If those who wanted to keep such memories alive were the perpetrators, would we be wrong in suspecting that they could not forgive themselves for what they had done and therefore needed living memories to keep blaming themselves? If they were the victims, would it not be likely that they wanted to hold onto these memories because they cherished resentment against perpetrators or at least wanted to hold it in reserve? If we remembered wrongs suffered in a secure world of perfect love, might not our memory be doing the bidding of the desire for revenge — either on ourselves or on others? Conversely, would there not be in that world something right about Nietzsche's coupling of nobility and obliviousness to wrongs suffered?

But, some may protest, *justice* demands that we remember eternally, and that is reason enough to remember. "Forget the past and it will be as if it never happened," is the advice of the evil Mephistopheles to Faust after he has abandoned Margarete, or, as he often calls her, Gretchen. Even if Gretchen and Faust were to reconcile and to inhabit a world of love, would it not be in some deep sense unjust toward both of them for non-remembrance to make Faust's abandonment "never to have happened"? He, the wrongdoer, would be thought of as though he were innocent, and she, the wronged, would be thought of as though she had not been harmed. The offense would have then been completely dissociated from the offender, and its harm would have been completely dissociated from the one who was offended. Would this not falsify their relationship? Would not this falsification be unjust — conveniently unjust to Faust and distressingly unjust to Gretchen? By what right would we detach the wrongdoing even from a judged, repentant, and transformed wrongdoer?

But that is exactly what forgiveness does! For herein lies the essence of Christian forgiveness: On account of his divinity, Christ could and did shoulder the consequences of human sin; so the penalty for wrongdoing can be detached from wrongdoers. And since on account of his humanity Christ could and did die on behalf of sinners, they, in effect, died when he died; so guilt can be detached from wrongdoers. When we forgive those who have wronged us, we make our own God's miracle of forgiveness. Echoing God's unfathomable graciousness, we decouple the deed from the doer, the offense from the offender. We blot out the offense so it no longer mars the offender. That is why the non-remembrance of wrongs suffered appropriately crowns forgiveness.

Grace-filled forgiveness and the non-remembrance of offenses is scandalous, especially when extended to vile evildoers — say, to soldiers who have slain children one by one before their mother's eyes but refused to let the mother die, preferring "her to remain alive but inhabited by death."[17] That many people feel a strong urge to reject forgiveness and non-remembrance is understandable. Moreover, no argument independent of belief in the God of infinite love who justifies the ungodly and fi-

17. Elie Wiesel, *From the Kingdom of Memory: Reminiscences* (New York: Summit, 1990), 186.

nally redeems and reconciles the world can be constructed to persuade those who want to keep a tight grip on strict retributive justice and insist on erecting an indestructible monument to wrongs suffered. But if God's reconciling self-giving for the ungodly stands at the center of our faith, then nothing stands in the way of opting for grace, with its pain and delight, of forgiving and ultimately releasing the memory of suffered wrongs.

It is important to get right the process by which we let go of memories of wrongs suffered. Such letting go is an act of grace, and it must be governed by the *logic* of grace. Faust, the wrongdoer, could never step into the paradise of non-remembrance on his own; for Gretchen's memory is an angel wielding a fiery sword at its entrance. Neither could he demand of Gretchen free passage; he has absolutely no right of admission, for he has *deserved* the remembrance of his misdeed. He can only beg to be admitted to the paradise from which the affliction of memory has been removed — he can only cast himself completely on her mercy.

But Gretchen could give to Faust the *gift* of admittance — and thereby translate both him and herself out of the world marked by transgression and into a world of love and felicity. What's more, it is my hope that she *will* give this gift to Faust if they both find each other in the forecourt of that world of love. Will someone force her not to remember? No — no one will even insist that she not remember. If she gives that gift, she will give it as all good gifts are given — voluntarily and joyfully. God will give her a new self made into a perfect dwelling place for the gift-giving and sin-bearing God — and it is through the power of that God that she will joyfully pass on to Faust God's gift of forgiveness and non-remembrance. Having found her proper self in God, who *is* love, she will flourish by doing what God's love does through her — forgive, reconcile, and no longer think of the injury.

Total Exposure?

So far in my proposal about the not-coming-to-mind of wrongs suffered in the world to come, I have examined two broad topics. First, I reviewed briefly what the great stream of the Christian tradition says about forgiveness, God's and ours. In that tradition, I pointed out, the non-remembrance of forgiven sins figures prominently. Second, I offered a series of considerations to show that nothing stands in the way of embracing the idea of non-remembrance, even if it does seem strange to us today. I argued that the idea is compatible with a plausible account of human salvation, of human identity, and of moral responsibility. Now it is time to point out at least some reasons *why* the Christian tradition so consistently couples full-fledged forgiveness with non-remembrance of wrongdoing. I will focus once again on the character of the world to come and inquire about the extent to which the eternal memory of evil suffered is compatible with the vision of the final consummation as a world of perfect love and undiluted joy — or whether it is compatible at all.

Engage with me in a bit of imagining. Will there be monuments to Hiroshima in the world to come? To the rape of Nanking and to Mao's brutalities? To Stalin's purges and the ravings of the Khmer Rouge? To the slaughter of indigenous populations by European colonialists? Will both victims and perpetrators gather around these monuments to commemorate this bloody history, while thanking God for delivering them from it? Maybe. But if so, would the world to come still be the world of perfect love and undiluted joy?

As I have argued earlier, if we *should* remember wrongs suffered, then we must remember *all* wrongs — each misdeed of every person, not only notorious atrocities and public crimes but also all the private misdeeds committed under the protection of impenetrable darkness and hidden behind the veil of silence, not only egregious private offenses but also all the trifling and infuriating nastiness — gossip, half-truths, slights, and more — that pervades every interaction between human beings, whose life is, on the whole, "brutish" even if it is no longer so short! It would be hypocritical and unfair to remember the wrongs of great public offenders but not the wrongs the rest of us perpetrated. So if in the world to come we *will* remember wrongs suffered, then, given that by definition all will be fair there, we will remember every evil deed and every evil thought that at the Last Judgment was recorded, brought to light, condemned, and then forgiven!

Let your imagination fly undaunted by the horror it would encounter right there in the city of "golden streets" and "bejeweled walls." Suppose I take a walk with a friend along a heavenly boulevard and see someone else walk by on the other side. Not wanting to speak ill of others, I say nothing to my friend. But both of us know: This is that despicable child molester who looked so respectable but who week after week abused his tender daughter or his fearful altar boy. Redeemed now, but back then.... Both my friend and I recall this truth, knowing all the while that we ourselves, with all of our small and great failings, lie exposed to the gaze of everyone else!

With the whole history of each inhabitant of the world to come — small and great sinners alike — permanently bathed "in the field of total visibility," would we not wish for some shadows and hiding-places to which to retreat from the unbearable assault that our own and others' memory of our wrongdoings would represent? Would we not exclaim, "If this supposed world of perfect love and felicity is such a horrid place of unceasing exposure of all forgiven sins, then I prefer a modest life-span in our world as it is, where, for all of its grave problems, I can at least enjoy the blessing of knowing that not all of my sins are universally known and perpetually exposed!" Indeed, with this kind of world to come as a prospect, one can understand why Gilles Deleuze — a fierce critic of Christianity who operated with some such vision of heaven — would rather burn in the lake of sulfur than stroll along the golden streets![18]

Do we not long to be accepted as we are, warts and all, someone may protest? Could not the world of perfect love be just such a world in which we are loved notwithstanding all of our imperfections? We do long to be accepted unconditionally. But we also want others to see past our warts and concentrate on what is beautiful about who we are. I hope that both of these longings will be satisfied. At the *transition* from the world as it is to the world to come, all of our imperfections will be known, and we will be loved nonetheless — and therefore forgiven, reconciled, transformed. And then *in* the world of perfect love we will shine in all of our beauty, our warts completely cured.

18. See Gilles Deleuze, *Kleine Schriften,* trans. K. D. Schacht (Berlin: Minerva, 1980), 114.

The Reality of Heaven and the Memory of Evil

Two more considerations contribute to a jarring disconnect between the memory of wrongs suffered and the loving character of the world to come. One concerns the *social vision* with which we are operating when we insist on the eternality of the memory of suffered wrongs. Certainly a world of perpetual remembrance of all evil deeds is compatible with perfect retributive justice, though such justice might arguably be closer to eternal damnation than to anything resembling eternal redemption. But could we imagine a world of perpetual remembrance as a world of love? We could imagine it as a world of the kind of love that struggles and suffers. All the blessed would then share in that extraordinary divine love, which loves despite knowing human beings' petty but often nasty transgressions and great crimes against each other and sins against God. But could we imagine such a world as one of felicity? Is it conceivable as a world of *joy,* and the world of joy *in one another* on top of it, which is what a world of love is said to be? I will not claim that this is impossible; but it seems to me rather implausible.

Here is what Elie Wiesel has to say about joy and the memory of horrendous wrongs. Addressing a prayer to God on behalf of the survivors of the Holocaust some fifty years later, he writes:

> Oh, they [the survivors] do not forgive the killers and their accomplices, nor should they. Nor should you, Master of the Universe. But they no longer look at every passer-by with suspicion. Nor do they see a dagger in every hand. Does this mean that the wounds in their soul have healed? They will never heal. As long as a spark of the flames of Auschwitz and Treblinka glows in their memory, so long will my joy be incomplete.[19]

Christian readers should not stumble over the first lines of this prayer and thus miss the import of its last sentence. For Wiesel's request for the Master of the Universe not to forgive killers and their accomplices ech-

19. Elie Wiesel, "A Prayer for the Days of Awe," *New York Times,* October 2, 1997, A19.

oes the psalmist's request that the sins of "wicked and deceitful men" may "always remain before the Lord" (109:15). Wiesel is a modern-day psalmist, not a follower of the Christ whose forgiveness knows no bounds. But the last line of the prayer makes a point on which the followers of this Christ will agree with Wiesel: Remembering horrendous evils and experiencing joy, especially joy in one another, are irreconcilable. A world to come that keeps alive the memory of all wrongdoings suffered — and not just of horrendous evils — would not be a place of uplifted radiant faces but one of eyes downcast in shame, not a place of delight in one another but a place enveloped in the mist of profound sadness. For Wiesel, the unforgiving and never-to-be-forgotten memory of the flames of Auschwitz precludes the experience of pure felicity. So it would be for everyone who remembered the wrongs of history truthfully and whose heart had not grown hard.

Second, the eternal memory of wrongs suffered implies the *eternality of evil* in the midst of God's new world. If wrongs suffered are permanently inscribed in the minds and identities of the citizens of the world to come, would this not represent a peculiar triumph of evil rather than its complete defeat?

Note that the memory of evil is what many evildoers want; they do evil to be remembered. In the movie *Amadeus,* Salieri speaks for many wrongdoers when, addressing the priest after killing Mozart, he says,

> Whenever they say Mozart with love, they'll have to say Salieri with loathing. And that's my immortality — at last! Our names will be tied together for eternity — his in fame and mine in infamy. At least it's better than the total oblivion he'd planned for me, your merciful God.[20]

Salieri killed *in order to* be remembered. Evildoers triumph when they and their deeds are remembered even when they themselves have been defeated — the reason the same psalmist who implores God not to for-

---

20. *Amadeus,* directed by Milos Forman, screenplay by Peter Shaffer (Republic Pictures, 1984).

give the wicked prays that the memory of them may be blotted out from the earth (109:15).

If we remembered wrongs suffered in the world to come, we would not only defer to the wishes of evildoers, we would also pay too much respect to evil itself. What incredible power evil would have if once you had wronged someone, you, the person you had wronged, and God would remain permanently marked by it! Would there not in the eternal memory of wrongs suffered resound a hellish laughter of the seemingly defeated and yet strangely triumphant underworld, triumphant because it has succeeded in casting eternally its dark shadow over the world to come? To be fully overcome, evildoing must be consigned to its proper place — nothingness. Non-remembrance does precisely that, as Kierkegaard insisted; "to forget," he noted, "is to take back into nothing."[21] Karl Barth thought no differently. "To the past and to *oblivion*" is where God's word consigns *das Nichtige,* that great destructive "something" that is also most properly nothing.[22]

Is the non-remembrance of wrongs suffered that I propose a flight from the unbearable memory into the felicity of oblivion? No flight is involved. According to my conception, each wrong suffered will be exposed in its full horror, its perpetrators condemned and the repentant transformed, and its victims honored and healed. Then, after evil has been both condemned and overcome, we will be able to release the memories of wrongs suffered, able to let them slip out of our mind. Will we let go of them *so as to be able* to rejoice with complete and permanent joy in God and in one another? No, that is not quite the right way to think about the not-coming-to-mind of memories of wrongs suffered. We will not "forget" so as to be able to rejoice; we will rejoice and *therefore* let those memories slip out of our minds! The reason for our non-remembrance of wrongs will be the same as its cause: Our minds will be rapt in the goodness of God and in the goodness of God's new world, and the memories of wrongs will wither away like plants without water.

21. Søren Kierkegaard, *Works of Love: Some Christian Reflections in the Form of Discourses,* trans. Howard and Edna Hong (New York: Harper & Row, 1964), 294.

22. Karl Barth, *Church Dogmatics* III/3 (Edinburgh: T&T Clark, 1977), 352; italics added.

An Imagined Reconciliation

I have often wondered what happened to Captain G. after the fall of 1984, when I was allowed to escape from under his inquisitorial "care." Where was he in the early nineties, when Mostar (the city in which he seemed to enjoy his job of poking around in people's lives) found itself caught in the whirlwind of a three-way war between Serbs, Croats, and Muslims? Did a communist defending the "brotherhood and unity" of the peoples of Yugoslavia morph into a nationalist fighting for the Serbian cause? Did he come out of the carnage alive? A hero? A four-star general? Or did he abandon the army out of disappointment that the socialist project for which he snooped on so many had so easily crumbled? What did he do after the war, during the years of uneasy and bitter peace? Did he withdraw to the mountains of his native Montenegro to nurse his wounds or drown his memories in Montenegrin vine brandy? Or, ensconced in his ancestral house, perhaps he is still proudly recounting to his grandchildren his great exploits in preventing secret plots against holy causes and wondering which one of these little ones will be found worthy to follow in his footsteps.

I have made a few attempts to track him down. The unsettling yet irresistibly attractive God of mine, intent on reconciling everyone and everything, kept nudging me to locate my nemesis and start the process of reconciliation. I searched the internet. I talked to a few friends with connections in the Yugoslav military. I came away empty handed . . . and relieved. But the Merciful Master of the universe ensconced deep in my conscience didn't seem satisfied. It wasn't divine anger that I felt, as though God were furious at me for failing to obey. Nor was it a sense of divine irritation, as though God were nagging, "How many times do I have to tell you to try harder?" It wasn't even disappointment, as though God were pointing out that Jesus Christ died to reconcile me to God and I couldn't even make peace with a fellow human being, for whom Christ also died. Instead, I simply sensed God's unwillingness to let the alienation and enmity have the last word. "Maybe you can do better," I heard a patient and persistent voice speak from the depths of my own heart — a voice that was my own, yet also that of Another. "And if not now, maybe later. . . ." Relieved from pressure but not from responsibility, I searched for ways to reconcile with Captain G.

Then the obvious occurred to me. Wherever Captain G. lived — presumably within the borders of the erstwhile Yugoslavia — he also showed up in my memory and frequented my imagination. There, I was mostly dealing with him without really engaging him. Early on, I would chase him away, and later, when his presence in my mind became more or less inconsequential, I would simply disregard him. Maybe, I now thought, I should try to reconcile with him in my imagination. I had made many — too many — attempts to forgive him on my own; maybe it was time to involve him in the process. Granted, even if I succeeded in reconciling with Captain G. on the screen of my mind, an imagined reconciliation could not permanently substitute for a face-to-face encounter of living and breathing human beings. Still, imagined reconciliation is something, and something is mostly better than nothing. I had no excuse. I had to begin.

The Commission

In my first attempt, I imagined Captain G. and myself before something like a Truth and Reconciliation Commission (TRC) not unlike the one in

216

South Africa, the best of them all. After the dismantling of apartheid, the TRC was set up to deal with politically motivated "gross violations of human rights." My case fell just below such violations, which in South African TRC parlance denoted murder, attempted murder, abduction, torture, and severe ill treatment. The South African TRC had to disregard less serious cases simply because time and resources were limited. In contrast, my imagination had no such limitations. I appointed Desmond Tutu, the wise and witty Archbishop and recipient of the 1984 Nobel Peace Prize, to preside over my own mental proceedings as he presided over the South African TRC.

Archbishop: And now, Captain G., to the case of Mr. Volf. . . .

Captain G.: My goal in his case was consistent with my professional duty. My job was to prevent the lure of Western democratic ideas and the force of ethnic loyalties from pulling the state apart. Religion was always suspect, and the Western powers were never to be trusted. Mr. Volf was a theologian and a son of a minister, and he was married to an American theologian who was a daughter of a theologian. I needed to find out where his loyalties lay and what his aims were. I put him under pressure — not too much. Just enough to make him talk.

Archbishop: You had no warrant for the interrogations.

Captain G.: He was in the military — I didn't need one! Besides, we were having "conversations." No real torture was involved, just significant psychological discomfort.

Archbishop: This Commission is set up to elicit full disclosure, not remorse. But you describe the case in such a matter-of-fact way. You appear to believe that what you did was right.

Captain G.: It's too bad that Mr. Volf had to suffer. He was innocent. Had I known so in advance, I would not have interrogated him. But the security business involves guess-work and sometimes necessitates the use of rough tools. Ask any security officer in the U.S.A., that "model" of Western democracy, and he'll tell you the same.

As I listened to the imagined exchange, I became more and more frustrated. On the positive side, Captain G. didn't deny his actions toward me, even though he stopped short of calling them mistreatment. That was something, for when wrongdoers deny their wrong acts they vi-

olate victims all over again. As it turns out, most wrongdoers do precisely that — at least until their backs come up against the wall of hard
facts. Even then, some continue with denials. As a case in point, take
Radoslav Krstic, an army general of the Republika Srpska. He was involved in the deportation of 30,000 women and children and the massa-
cre of more than 7,000 Muslim men in Srebrenica in July of 1995. During
his trial at The Hague, he denied that he issued the command to kill.
When the tape of his own voice issuing exactly such a command to an
army major was played back to him in the courtroom ("Liquidate them
all!") he insisted that the tape was a fake. He had done nothing wrong.
True, General Krstic had much to lose if he admitted to his crimes, for he
was on trial, whereas Captain G., whom I had placed before the TRC,
stood only to gain from confessing, since the TRC was set up so that people could trade truth for amnesty. Still, self-interested as it was, Captain G.'s acknowledgement of what he did was significant to me.

Yet paradoxically, that acknowledgement made me feel rather worse
than no acknowledgement at all. Captain G. admitted enough to gain
amnesty but not enough to appear in any significant way as a wrongdoer,
or, more importantly for me, to show that he cared for how it *felt* to be
mistreated. As he presented the case, mistreatment was just one in the
series of unfortunate mistakes that a person in his position was bound to
make. Neither did I gain much from the public nature of his acknowledgement. Some offenses positively demand public acknowledgement,
and some victims crave it; but I didn't need it, especially not when it
came with what amounted to a self-justification. He did his job, and that
job inherently involved sometimes aiming at the wrong target. The way
he saw it, he did the right thing — just to the wrong person.

Partial and therefore false truth and acknowledgement mixed with
self-justification — that may be enough for official amnesty and national
unity. But the cocktail is poisonous when it comes to forgiveness and social reconciliation. I came to the imagined hearings having extended forgiveness. That's what the faith I embrace demands of me — to take the
initiative to forgive even before the wrongdoer has repented. During the
hearings, Captain G. not only failed to embrace my gift of forgiveness —
he mostly hurled it back into my face. "Your gift is an insult, for I did not

do the wrong that you, by forgiving me, claim that I did," he implied. So reconciliation became impossible.

Reconciliation requires more than truth, more even than full disclosure. It also requires moral judgment, and along with moral judgment the wrongdoer's acceptance of moral responsibility — as well as the victim's willingness to release the wrongdoer from a genuine moral debt. In my imaginary TRC, Captain G. was willing to tell just enough truth and accept just enough responsibility to gain amnesty. The same was true of many wrongdoers in the TRC over which Archbishop Tutu presided in the flesh. For such wrongdoers, the TRC was all about getting out of the legal consequences of their misdeeds, not about their own transformation or reconciliation with victims.[1] If I was going to make progress on the path of reconciliation with Captain G., I would have to imagine an alternative scene, one that would allow both of us to unearth more of what happened and examine the moral dimensions of our actions and motivations.

In a Pub

Our next meeting, my second imaginary attempt at reconciliation, took place in a far corner of a dimly lit and largely empty pub. There, I thought, we could talk as human beings free from the trappings and limitations of a commission. In that more personal setting, I almost didn't recognize him. But even aged by twenty-five years, his dark, piercing eyes were unmistakable, though somewhat mellowed.

"Hallo, Miroslav." He greeted me with what seemed like a faint smile.

"Hallo, Captain G.," I said coldly and emphatically, irritated by the familiar greeting. I could not quite tell whether his tone was a sincere expression of a hoped-for reconciliation or an ironic reminder of the mock-

---

1. On the conditions for the applicants for amnesty in the South African Truth and Reconciliation Commission, see Desmond Tutu, *No Future Without Forgiveness* (New York: Doubleday, 1999), 49f. When relationships were truly healed during the proceedings of the South African Truth and Reconciliation Commission — and they often were at least partially healed — it was because both the perpetrators and the victims went beyond the condition of truth-telling set up by the Commission.

ing familiarity he feigned by using my first name during interrogations. Then I added, "I would prefer that you address me more formally. Abuse is not a form of intimacy."

"Yes, I know. The winter of 1984 was not pleasant for you. I bore upon you rather heavily. It was not out of personal malice, you know."

"It was evil," I corrected, thus suggesting what it was that I wanted to hear from him.

The exchange was not a promising start to our reconciliation. I had called for this meeting, and I had handed him the gift of forgiveness — and have vowed to forgive him again if I ever take away with the left hand the forgiveness I've given to him with the right. Yet sitting there opposite him, I was angry.

"Let me tell you a bit of my story," he continued.

"Please, spare me *your* story!" I thought to myself, disgruntled at his taking charge once again and making the meeting revolve around himself.

"I was just a kid when I threw in my lot with the Yugoslavian military. I was fifteen, driven from home by poverty and abuse and attracted to the military by vague ideals of the socialist revolution and, I admit, easy living. It was an achievement when I graduated from the military academy and became a security officer. My job was to expose the enemies of the people. And you did seem like a good candidate — religious, westernized, married to an American, a critical student of Marx, and, not to forget, a pacifist. I had to find out whether you were endangering the state. That was my job."

"It's a bad job if you must violate people to do it well," I insisted.

"But that's the job I had. It wasn't that I just had to feed my family and couldn't afford to lose my job. I was part of a system, with rewards and punishments and justifications of its actions. I had no place to stand outside."

"And that's supposed to excuse you! You think that circumstances relieve you from the responsibility to act like a human being?"

"I didn't mean it that way," he said.

"So if you'd been in Eichmann's shoes you'd have done Eichmann's deeds? Right! First, you *could* have found a proper place to stand outside the system. Second, what happened to your conscience? Didn't it tell you that you shouldn't mistreat fellow human beings? Third, being part of the system doesn't explain that spark of delight in your eyes as you were watching me, humiliated and trembling in fear."

"I know, I know," he added with a touch of meekness in his voice. "The evil got the better of me."

"Well, it shouldn't have," I said, anger having now overwhelmed my better judgment. "You should have resisted. That's part of what it means to be a human being — to resist being made an instrument of evil and to strive to do what is right."

"Don't act like such a saint yourself," he suddenly interjected. Having lost his patience and any semblance of meekness, he once again morphed into the Captain G. of my accursed memory. "I know things about you that others don't."

"That's just empty posturing. And if you do know such things, you should be ashamed of yourself for violating my privacy! You dare to question my saintliness — *you* of all people! And even if I'm not a saint, what's that got to do with your mistreatment of me? Because I'm not a saint, it's okay for you to be a devil? You should come to me crawling on your knees begging for forgiveness, and all you do is tell me about your 'circumstances,' the power of evil — all good reasons why you, a poor victim, have wronged me. *I* should feel sorry for *you!?*"

"It could have been worse for you, you know, had I not. . . . Oh, what's the use? It was a waste of time to come here."

"It certainly was, if you expected me to tell you what a fine fellow you really are, one who just happened to have been a victim of the system. Your mother might excuse your actions on the basis of circumstance, or perhaps some of your befuddled and stodgy Stalinist friends would. But *you* were *responsible*. This talk of 'circumstances' is just a lame excuse." I was fuming. I got up, left some cash on the table to pay for the drink, and walked away. The more I dwelled on the memory of what he did to me in 1984 and on how he viewed his own misdeeds in my imagination, the angrier I became.

It didn't take me long, however, to realize that I was partly responsible for running the reconciliatory process into the ground. Perhaps he had chosen the wrong way to open up the conversation, but after his greeting, I didn't give him a chance, even though he was trying. I was aware that I was working against my own goals, yet the conversational slope I was trying to climb was too slippery. My attempts to scale it just made me slide down faster and faster. I zeroed in on the heart of the problem; he tried to make me see the larger context. My need to apportion blame collided with his need to explain his behavior. I feared, maybe rightly, that his explanations were justifications; he feared, maybe rightly, that my accusations were vilifications. So the process derailed despite my commitment to reconcile.

We two could not reconcile on our own, I decided. We needed a mediating party — someone who could understand both of us and interpret us to each other, someone who could keep us honest, who could see through our evasions and manipulations, who could deal with our worst fears and enflame our best hopes. A good therapist could serve some of these needs — one who knew the intricacies of the human psyche and was skilled at helping us transcend ourselves and our past, maybe insert our personal histories into a larger frame of meaning. But this therapist would have to be interested in our reconciliation, not just in our individual healing — indeed, a therapist committed to the belief that Captain G. and I would be fully healed as individuals only when we were reconciled to each other.

But therapy by itself fell short of what was necessary for our reconciliation. I, at least, needed someone to keep reminding me of the new identity and new possibilities provided by God to set me free from the debilitating power of the past. As much as a therapist, I needed a spiritual director to challenge me — sometimes gently, sometimes forcefully — that Christians have no option when it comes to reconciling, since failing to reconcile with fellow human beings, for whom Christ died to reconcile them to God and to each other, is to reject God's work on our behalf.

But what kind of therapist/spiritual director could possibly know enough — and know the truth — about what actually transpired between Captain G. and me, and about the context of these events in each of our lives, to help bring about complete reconciliation? We participants in the events could share with this third party only shards from the past, partial truths partly decontextualized and spun from our own perspectives due to our human limitations and narrow interests — surely insufficient data for even a highly skilled therapist-director to work with. To whom could I turn to keep the process of reconciliation with Captain G. on the right track and take it to its destination? I could think of none less than *God*.

Invisible Guest

I gave Captain G. another call.

"I'm sorry I stormed out of our last meeting. I've done some thinking about our encounter. Maybe we should try one more time," I said somewhat tentatively to the incredulous voice at the other end of the telephone line.

"And what makes you think we won't part in the same way we did the last time, more angry with each other than when we started talking?" he inquired reasonably.

"Well, I'm thinking of asking a guest to join us — an Invisible Guest, but a real one nonetheless."

"Spare me the clumsy indirectness. You know that I don't believe in God."

"That's your right. But I'm not suggesting that we discuss whether or not God exists or whether it's good to believe in God. I know very well that you don't think religion is a force for good. But even if you don't believe in God, I do. And for me, at least, a sense of the presence of God — a giving and forgiving God, a God of truth and justice who loves you no less than me — might make a difference in our encounter."

"Your invisible guest amounts to no guest at all, as far as I am concerned; but if that imaginary crutch helps you, it's fine with me."

"Crutch? You might as well call the air I breathe a 'crutch.' But I won't argue with you. You were schooled in the Marxist critique of religion. So perhaps *you* can think of my guest as a screen onto which I've projected the commitment to be truthful, no matter whether truth favors you or me; the desire to repair and restore the human bond between us; the pledge to forgive while not disregarding justice; the belief in the possibility of human goodness, notwithstanding our fragility and flaws; the hope in future wholeness and reconciliation."

"That may be a bit too much for a 'Guest-on-the-screen' to accomplish," he grumbled skeptically. "You'd probably need a real God, and a Christian God on top of it, to achieve all that."

"I think you're right. And that, among other things, is why I believe. Do you agree to meet once more?"

He did. As I was waiting for him a few days later, I ran through the best-case scenario of our imminent encounter, but I knew full well that in reality it might turn out differently, very differently. Here is what I decided I *wanted* to happen between us, in the presence of the One I believed was as much his Guest as mine.

Once More in a Pub

"You were right," I said after we had exchanged the obligatory pleasantries. "I *am* a flawed human being. I shouldn't have implied anything different. I wrong people all the time, mostly not out of malice but out of culpable laziness, which squelches my energy for doing good. I did not mean to paint you as a demon from an abyss and myself as an angel from on high."

"I am sorry," he said. "I should never have interrogated you years ago. I should not have inflicted psychological pain to extract information. Even if the system allowed it — indeed encouraged it — I had no right to do so. I regret that I wronged you."

"I forgave you . . . and have also taken my forgiveness back as many times as I have given it to you — no testimony to my great virtue."

"Earlier, when I mentioned that I had no place to stand outside the military system for which I worked, when I spoke of the need to feed my family, when I suggested that the evil had taken hold of me, I wasn't trying to *justify* what I did. I merely wanted you to understand my actions in their context, to see my wrongdoing not simply as diabolical meanness

224

but as the consequence of wrong seeing, as 'culpable laziness,' as you put it about yourself, as weakness, as misplaced belief in the rightness of my cause, and much more."

"In that regard you and I are more similar than we are different."

"You mentioned a sparkle of enjoyment in my eyes as I was pummeling you with threats. You were right. That's what I am most ashamed of. I shudder now when I hear a war criminal say, 'It's nice to kill people,' as I read that someone from our region said recently. Yet I cannot deny that I felt a rush of joy at humiliating others and causing them pain. I am doubly ashamed that you noticed that perverse joy. I myself don't know what happened. The best explanation I can give is to repeat what I said earlier, namely, that evil got the better of me. Deep down I knew that what I was doing wasn't right, even while I felt satisfaction in doing it. Maybe the system of which I was a part did play a role in this perversity. It told me that what I was doing was not only right but also necessary. The system made it seem right for me to do what was wrong, and my own inexplicable satisfaction in wrongdoing along with the benefits I was drawing from the system kept me going. Please forgive me."

"I do forgive you; but more importantly, God forgives you. You should ask for God's forgiveness, too; or rather, you should receive the forgiveness that God gave you."

"I don't care about God's forgiveness; I do care about yours. Remember, I don't believe in God."

"But you see," I interjected, "I believe that on my own I have no power and no right to forgive you. You haven't broken some arbitrary rule *I* have made. By wronging me, you've transgressed the moral law *God* established to help us, God's beloved creatures, to flourish; so you have wronged God. Ultimately, only God has the power and the right to forgive, and only God's forgiveness can wash you clean of your wrongdoing. When I forgive you, I mostly just echo God's forgiving of your sin."

"You won't be surprised to hear me say that I don't think in those terms — I'm no theologian, as you know. But all's well that ends well. So far as I'm concerned, the important thing is that you have forgiven me and taken away that burden of my past."

"You may feel that I have taken away your burden, but actually, whether you believe it or not, God is the one who has shouldered the burden of your past. That is why I am both obligated and able to forgive you."

"I repeat: To me, that *you* have done so is all that matters."

"I understand. But you also should understand that what I have done is possible only because of God. I don't mean that God just made my forgiveness happen, like some magical trick. To be frank, I am sometimes angry at God for forgiving you. At those times I ask, What right does the Almighty have to forgive someone for an offense against *me?* And why should I have to remember the offense against me as an offense forgiven by God? What's even more unsettling, since my faith teaches that in Christ God has reconciled my offender and me to each other, I have to think of us as already in some sense reconciled. That seems preposterous! But then I remind myself that when you wronged me you sinned *most* egregiously not against me but against God, and God forgave you of that sin just as God forgave me of my sin. Then remembering your wrongdoing as forgiven by God helps me to forgive it myself. And then remembering our reconciliation by God in Christ helps me to reconcile with you face-to-face."

"It sounds like the Christian faith works for you. And we did make some progress this time," he observed.

Captain G. and I parted amicably, but I knew I'd have questions in his absence — questions about how genuine and above all how deep this reconciliation was. But for the time being I was pleased with what happened. So went the best-case scenario I played out in my head.

A Puzzlement

I told a friend about the encounters I'd imagined between Captain G. and me and about my labor of reconciliation. She was puzzled.

"Your brand of reconciliation seems cheap to me," she said.

"Why cheap?" I asked, just to hear her say what I knew was on her mind.

"You're letting him off the hook! He and the likes of him should have charges pressed against them. Your Captain G. should be punished: You harm others, you pay. It's that simple. Otherwise you'll have evildoers growing like weeds."

"Punishment is too petty, and it doesn't help that much. I want more. I want Captain G. *dead!*"

"What?! Where did that come from? You seem to me to want the ultimate punishment for him, not no punishment. I fail to see where reconciliation fits in to that picture! Which is it: death or unconditional forgiveness? Isn't there some middle ground between the two extremes?"

"No, there isn't — at least not good middle ground. Those extremes may sound incompatible, but they aren't. This 'death' that I'm talking about is the word the Apostle Paul uses when he speaks of human transformation. He describes it as dying and rising with Christ. I want Captain G. to become a new person — dead to his old self and alive to his new self. I believe that Christ took all of our deserved punishment upon himself when he died on the cross. The only 'punishment' left for Captain G. to undergo is this 'death' to his old self."

"And what if he doesn't want to die?"

"Then we'll want to make sure that he doesn't pose a danger to others. What I am against is retribution. It's incompatible with forgiveness and reconciliation. I am *for* transformation and, when necessary, containment and discipline, including incarceration. Do you think that's cheap?"

"He hasn't paid for what he's done! Isn't that cheap?"

"On the contrary — as expensive as it gets. In Christ, *God* was judged in his place!"

"God certainly comes in handy for you — does all the important work."

"Would you have me believe that the Source of all that exists and the merciful Guide for all who walk the path of life just sits in a far corner of heaven twiddling the almighty thumbs? Either God exists and is then at the center of everything and affects it all, or God doesn't exist. It is foolish to believe in a God who does nothing. An idle God is a false god."

"There are worse ways for God to be false."

"I agree. But I wouldn't count shouldering the sin of the world among the ways of being a false god — and certainly not a cheap form of reconciliation!"

After the Judgment

After several more imagined encounters with Captain G., I fast-forwarded my imagination to the end of history. The end of history? Yes — for people who take seriously their belief in God think of time in terms of that ultimate framework. The next few years, retirement, even one's last breath and last heartbeat are simply stops along the journey to the end of history. And further still, their framework of time reaches beyond history to the life everlasting, which itself is enveloped in God's eternity — the ultimate horizon of my hope. But what has the end of history got to do with Captain G.?

In my imagined encounters with him in the here and now, our efforts at reconciliation kept taking one step forward and then a half step backward as we revisited the old "stuff" from new vantage points, but with little gain. When we did make progress, it was often more in form than in substance. Why? Because we are finite beings with limited knowledge, and frequently we each pursued our narrow interests at the expense of the other. Since neither our thoughts nor our feelings fully matched, even seeming agreement on the "facts" of our past was eventually exposed as disagreement. So even at our best, our peace was incomplete, flawed, and fragile.

But from the start I had hoped for more than such frayed reconciliation. As I embarked upon the process, I had not just been pushed from behind by the conviction that on the cross God reconciled estranged human beings to each other. Equally importantly, I had been pulled from ahead by the hope that God's reconciliation will become complete and uncontested reality on the Day of Final Reconciliation, the Day of Judgment and Embrace, the Day that would be the last day of the old world and the first of the new. Reconciliation that has been partial and fragile now will be complete and unassailable then.

"Imagine," I said to Captain G. one day, "that we both find ourselves on the other side of that Divine Courtroom, the place through which all mortals must pass before they can enter God's new world, which Christian tradition has always described as a world of love. What do you think would happen then?"

"That scenario strains my atheist imagination. And besides, God wouldn't want atheists there."

"If you were there, you wouldn't be an atheist. As to your atheist imagination, you don't have to be a Christian — or even believe in God — to imagine a world of love."

"You tell me what would happen," he responded, unwilling to venture on the path down which I was pointing him.

"Okay. I'll answer my own question by borrowing from Franz Kafka."

"I'm not familiar with him," he said.

"He's a Jewish writer. His book *The Trial* might interest you. It is about being treated as guilty without ever being told what you are guilty of. At one point in the book Kafka distinguishes between an 'actual acquittal' and an 'apparent acquittal.' In what he calls 'apparent acquittal,' the court certifies the innocence of the accused, but no file is ever lost and the court forgets nothing, so the case can be resumed at any time. It is different in the case of an actual acquittal. 'In an actual acquittal,' writes Kafka, 'the files relating to the case are completely discarded, not only the charge, but the trial and even the acquittal are destroyed, everything is destroyed.'"[2]

"So let me guess — " Captain G. said, "if I were to be counted among the eternally blessed, at the Last Judgment I would receive an 'actual acquittal.'"

"Yes. I would too — as would everyone who ever entered the coming world of love. And in addition to the destruction of everything pertaining to the wrongdoing, the *conditions* that made the wrongdoing possible would also from that point on be nullified."

"That seems an absolutely extraordinary vision — every wrongdoing of the past simply eradicated and all wrongdoing in the future made impossible. I can imagine that. What then?"

2. Franz Kafka, *The Trial,* trans. Breon Mitchell (New York: Schocken Books, 1998), 158.

"To tell you the truth, I'm not sure. That's the point at which we all need to rein in our imagination. I figure I'll just let myself be surprised. But I think of that life as like being absorbed in a piece of arrestingly beautiful music — music that captivates my entire being and takes me on an unpredictable journey. That's what that world of love will do for its inhabitants. It will bar the pathways through which the wounded past, a past marred by wrongdoing and suffering, enters the present, and it will set them free to explore the truth, the goodness, and the beauty of that world — each on their own and all together."

In a tone that seemed to oscillate between incredulity and longing, he said, "I hope you are right."

Afterword

I was tempted to put a warning label on this book: "WARNING: CON-TENTS MAY BE HAZARDOUS TO SOME OF YOUR CHERISHED NOTIONS."

Cherished Notion No. 1: "We should remember wrongs solely out of concern for victims." No one would put it quite that way, of course, but for almost half a century in our broader culture we have stressed the overarching importance of remembering for the sake of victims. We remember their misfortunes to honor them, protect them, render justice to them, keep them in a sense "alive," and more. And justly so. We would make a grave mistake if we let our memory fail the victims of wrongdoing. Yet in this book I argue that we should also remember in a way that is fair, even generous to the *perpetrators* of wrongs. Such concern for their good may be the most puzzling, maybe even the most offensive aspect of the book. I do give reasons to justify generosity toward perpetrators — reasons as good as a Christian theologian can give, I think. But I do not give extensive arguments to support those reasons. For such support I invite readers to dip into my two previous books, *Exclusion and Embrace* (1996) and *Free of Charge* (2005).

Cherished Notion No. 2: "We should forever remember wrongs suffered." Over the course of roughly the last half-century, we have come to believe that letting go of the memories of wrongs suffered at any point would betray victims and endanger the wider community. In contrast to this widespread opinion, in the last part of the book I suggest that under carefully defined conditions it may be salutary to release memories of wrongs. This suggestion may very well be the most controversial aspect of my argument in the book. But perhaps this issue is worth stirring up some controversy about. After all, for millennia the Jewish and Christian traditions have envisaged, even looked forward to the "end" of the memory of wrongs. That traces back to Jewish and Christian sacred texts. And I am convinced that any idea about the shape of human living rooted in both Jewish and Christian sacred texts and persisting over millennia merits serious consideration, especially if it has been discarded only recently. After all, I consider these texts to be the Holy Scripture of the faith I embrace. Persons who opine that the Hebrew and the Christian Bibles "contain mountains of life-destroying gibberish" will demur,[1] of course. But it's a mistake to think that our scientific explanations and technological advances, extraordinarily important as they are, can make us wiser than previous generations about how to lead truly human lives.

Both ways in which this book disturbs conventional opinion are rooted in a single conviction: the proper *goal* of the memory of wrongs suffered — its appropriate *end* — is the formation of the communion of love between all people, including victims and perpetrators. Imagine this book as a suspension bridge in which the roadway hangs on a concrete arch anchored on both sides of the divide. The roadway is the reflection on memory. The arch that upholds the roadway is the process of reconciliation. The anchors that support the process of reconciliation are on one side the death of the One for the reconciliation of all, and on the other the hope for the world to come as a world of love. Perfect love is the goal of memory. And when that goal is reached, the memory of wrongs itself can end. Put simply, love is the "end" of memory in the twofold sense of that term.

Although the book may be hazardous to recent conventional "wisdom" about the memory of wrongs, it is, I believe, good medicine for our

---

1. Sam Harris, *The End of Faith: Religion, Terror, and the Future of Reason* (New York: W. W. Norton & Company, 2004), 23.

cultural health and personal flourishing. The warning appropriate to this book isn't like the one on a life-endangering pack of cigarettes — it's like the one on a life-enhancing bottle of medicine apprising the taker of the temporary discomforts that accompany its curative effects.

Acknowledgments

———《⁄》———

Like a painting in progress, this book has been long (too long!) in the making — started, sidelined by other creative endeavors, then taken up again and tinkered with, only to be left unfinished again for a while. Now that my "painting" is finished, I find myself at a loss for how to thank all those who, over the past eight years or so, have contributed to its creation, whether by nudging me in one way or another to work on it or by engaging me as I thought about the subject matter and wrote. My memory has simply not been able to keep track of the many benefactors who in these ways helped to produce this book. May their good deeds be remembered by the One to whom no good deed is lost!

I have presented the substance of various parts of the book in named lectureships, listed here in the order in which I participated in them: Gray Lectures, Duke University Divinity School (2001); Stob Lectures, Calvin College (2002); Princeton Lectures on Youth, Church, and Culture, Princeton Theological Seminary (2002); Reid Lectures, Westminster College (2002); Robertson Lectures, Glasgow University (2003); Raynolds Lecture, Princeton University (2004); Dudlean Lecture, Harvard University Divinity School (2004); and Kelleen Chair Lectures, St. Norbert College (2006).

Though the book contains considerably more than was delivered in that venue, I am delighted to have it appear in the ongoing series of annual Stob Lectures that Eerdmans publishes in conjunction with Calvin College and Calvin Theological Seminary. The series honors the late Henry J. Stob, longtime distinguished professor of philosophical and moral theology at Calvin Theological Seminary and, before that, professor of philosophy at Calvin College. Though I never met Professor Stob personally, the fact that he played so important a role in the history of an academic community I deeply respect and with which I have had a number of happy associations gives me particular pleasure in having my book associated with him.

Independently of named lectureships, I have also spoken on the topics covered in this book in a number of academic venues, such as the annual meetings of the American Theological Society (2003) and the American Academy of Religion (Philadelphia, 2005), the universities of Sarajevo and Beijing, Renmin University (Beijing), and Yale Divinity School, where I teach. To audiences and conversational partners in all these places, as well as to those I have failed to mention, I offer sincere thanks for concentrating, stimulating, and challenging my thinking.

Many individuals have also helped me in the process of writing this book. Peter Forrest and Sean Larsen served as my research assistants, and Linn Tonstad commented on the manuscript. My "team" at the Yale Center for Faith and Culture — Joseph Cumming, Linda LaSourd Lader, Dr. David Miller, Dr. Chris Scharen, and Travis Tucker — discussed the entire manuscript with me. None of that wonderful and hard-nosed group will begrudge me if I single out Linda, who having gone through the manuscript with extraordinary care asked penetrating questions not just of sense but also of sensitivity and offered wise suggestions (and issued commands!). Professor Kendall Soulen critically and helpfully engaged an earlier version of the last part of the book. I learned a great deal from the three respondents at the American Academy of Religion's session on my work on memory: professors Sarah Coakley, Nicholas Wolterstorff, and Michael Wyschogrod. And Professor Hillel Levine of Boston University gave me not only an invaluable Jewish perspective on what I have written but also brought to bear his own incomparable experience in the practice of reconciliation. Without Connie Gundry Tappy, my editor, the manuscript would not be half as readable as it is now. After my many unkept promises to deliver the manuscript to Eerdmans, editor-in-chief Jon Pott must have thought that he would never see it either. I want to thank him for his gentle and steady nudging hand as well as his editorial wisdom.

I owe to all these people a great debt of gratitude. And I owe it as well to one more person — one who has not seen the manuscript and will not read the book. Susan Bergman, the author of the fine novel *Anonymity* (1994), suggested in one of our exchanges that I weave into this book the story of my interrogations. She died of brain cancer at the beginning of 2006 without ever seeing a word of what I wrote.

Finally, I owe more gratitude than I can ever express, and for more than I will ever know, to my family — Judy Gundry-Volf, my wife, and Nathanael and Aaron, our two sons. Now that this book is finished, however, I want more to beg their pardon than to thank them — pardon for having to send one or the other boy out of my office because I was working on "the book," for having at times neglected family obligations because my mind was preoccupied with writing on top of other duties, for leaving the three of them to fend for themselves while I was away lecturing on memory, and more. I hope that today they will remember my fatherly and husbandly failings with mercy and one day even find that these shortcomings do not come to their minds.

This book is dedicated to Tim Collins. Happy 50th, my friend!

Index